THE GOSPEL CHURCH SECURE

The Official History of the Methodist Sacramental Fellowship

Norman Wallwork

CHURCH IN THE MARKET PLACE PUBLICATIONS
2013

Church in the Market Place Publications

British Library Cataloguing in Publication Data
A record for this book is available from the British Library

ISBN 978-1-899147-92-2

Typeset in Bookman Old Style
by RefineCatch Ltd, Bungay, Suffolk

Printed in Great Britain by
Cambrian Printers, Aberystwyth

FOR GEOFFREY THACKRAY EDDY

Doyen of the Fellowship
in the seventy-fifth year of his membership

GREAT is our redeeming Lord
 In power, and truth, and grace;
Him, by highest heaven adored,
 His church on earth doth praise.
In the city of our God,
 In his holy mount below,
Publish, spread his name abroad,
 And all his greatness show.

For thy loving-kindness, Lord,
 We in thy temple stay;
Here thy faithful love record,
 Thy saving power display.
With thy name thy praise is known,
 Glorious thy perfections shine;
Earth's remotest bounds shall own
 Thy works are all divine.

See the gospel church secure,
 And founded on a rock;
All her promises are sure;
 Her bulwarks who can shock?
Count her every precious shrine;
 Tell, to after-ages tell:
Fortified by power divine,
 The church can never fail.

Zion's God is all our own,
 Who on his love rely;
We his pardoning love have known,
 And live to Christ, and die.
To the new Jerusalem
 He our faithful guide shall be:
Him we claim, and rest in him,
 Through all eternity.

Charles Wesley (1707–88)

Contents

Foreword

The title of this book may appear at first sight a touch triumphalist in tone but this is not reflected in the story it tells. This is the history of a Fellowship rather than a campaigning organisation. That is not to belittle its achievements, either in the life of the Methodist Church or more widely.

The early controversies and opposition which the Fellowship faced may now seem a world away. This is only because many core aims of the MSF have now become firmly embedded in Methodism as a whole. Most significantly this is seen in the much more regular celebration of Holy Communion which is now an integral part of the Sunday service instead of being 'tacked on' at the end of a preaching service.

Methodists have always been encouraged to live on a larger map – following John Wesley's famous dictum, 'I look upon all the world as my parish.' This has usually been interpreted in terms of geography rather than ecclesiology, but the MSF has helped Methodism re-discover and celebrate its vital part within the one holy, catholic and apostolic church.

As Methodists we sing our theology. Charles Wesley reminds us that 'vying with that happy choir, who chant thy praise above, we on eagles wings aspire, the wings of faith and love.' This lively sense of the communion of saints is vividly reflected in these pages, not least in the celebration of some of the Fellowship's memorable and influential members.

Many of these have greatly influenced my own journey of faith. It is because of them that I have always valued my membership of the MSF. The Fellowship has nourished me personally and spiritually. I have been pleased that, in recent times, the Fellowship has widened its appeal beyond those who might naturally regard themselves as 'High Church Methodists.'

The MSF has also been a place where scholarship, learning and debate have been enjoyed. These have been shared with the Church at large. I very much hope that, through its lectures and publications, the Fellowship will continue to be a means of grace for the broader Methodist community.

We owe a great debt of gratitude to Norman Wallwork who has brought this history to fruition. His own part in the development of the Fellowship has been significant. He has been its energetic Chairman, a great encourager and a stimulating writer and speaker.

I believe the author has shown that the contribution of the Fellowship remains an important one. There is always a temptation to be congregationalist and insular. The larger vision of the Gospel Church in its fullness remains vital. A church whose social action, evangelism and ecumenism are deeply rooted in the worship of the triune God is all of a piece.

Father, God, thy love we praise,
Which gave thy Son to die;
Jesus, full of truth and grace,
Alike we glorify;
Spirit, Comforter divine,
Praise by all to thee be given;
Till we in full chorus join,
And earth is turned to heaven.

David Walton
Vice-President of the Methodist Conference, 2008

Preface

Like one of the alleged reasons for the writing of the gospels, the time has come for the Sacramental Fellowship to set down its origins and development while there are still living links to the people and events surrounding its beginnings and some of the key chapters of its history. In eighty years there have been relatively few lapses in the keeping of the Fellowship's minutes and records. To A S Gregory and to David Owen in particular the MSF owes a great debt for the careful preservation of much of its archival material.

The number of religious publishing houses is in rapid decline. Those that remain must of necessity be ultra-cautious about the books they accept for publication. Generous legacies from the estates of Kenneth Warburton, Cedric Hallam and Colin Penna meant that, from the outset therefore, this history of the MSF could be placed in the hands one of its own members, Robert Davies of Church in the Market Place Publications. At every stage of the production the editors of the Fellowship have been grateful for the advice and encouragement received from Mr Davies and for the skilled and friendly help of the typesetter, Mr Kevin Eaton of RefineCatch Ltd. The Fellowship is also grateful to the Reverend Susan Keegan Von Allmen, the Superintendent of the West London Mission Circuit, for permission to use the photograph of Hinde Street Methodist Church which appears on the front cover of this book.

I owe the greater part of my Christian, Catholic and Methodist formation to the Methodist Sacramental Fellowship and my debt is incalculable. I was drawn into its life through the witness of Stella Buckley, when she was Deputy Head of Penrith Grammar School. I received her constant encouragement as one of her fifth and sixth-formers, as we shared the Sunday morning fellowship of 'the back pew' in Wordsworth Street Methodist Church, and as I was introduced by her in person to the patriarchal J E Rattenbury and to the newly retired A S Gregory.

The version of this book that was finally handed over to the type-setters, printers and publisher owes a huge amount to Margaret Wallwork's in depth knowledge of the MSF and to her scrupulosity in challenging, correcting and preparing every aspect of each chapter as it was received from the author.

I would like to thank David Walton for graciously and readily agreeing to write the Foreword to this history. I wish also to record the loving encouragement and enquiry of William and Richard Gallois and of Barbara, my wife, who have been a constant and vital support to me as I have sat day after day in my 'executive hermitage' working on 'the book.'

Cowley, Exeter, 2013

Introduction

When, as a student, I made my first enquiries about the MSF to A S Gregory, one of the founders of the Fellowship, he replied, 'You speak of the future of Methodism. I believe Methodism has no future outside the Catholic tradition.' He didn't mean that Methodism should pack up its tents and knock on the doors of the Vatican! But he did mean that Methodism's long-term destiny lay within a renewed and transformed Catholic (and Orthodox) Church acknowledging one collegial magisterium and one ecumenical primacy.

The history of the MSF began with its right to exist. Its vocation was then to challenge and change the inward and outward life of Methodism. Finally the Fellowship itself underwent a transformation from a high Wesleyan ginger group into a fully-fledged Catholic presence within the Methodist tradition.

Beginning with the Wesleys there has been an unbroken succession of teachers, preachers and writers who have proclaimed the presence and sacrifice of the incarnate Christ in the preached word and the celebrated sacrament. Central to everything has been the faith of the scriptures and of the historic creeds. At the heart of Methodism was the memory of a life of disciplined prayer.

The theological rigour that forged the united Methodist Church and the Deed of Union of 1932 claimed that Methodism cherished its place in the one holy, catholic and apostolic church. The issue facing the founders of the MSF was how to invite and encourage Methodism to put such a theory into practice. When they first appeared in the new Methodism they found they had to fight to stay in existence, let alone to issue a challenge.

Once the storm over the Fellowship's right to exist had abated there began the long witness and struggle to make Holy Communion central in the life of the Methodist people. The Fellowship's prayer and work for the visible unity of the

Church had only just begun. From the start every member committed themselves to a life of disciplined daily prayer. The Aims of the Fellowship were hugely strengthened by the emergence of the liturgical movement, the rise of the ecumenical movement and the blossoming of Biblical scholarship.

Internally the MSF was to undergo its own transformation. Although its first members were drawn from all branches of pre-union Methodism, the Fellowship's early agenda was inevitably 'High-Wesleyan,' urging a full celebration of the Cranmer-Wesley communion order, a re-discovery of calendar and lectionary, and rapprochement with the Church of England. But halfway through its existence the members of the Fellowship found themselves living on a larger map and facing a bigger agenda. The liturgical movement, liturgical theology and the LIMA document of the World Council of Churches meant seeing the Communion of the Lord's Supper in the light of a richer eucharistic faith and practice, and ever more profoundly at one with the Orthodox Liturgy and the Catholic Mass. Baptism and Christian initiation also became a richer and more visible journey. Ecumenical theology also introduced wider concepts about corporate and ministerial priesthood.

Members of the Fellowship also found themselves drawn into the life of the Ecumenical Society of the Blessed Virgin Mary and the Ecumenical Marian Pilgrimage Trust. Methodist-Roman Catholic dialogue saw, in the Methodist understanding of Christian Perfection and Prevenient Grace, a profound connection with traditional doctrine and devotion relating to the Mother of Jesus.

The latest source of enormous encouragement to the MSF has been the international emergence of Canonical Theism, under the inspiration of William Abraham:

> Canonical theism is dispersed in the Scriptures, the Nicene Creed, the iconography, the liturgy; it is enacted in the life of the saints; it is summarized and worked through in the work of the Canonical teachers of the Church prior to the great

schism; it is implicitly received in baptism; and it is handed over in ordination to the diaconate, priesthood, and episcopate from generation to generation. The intellectual core of Canonical theism is a rich vision of God, creation and redemption.[1]

The Prayer of the Fellowship

Almighty God, who raised up your servants,
John and Charles Wesley,
to proclaim anew the gift of redemption
and the life of holiness;
pour out upon us
the gift of your Holy Spirit,
that we may honour you in word and sacrament,
and serve you in the needs of our neighbour;
through Jesus Christ our Lord. Amen.

1
Wesleyan Legacy

John Wesley

Within the Methodist family both 'catholics' and 'evangelicals' have claimed Wesley as one of their own but he does not easily fit into either contemporary version of these traditions. Gordon Rupp cautioned Methodists about using John Wesley as a ventriloquist's dummy and putting into the venerable father's mouth isolated quotations or passages to reinforce their own views and opinions. In any case, as Jabez Bunting's public adversary, Dr Joseph Beaumont, wryly observed, 'Wesley, like a strong and skilful rower, looked one way, while every stroke of the oar took him in the opposite direction.'[1]

Wesley was indeed a contradictory man. Staunch defender of the 1662 *Book of Common Prayer* as he was, in his own abridgement of it Wesley retained, revised and omitted its contents at will.[2] Faithful churchman that he was Wesley frequently used extempore prayer. Committed Episcopalian, that he insisted he remained, Wesley finally lodged himself in a three-fold ministry of superintendent, elder and deacon, and a doctrine of presbyteral succession. Immersed in the patristic tradition, that he never ceased to admire and love, Wesley's final authority was the Bible.

> Permit me to speak plainly. If by catholic principles you mean any other than scriptural, they weigh nothing with me. I allow no other rule, whether of faith or practice, than the Holy Scriptures; but, on scriptural principles, I do not think it hard to justify whatever I do.[3]

Ted Campbell, in his study of Wesley and Christian Antiquity, concluded, 'the boundary between reality and hope was frequently blurred in Wesley's understanding.'[4]

For many decades a good number of Methodists have erroneously maintained that Wesley's theology and churchmanship were significantly resourced alike by Scripture, tradition, reason and experience. Albert Outler, with whom the language of this 'Wesleyan Quadrilateral' originated, while holding that a Methodist theologian must be critical and faithful to Scripture, acquainted with the Christian past, logically analytical and the possessor of an inward faith, later confessed, 'more than once, I have regretted having coined [the phrase] for contemporary use, since it has been so widely misconstrued.'[5] The perceived wisdom now among Methodist writers is that the authentic Wesleyan tradition is one that regards Scripture as the normative source of God's self-disclosure. Scripture's proper role is to critique tradition, reason and experience but only in so far as it is in constant and serious dialogue with them.[6]

John Wesley's changing churchmanship is well expressed by Frank Baker:

> [Wesley's] view of the ideal church as a sacramental institution with an evangelical mission was slowly transformed into that of a missionary society performing sacramental functions, with the Church of England fulfilling the one task and the Methodist societies the other.[7]

A much cited example of Wesley's changing churchmanship was his move from affirming the Lord's Supper as a 'confirming' ordinance to a 'converting' one.

> ... among us it has been diligently taught that none but those who are converted, who have received the Holy Ghost, who are believers in the full sense, ought to communicate. But experience shows the gross falsehood of that assertion that the Lord's Supper is not a converting ordinance. Ye are witnesses. For many of you know that the very beginning of your conversion to God (perhaps in some *the first deep conviction*) was wrought at the Lord's Supper.[8]

Wesley believed that those 'seekers' who still fell short of 'believing faith' should come to the Lord's Supper. He argued that the 'unconverted' disciples had received the Supper at the Lord's own hand *before* they had received the Holy Spirit.

Again and again in his Journal Wesley testifies to those who, at the sacrament, 'found rest to their souls' or 'had their sins taken away' or were 'first wounded, and then healed.' Wesley cited one who attended an Easter celebration of the Lord's Supper, went home and testified, 'Now my sins are forgiven. I am not afraid to die now; for I love God, and I know he loves me.'

The strength of Wesley's churchmanship was well disclosed in the expectations he set before his first 'Helpers' when he bade them observe and enforce both the 'institutional' and 'prudential' means of grace. The *Instituted Means of Grace* were (1) Private, Family and Public Prayer (2) Searching the Scriptures by constant reading, meditating at set times and being present at the daily Preaching Service (3) Attending the Lord's Supper at every opportunity 'with due preparation, solemn prayer, careful examination, deep repentance, self devotion and discerning the Lord's body' (4) Fasting every Friday (5) Engaging regularly in Christian Conference including planned conversation that is begun and ended with prayer.[9]

The *Prudential Means of Grace* included: (1) Attending the classes and the small intimate Methodist band meetings; (2) Meeting with other members; and (3) Visiting the sick. To these 'prudential' means of grace, Wesley added four others for the building up of the faith of the Methodists, namely doctrinal and experiential hymn singing, the Love Feast, the Watchnight Service and the Covenant Service.

The great store which John and Charles Wesley set upon all the means of grace never prevented them from seeing the chief means of grace in the Eucharist:

> The Prayer, the Fast, the Word conveys,
> When mixed with faith, thy life to me,
> In all the channels of thy grace,
> I still have fellowship with thee,
> But chiefly here my soul is fed
> With fullness of immortal Bread.[10]

Charles Wesley

There are Methodists who, in matters of churchmanship, regard themselves as the lineal descendants of Charles Wesley, rather than John. In January 1774 Charles wrote to his brother, reporting what he had said about him to a Welsh clergyman, Mark Davis:

> All the difference betwixt my brother and me was that my brother's first object was the Methodists, and then the Church; mine was, first the Church, and then the Methodists.[11]

Charles was stricter than John in refusing quarterly membership tickets to 'counterfeits and slackers.' He disliked John's licensing of the Methodist preaching houses as Dissenting chapels and opposed John's Bristol ordinations of 1784, employing the famous phrase, 'ordination is separation.' When it came to taking on new travelling preachers, Charles was far more cautious than John with regard to the doctrines they held, the education they had received and to inquiries about their personal histories. Charles was appalled when some of the lay itinerants took it upon themselves to preside at the Lord's Supper.

John Wesley's Conference obituary for his brother remains an enigma: 'His least praise was his talent for poetry.'[12]

Charles Wesley's hymns reveal the breadth, depth and height of his scriptural, patristic and Anglican churchmanship. Though most of the hymn collections were published under the name of both brothers, practically all the poetry comes from the pen of Charles. Hymns on God's everlasting love celebrate the universality of Arminian grace. Those on the Trinity proclaim the fullness and mystery of patristic faith. Those on Jesus Christ celebrate his humanity, his divinity and his saving work. Those on the Holy Spirit invoke the immanent power of Pentecost and the doctrine of assurance. Those on the Atonement bring all Calvary before our eyes. Those on the Lord's Supper celebrate the Real Presence and the Eucharistic sacrifice. The hymns of 'experimental and practical divinity' carry the believer from conviction to conversion, from new birth to saving faith, from prevenient grace to perfect love, and from the communion of saints to the beatific vision.

After the Wesleys

At least three times, following the death of its founders, Wesleyan Methodism was compelled to establish and assert its own ecclesiology The first occasion was in the years up to and following the 1795 Plan of Pacification, when 'the Wesleyan Body' began to accept that it was independent of the Church of England, that its Itinerants were evolving into ministers of word and sacrament, and that the Lord's Supper was being celebrated in Methodism's own preaching houses and chapels. The second occasion was in the wake of the Oxford Movement, when Wesleyans in particular were either being 'unchurched' by Tractarians or felt, as in the case of Jabez Bunting, that they were now the authentic inheritors of the English Protestant Arminian tradition. Wesleyan scholars and leaders began to expound a 'high' view of 'the pastoral office' held by their itinerant preachers and to defend the authenticity of their own sacraments. The third occasion was the fear of some Wesleyans that their distinctive churchmanship and their hopes of re-union with the Church of England would be diluted with the advent of Methodist Union in 1932.

Thomas Jackson and a Revival of Apostolic Christianity

Thomas Jackson was born in 1783. He was received into Full Connexion in 1808 and died in his ninetieth year in 1873.[13] Jackson's early ministry brought him into contact with those of Wesley's preachers who had begun their distinguished ministries under their venerable father's shadow, those of the calibre of Thomas Coke, Samuel Bradburn, Joseph Benson, Adam Clarke and Richard Watson. In the second half of his itinerancy Jackson exercised his own influential ministry, intimately associated with the two Wesleyan giants, Robert Newton and Jabez Bunting. In the 1830s and 1840s Jackson defended the evermore independent character and nature of Wesleyan Methodism as an ecclesial reality owing an unpayable debt to the Church of England, but now both separate and faithful. In a memorable speech to the Wesleyan Conference of 1834, *The Church and the Methodists*, Jackson spoke of the Church of England's 'truly sublime and evangelical liturgy' and, in the most able of his pamphlets, *Answer to the question, Why are you a Wesleyan Methodist?* Jackson defended Wesleyan polity by asserting, 'The external order of the Wesleyan ministry is Presbyterian with the advantage of a modified episcopacy, for every Superintendent of a Circuit has the oversight of his colleagues.' In his *Wesleyan Methodism a Revival of Apostolic Christianity* Jackson declared:

> There is ... an Apostolic Succession ... in which every minister should be careful to stand ... a ministry characterised by Apostolical truth, by Apostolical zeal and faithfulness, by Apostolical efficiency and power, by Apostolical labour and self-denial, and by Apostolical success. In this succession we believe that our fathers stood and we ourselves are in it as far as we are actuated by the same spirit, and tread in the same steps.[14]

Benjamin Gregory and 'The Holy Catholic Church, The Communion of Saints'

Benjamin Gregory (grandfather of T S and A S Gregory) entered the Wesleyan ministry in 1840, was Connexional Editor from 1868 to 1893 and died in 1900. He played a leading part in the 1882 Wesleyan revision of the *Book of Common Prayer, Public Prayers and Services*, and late in life wrote his key account of the troubled Wesleyan years, *Sidelights on the Conflicts in Methodism, 1827–52.* His Fernley Lecture of 1873 was entitled *The Holy Catholic Church, The Communion of Saints*. One of Gregory's underlying aims in his book of 300 pages was to avoid any sense that there was a '*specific Methodist* idea of the *Catholic* Church!'

Gregory argued that Methodists, Baptists, Episcopalians and Presbyterians were all 'true Catholic Christians.' Christian was the genus and Methodist was the species.[15] He took the view that, when Methodists sang the *Te Deum*, they were thinking not only of their fellow Methodists throughout the world but also of every 'misled Roman Catholic' and every 'exclusive coterie of Plymouth Brethren' loyal to their Saviour.[16] Jackson wrote that Methodists felt their oneness with the 'Patriarchal Church' without which every Methodist would be 'consciously incomplete.'[17]

'A Methodist's oneness with the Church above,' said Gregory, 'is no longer a matter of faith and feeling, but of consummated experience.' Gregory also argued that 'the throwing open of the Communion to all respectable comers' was 'at variance' with the vital principles of Methodism and of Apostolical Christianity.[18]

William Burt Pope and 'The Power of the Keys'

W B Pope, who was the outstanding Methodist theologian of the nineteenth century, entered the Wesleyan ministry in 1841 and re-published his 1875 classic, *A Compendium of Christian Theology*, as a second, revised and enlarged edition in three volumes in 1880. Pope drew widely from patristic, reformed and eastern traditions. The major part of the third volume of the Compendium is dedicated to 'The Administration of Redemption' and within it to 'The Christian Church,' where Pope describes Methodism as being Presbyterian in its theory but possessing an episcopacy 'of the earliest type' through its Superintendents. Methodism's diaconate was exercised through various lay officers and the Lord had left the 'Power of the Keys' to be exercised through 'the general government of His body.'[19]

Herbert B Workman and 'The Place of Methodism in the Catholic Church'

H B Workman was born in 1862 and entered the Wesleyan ministry in 1885, retiring as Principal of Westminster Training College in 1930 and living until 1951. He was one of Methodism's finest church historians and among his classic works were *Persecution in the Early Church* (1906) and *The Evolution of the Monastic Ideal* (1913). In 1921 Workman re-published his 1909 essay, *The Place of Methodism in the Catholic Church*. Workman argued that Methodism followed the great Christian tradition in Wesley's union of authority and experience, in its commitment to the creeds, to holiness and to Christian conversion, in its use of the laity as under Francis of Assisi and Wyclif, in its right understanding and practice of Christian mysticism, and of the Quietist and Puritan traditions. Workman argued that Wesley was an inconsistent Episcopalian, who left behind him a church of Presbyterian order.[20]

The Wesleyan Guild of Divine Service

About 1900 a group of Wesleyan ministers and laymen formed the 'Wesleyan Guild of Divine Service.' The earliest known reference to the Guild is 1902 and the last information dates from 1914. In 1905 the Guild published a manifesto, *Methodist Worship: A Plea for Toleration*, by James Johnson, to which the preface was written by the prominent Wesleyan, Thomas Bowman Stephenson, founder of the National Children's Home and Orphanage and the Wesley Deaconess Order. Its twenty-seven pages pleaded with Wesleyan Methodists to adopt a friendly attitude to liturgical worship, and provided affirming quotations from John Wesley, Thomas Coke, Adam Clarke, Jabez Bunting, Robert Newton, Thomas Jackson, Richard Watson, William Arthur and Hugh Price Hughes, to show that services in the Prayer Book tradition were scriptural, Methodist and sufficiently broad and rich to provide a proper and full diet for Wesleyan morning congregations. Both Hugh Price Hughes and James Harrison Rigg were quoted as giving full approval to the Guild's aims and existence. Daniel Hone, an erstwhile Methodist, and a co-founder with John Kensit of the Protestant Defence Brigade,[21] wrote a repudiation of Johnson's Guild of Divine Service manifesto, dubbing it 'the Guild for Corrupting Methodism with Ritualism.'[22]

From Hone's list of condemnations it is clear that the Guild wished to promote greater interest and reverence in all things connected with divine worship, wanted the people's fuller and more intelligent participation in prayer and praise, advocated kneeling for prayer, standing for singing, urged a proper, full and decent administration of the sacraments according to prescribed forms, the reading of the proper lessons, the receiving of the 'offertory' at the communion table, a fuller and more profitable observance of the church's year and a greater frequency of Holy Communion. It is also clear from Hone's pamphlet that the Guild had a list of negative concerns and advocated the use of churches only for worship, the restricting of the Lord's Table to its proper use, the cessation of 'all entertainments' on Good Friday, the limiting of pulpit announcements to the spiritual work of the church and the exclusion of 'sensational advertisements' from all forms of church notices.

The Guild had the support of such Wesleyan worthies as Agar Beet and H H Fowler, and among its committee members were Herbert B Workman, Ernest J B Kirtlan and Sidney Benjamin Gregory (uncle of T S and A S Gregory), with Kirtlan and Gregory carrying the succession into the MSF, where their names appear in the early membership lists of the Fellowship.

Henry Lunn and 'The Secret of the Saints'

One of the richest veins of 'high Wesleyanism' was a deepening spirituality exemplified in the writings of an early member of the MSF – Sir Henry Lunn. Originally a Wesleyan minister, medical missionary and also a Liberal politician,

Henry Lunn resigned his Wesleyan ministry in 1893 (after quarrelling over the select and segregated living conditions of Methodist missionaries abroad). But he then became an early ecumenist, hosting the high-level and pioneering Grindelwald Conferences on Christian unity and editing the *Review of the Churches* (1891–96).[23] In 1910 Lunn was confirmed as an Anglican and regarded himself as 'A Methodist member of the Church of England.'[24] As well as being a pioneer ecumenist he published three remarkable books of devotion to introduce his fellow Wesleyans to the classics of Christian spirituality. The first, *The Love of Jesus* (1911), ran to at least eleven thousand copies by 1933, was favourably reviewed in both the *Church Times* and the *Catholic Times*, and was specifically addressed to 'the people called Methodists.' Lunn contrasted the discipline and fervour of the Methodism of his youth with the half-heartedness of Edwardian Wesleyanism. The writer invited his readers to return to the spirituality of Aldersgate and of early Oxford Methodism, at the heart of which were daily offices of prayer, fasting and frequent communion. Lunn provided simple offices for morning and evening, with evening confession, extracts from Lancelot Andrewes, the Prayer Book collects, some devotions to the Passion, portions of Wesley's *A Companion for the Altar* (extracted from Thomas à Kempis), a selection of the Wesleys' *Hymns on the Lord's Supper*, a Preparation for Holy Communion, the Wesleyan Communion Office and guidance on Bible study, fasting and the use of money. The dedication in *The Love of Jesus* ran, 'To the memory of my friend, colleague, and teacher Hugh Price Hughes President of the Wesleyan Methodist Conference, 1898 in gratitude and affection I dedicate these pages.'

Lunn's *Retreats for the Soul* (1913), which sold eight thousand copies in five years, revealed the compiler's commitment to and benefits from the Anglican retreat movement. The book began by demonstrating the need for retreats, the promises they held for participants and the methods to be adopted in a good retreat. At the end of the book were time-tables for various retreats, including a

Methodist Retreat at Swanwick held in 1912 and a retreat for Methodist Oxford undergraduates held the following year at an Essex retreat house. The major section of *Retreats for the Soul* consisted of extracts from the spiritual classics, including Lancelot Andrewes' *Preces Privatae*, Thomas à Kempis' *The Imitation of Christ*, Lorenzo Scupoli's *The Spiritual Combat* and Brother Lawrence's *The Practice of the Presence of God*, and finally there was an anthology of hymns and Christian verse.

The trilogy concluded with *The Secret of the Saints* (1933), which Lunn wrote to support the work of the 1930 Wesleyan Methodist Conference Committee on Corporate Prayer, of which he was a member. Gordon Wakefield regarded *The Secret of the Saints* as the most original of Lunn's trilogy and a book 'as truly catholic as Wesley's *Christian Library*,' which was part of its inspiration.[25] In his Preface Lunn wrote, 'If we would be true Christians of the Catholic Church, we must enter into a Catholic affection for all … be equally glad of the light of the Gospel, wherever it shines or from whatever quarter it comes.'[26] The chapters featured the need of an apostolate of prayer, the masters and mistresses of meditation across the ages, how to pray and the art of meditation concluding with 'The Discipline of Love,' 'The Vision of God,' a series of meditations and an appendix from Gilbert Shaw's *A Pilgrim's Chapbook*.

Walter James and 'The Unveiled Heart'

Before and after Methodist Union the daily devotions of hundreds of Methodist ministers were fed and sustained by a tiny book of less than 130 pages. *The Unveiled Heart* by Walter James was published in May 1909. Ten thousand had to be printed in that first year. The book ran to at least ten editions and ministers were still buying it as they entered college and circuit in the 1920s.[27] Walter James was ordained into the Wesleyan Methodist ministry in 1907 at the age 27 and died eighteen months later in September 1908.[28]

On each right hand page of *The Unveiled Heart* were two or three very short extracts from scripture or from an ancient or contemporary spiritual classic, with references to the morning and evening psalms. On each of the left hand pages, in succinct prose, was one of forty-nine prayers about the inner conflict, hopes, failures and longings of one struggling to be a faithful and an effective minister. Morning by morning a whole generation of Wesleyan and Methodist ministers took these searching prayers with them into their place of private devotion.

Samuel Chadwick and 'The Path of Prayer'

Samuel Chadwick was born in 1860 and entered the Wesleyan ministry in 1886. During his ministry he became Methodism's most outstanding evangelical preacher and a city centre missioner, linking holiness and social action. At Oxford Place, Leeds, being an expert in Catholic spirituality he led Lenten devotions. Possessed of a Franciscan spirituality, he developed his 'Cliff Trekkers' as unencumbered evangelists. The church historian, John Munsey Turner, referred to Chadwick as a 'high church evangelical Methodist.'[29]

In 1931 Chadwick published *The Path of Prayer*, which ran through thirteen impressions in six years and was republished in 1948. The most startling sentences in the book come in the chapter 'Praying One for Another' and in the section 'The Intercession in Heaven:'

> Prayer finds its expression and availableness in terms of Christ and His finished work. He takes the prayers of the earthly altar and adds to them the fires of the heavenly, and they become acceptable through his name. So much is revealed, and we have no authority to go beyond, but it makes clear that in the fellowship of the saints there is prayer in Heaven, and there is no logic by which the redeemed can be excluded from the ministry of intercession.[30]

Thomas H Barratt and the Lord's Supper in Early Methodism

In 1923 Thomas Barratt, Wesleyan scholar, tutor and college principal, wrote an article in the *London Quarterly Review* under the title *The Place of the Lord's Supper in Early Methodism*, which was re-published in *Methodism: Its Present Responsibilities*, after the movers and shakers from all three of the uniting Methodist bodies had met in Bristol in 1929, on the eve of Methodist Union, for The Methodist Church Congress.

Barratt began his paper by reminding Methodists that Wesley's 1733 Oxford publication, *The Duty of Constant Communion*, had been re-published by him fifty-five years later with a note that he had not seen fit to alter any of its sentiments. In the first and most celebrated part of his paper Barratt demonstrated how Wesley practised what he preached in regard to 'constant' communion in the midst of an 18th century Anglican practice of profoundly infrequent communion. In 1740 Wesley was communicating, on average, every four days. For the last eight years of his life he communicated, on average, every five days and, by the time he received communion for the last time before his death, he had taken communion fifteen times between 1st January and 16th February 1791. It was Wesley's custom to preside at the Lord's Supper on Sunday mornings or, as a preparation for the Lord's Day, to celebrate the sacrament in private homes on Saturday evenings. Barratt also reminded his readers of Wesley's custom of holding a Communion service on each of the twelve days of Christmas.[31]

Barratt then inquired into Wesley's expectation about the duty of constant communion among the Methodists themselves. In the Preface to his abridgment of the Prayer Book, *The Sunday Service of the Methodists*, Wesley had written, 'I advise the elders to administer the Supper of the Lord on every Lord's Day.' Wesley's *Journal* records numerous occasions when he or Charles presided at crowded communion services in London and Bristol, when it took several hours to communicate five or six hundred people. In

1770, in Bristol, John and Charles began the Sunday communion at 9 o'clock because 'we judged it best to have the entire service.' More than once there were over a thousand communicants in Leeds and Manchester, with several clergy assisting, and Wesley recorded similar figures in Newcastle and Macclesfield.

Barratt's third inquiry dealt with the notion that, after his evangelical conversion, Wesley viewed the Lord's Supper differently. Barratt saw that this was partially true. Wesley did remove some sacerdotal references from his revision of the Prayer Book communion office. As an itinerant Wesley did admit non-confirmed believers to communion. He encouraged Dissenters at his celebrations to sit or kneel as they thought best. Most importantly of all, Wesley held, contra the doctrine of *ex opere operato,* that even though the Lord's Supper was ordained of God, it profited nothing if the communicant refused to trust in God alone.

J Ernest Rattenbury

Rattenbury, who was born in 1870, was the grandson, son and later brother and uncle of Methodist ministers. He noted in an article for the *Methodist Recorder* on *The Methodist Prayer Book*:

> At my baptism, I received as a present from my grandfather, The Bible, the Book of Common Prayer, and the Methodist Hymn Book, joined together in one magnificently bound volume, which has always been to me the symbol and substance of my Methodist heritage.[32]

Prior to his exceedingly long and fruitful retirement (1935 to 1963) Rattenbury was a city missioner, a successor to another high church Wesleyan, Hugh Price Hughes, and had devoted the last eighteen years of his inner London ministry to the development of the West London Mission and the opening of the Kingsway Hall. Elected to the Wesleyan Legal Hundred in 1914, as a leading figure in the unofficial Wesleyan-Anglican discussions at Kingsway Hall in 1917 Rattenbury set his face against Methodist Re-Union for ten years between 1918 and 1928. He opposed the 'Tentative Scheme' of 1920 and was a leading light of 'The Other Side' which held out against Methodist Re-Union for a considerable time, believing it would inhibit re-union with the Church of England.[33]

About 1920 Rattenbury published a pamphlet on *The Sacrament of the Lord's Supper*, in which he began to pursue his magnificent obsession as an evangelical sacramentalist, namely the eucharistic faith and practice of the Wesleys:

> The Sacrament of the Lord's Supper, variously named the Holy Eucharist and the Holy Communion, is the central symbolic service of the Christian Church, and has always held a central position in the Wesleyan Branch of that Church. John and Charles Wesley were responsible for a great sacramental revival in the Church of England in the eighteenth century.[34]

Having demonstrated the Wesleys' dependence on Dean Brevint's *The Christian Sacrament and Sacrifice* for the pivotal doctrines of the real presence and the eucharistic sacrifice in their 166 *Hymns on the Lord's Supper* (1745), Rattenbury employed the central section of his pamphlet as a devotional commentary on the Prayer Book communion office, concluding:

> Then we pass into the inmost courts of the temple ... and prepare ourselves to receive the precious, personal benefits of [Christ's] love ... falling on our knees, we make our humble confession ... the minister prays that we may be absolved from our sins ... to comfort and strengthen us he cries, 'Lift up your hearts!' ... with all the triumphant host we feed on the bread of angels ... the minister voices our love in the prayer of humble access ... consecrates the bread and wine acting as our representative ... and God himself comes to us.[35]

As he concludes his pamphlet, Rattenbury declares 'the Holy Eucharist' to be the most evangelical of experiences as it proclaims the finished work of Calvary and invites the worthy communicant to surrender all to Christ. Ernest Rattenbury would spend another forty years expounding the eucharistic faith and practice of the Wesleys, and inviting his fellow Methodists to rediscover the depths of their sacramental legacy. This he would do in three major books. First in his pre-Union Quillian Lectures of 1928, *Wesley's Legacy to the World: Six Studies in the Permanent Values of the Evangelical Revival*, then in his 1941 Fernley-Hartley Lecture on *The Evangelical Doctrines of Charles Wesley's Hymns* ('Dr Rattenbury never preached Christ more truly than in this noble and learned book' – Bernard Lord Manning) and then in his great classic of 1948, *The Eucharistic Hymns of John and Charles Wesley*. Of this, the most monumental of his trilogy, Bishop Ole Borgen wrote:

> For the first time Methodism is presented with a critical-analytical treatment of the greatest treasure of sacramental hymnody that any church ever possessed, a treasure Methodism has largely chosen to ignore.[36]

For reasons that will become clear, Dr Rattenbury dedicated *The Eucharistic Hymns of John and Charles Wesley* 'To the Members of the Methodist Sacramental Fellowship'!

2

Gregorian Voices

The Gregory Family

Benjamin Gregory (1772–1849) who, according to tradition taught himself to read by studying the gravestones in the churchyard, entered the Wesleyan ministry in 1799. He had two sons, six grandsons and five great-grandsons who, together with himself, made up the family dynasty of fourteen Gregorys who became British Wesleyan ministers. Two other great-grandsons of the first Benjamin Gregory entered the ministry of the Methodist Episcopal Church of the USA.

Benjamin Gregory (1820–1900), 'The Great,' entered the Wesleyan ministry in 1840 and was the most illustrious of the five ministerial relatives who all bore the name Benjamin Gregory. From 1868 to 1893 he was Connexional Editor of the Wesleyan Methodist Church. He also played a leading part in the 1882 *Book of Public Prayers and Services* which (in the wake of the Tractarian Movement) provided Wesleyans with their own version of the *Book of Common Prayer* and a revision of Wesley's *Sunday Service of the Methodists*. A fascinating account of twenty-five years of Connexional troubles, turmoil, tensions and tit-bits is vividly recorded in his 1897 publication, *Sidelights on the Conflicts in Methodism, 1827–52*. As we have already noted, his Fernley Lecture of 1873, *The Holy Catholic Church, The Communion of Saints*, rigorously defended Methodism's authentic place within the life and ministry of the church universal. He was President of the Wesleyan Conference in 1879.

Sidney Benjamin Gregory (1867–1947) was nephew of the above and a committee member of the 'Wesleyan Guild of Divine Service:' he joined the MSF in the 1940s and was the uncle of A S Gregory and T S Gregory, two of the key figures in the founding of the MSF.

Stephen Herbert Gregory (1870–1950) was a younger brother of the above and a Wesleyan missionary in North India: he also joined the MSF. He was the father of T S Gregory and, in October 1934, it was he who suggested to his son and to R C Simmonds the name 'Methodist Sacramental Fellowship.'[1]

Arthur S Gregory (1895–1989) was the last of the fourteen Wesleyan ministers of the Gregory family. Together with his cousin T S Gregory he was a co-founder of the MSF and, for many years, an officer and Vice-President of the Fellowship. After Kingswood School he read Classics at Trinity College, Oxford, became Assistant Tutor at Handsworth Theological College and entered the circuit ministry in 1926. He was an accomplished musician and an outstanding authority on hymns and church music. As well as being a founder of the MSF he was a founder of the Methodist Church Music Society, and was the only minister to serve on both the 1933 and the 1983 hymn book committees. On the 1933 committee he was notorious for his insistent dislike of the tune *Beatitudo*, eliciting the famous retort from the chair, Luke Wiseman, 'I think we all know Mr Gregory's *attitudo* to *Beatitudo!*' A S Gregory's *Praises with Understanding*, published in 1936 and revised in 1949, became a notable landmark in Methodist hymnology. The final and deeply moving section of the chapter, *Hymns on Eternal Life,* with its profound insights into Charles Wesley and the communion of saints, was written by the author's cousin, T S Gregory.

Theophilus S Gregory (1898–1975), described by Reginald Kissack as 'the culmination of all the Gregorys'[2] was, in some ways, the John Henry Newman of Methodism: he was remembered both as a highly gifted Methodist minister and as a well-respected Roman Catholic editor of the *Dublin Review*, and also as a BBC Third Programme editor and broadcaster. At Kingswood School he was said to have 'read everything' and was awarded a scholarship at New College, Oxford, which he did not take up until he had seen war service in France, where he won the Military Cross. After a year as the Assistant

Tutor at Handsworth Theological College he began his Wesleyan circuit ministry. (His younger cousin A S Gregory later followed him as the Assistant Tutor at Handsworth and neither of them had any formal theological or ministerial training before beginning their circuit work.) T S Gregory served in Bicester from 1922 to 1924, in the West London Mission from 1924 to 1926, in York from 1926 to 1929 and in Sidcup from 1929 until his 'resignation' in 1935. Beyond his own congregations, where one of his flock recalled him simply as 'astounding,' he had a profound influence on such young figures as Gordon Rupp, Kingsley Lloyd and Marcus Ward, each of them destined for distinction in the Methodist ministry. Those who listened to the prayers and preaching of 'TS' felt 'he touched other worlds and that they were entering the holy of holies beyond their earthbound lives.'[3] One of those who sat at his feet in York was the schoolboy Christopher Hill, later Master of Balliol, who dedicated his Ford Lectures of 1962 to T S Gregory, acknowledging 'a thirty-five year old debt which can never be repaid.'

The Methodist School of Fellowship

In the 1920s T S Gregory became a spiritual director and an unforgettable speaker at the annual Methodist School of Fellowship at Swanwick, in a unique and memorable galaxy which included W Russell Maltby, J Alexander Findlay and R Newton Flew. In 1933 T S Gregory took his place with William Temple and Dom Bernard Clements as a leading contributor to the SCM International Ecumenical Conference in Edinburgh. But alongside T S Gregory the ecumenical Methodist, the spiritual director and the preacher 'who touched other worlds' was the restless thinker, haunted by the 'now' of the incarnation, the Real Presence and the Eucharistic Sacrifice, and wondering if these central Christian mysteries (plumbed and celebrated as they were by his beloved Charles Wesley) any longer made sense to his contemporary Methodists – a concern brought into sharp focus by the impending event of Methodist Union.

In his obituary for T S Gregory, Marcus Ward wrote:

> When I became assistant Tutor at Richmond [Theological College] in 1930 T S [Gregory] was minister at Sidcup and he called on me for frequent help in the newly established congregation at New Waltham. I saw a good deal of him and could not avoid noting the growing sense of disenchantment with contemporary Methodism and the way in which the future was being shaped in the plans for Union. There were many of his friends in the London area who shared my anxiety and probably understood it better than I did. So it came about that a group of us met regularly on Mondays with TS in my room at Richmond, as being a convenient centre. To put it crudely the idea was to keep TS in Methodism, persuading him that the traditional and catholic values of old high Wesleyanism still existed and could and would continue to exist. Clearly in a sense we failed ... [yet] in a sense the MSF abides as his memorial. The little group did not dissolve with his departure. It became the nucleus of the society which took shape as MSF enshrining the values of Methodism which TS loved to the end and to which he contributed so very much.[4]

The Path to Rome

Though the last five of his fourteen years in the Methodist ministry were intertwined with the formation of the MSF, the personal pilgrimage of T S Gregory led him irrevocably to Rome. One of his 'Catholic Methodist' friends ruefully remarked that he took his friends on to the station platform, left them in the waiting room and then boarded a train all by himself! There was a rumour that, in the protracted three-year process of finding a full-time successor to W E Orchard following the famous Presbyterian's conversion to Rome, the Church Meeting of the Congregational King's Weigh House, Mayfair invited T S Gregory to be Orchard's successor, only to be told by TS that he was likely to be following the good Doctor on the same journey!

Towards the close of his Sidcup years T S Gregory began writing his Apologia, *The Unfinished Universe*. The Preface begins:

> I wrote this book as a Methodist minister, and began work upon it without any suspicion that I should ever become anything else. There are questions – so it seemed to me – which must assail any sincere Christian in these days, some of faith and others of practice; and it was in attempting to find a Christian answer to them that I was led into the Catholic faith. This book is therefore the story of my conversion; and perhaps I may be pardoned for offering my good wishes to it, as to a friend who has shown me much kindness.[5]

Those who have struggled to follow the reasoning and philosophy of its 300 pages testify to its superb language, its terrifying erudition and its profound theology, but also to encountering considerable density and inaccessibility and perhaps, like Francis Drake's dictum, it is only those who have 'continued in the same until it be *throughly* finished' to whom it has yielded its true glory. In the process of the book's completion T S Gregory informed his District Chairman, J Scott Lidgett – no less, that he felt in his mind and heart he was being drawn irresistibly to Rome. 'Stop preaching at once,' ordered Lidgett. Lidgett then arranged for a student from Wesley House, Cambridge – Gordon Rupp – to occupy Gregory's pulpit. Rupp later wrote, 'I found the splendid people in that wonderful circuit up in arms, but against the Methodist Establishment and in sympathy for a minister they loved and whose memory has been held in esteem and endearment in after years.'[6] Unusually for the time, T S Gregory had already served in his appointment for six years.

T S Gregory and the Wesleys

T S Gregory had forty years before him as a Roman Catholic but, particularly following the relaxed rules about Roman participation in the life of the 'separated brethren' after Vatican II, he was able to make a number of contributions to his beloved Methodism. In 1957 he was invited by the Methodist Connexional Editor, J Alan Kay, to contribute to a symposium, *Commemorating Charles Wesley*, for the 250th Anniversary of Charles Wesley's birth. Gregory's article typically spoke of Charles Wesley as the poet of the mystery of the divine incarnation in the flesh of his own time and country. Wesley was testifying to something beyond speech that swept his soul to that happiest place, to Calvary, not watching the drama of redemption but as crucified with Christ, as bearing the marks of Jesus, as eternally held in his heart. In 1963 he wrote for David Francis in *The Preacher's Quarterly* on 'Preaching is Praying' in which he observed:

> The evangelical preaching of the early Methodists was not preaching in the traditional sense at all. They were not eloquent Dissenting sermons with headings to be sent off to the printer nor like John Wesley's sermons capable of publication. Their intention was to bring [men] face to face with God their Saviour and to restore a broken communication between earth and heaven ... the Methodist movement was teaching the English to pray as they have never been taught before or since.[7]

A Methodist Roman Catholic

In 1965 T S Gregory returned to his beloved Methodist School of Fellowship to preside for the week at early morning prayers. To those who were present in the chapel at Swanwick, 'the forgotten flame of Wesleyan spirituality was rekindled.'

> Giving thanks – is telling the truth about God to God ... Forgiveness – is God telling the truth about me to me ... by forgiveness God takes away the cheating and brings me home ... The depth of grace is God giving himself ... Jesus, the un-Crucified was the last of the idols ... only in Christ crucified could we see God ... In the cross is nothing but God *crucified before our eyes where we our Maker see ... O let me kiss thy bleeding feet ...* Unveil our face and transform us into Thy likeness, that the Love who is eternally between the Father

and the Son may be our life with all Thy saints in earth and heaven.[8]

Gordon Wakefield had already arranged for T S Gregory to write the Methodist Lent Book for 1966, which bore the title *According to Your Faith*. The book, which was dedicated 'To the Methodist School of Fellowship and to those above all who being now made perfect are now with us perfectly,' is a further exposition of Charles Wesley as the poet of Christ's all prevailing and ever present incarnation and passion.

> There is but one road to the stature of Christ, to have the mind that was in him, issuing in his tremendous mystery of obedience, to live as he lives not by means of an artificial imitation but in an actual participation of him in and through all my experience of earth and time and humanity – *Still the Lamb as slain appears / Still he stands before the throne / Ever offering up my prayers / These presenting with his own.*[9]

T S Gregory was consistent in maintaining that Methodism was not a Church and went wrong in trying to be one. Its true vocation was to be a religious order within the whole church, cutting across the traditions. For Gregory, Rome was 'the fundamental Christ event' – the continuation in time and space of the life of the incarnate Christ.

> Roman Catholicism is the only Church theologically great enough to contain the Wesleyan gospel. Methodism will never be really at home until it becomes Roman Catholic.[10]

The Death of T S Gregory

T S Gregory retired from broadcasting and journalism to Badby, Daventry.

> It was a quiet life, though [he] loved observing the birds and the flowers, the foxes and the dexter cattle. [T S was the neighbour] of a Passionist convent where he taught the New Testament once a week to the small community. He went to early Mass each day, crawling breathlessly up the hill. He had smoked heavily and changing to a pipe did him little good.

Often he was the only person on the lay side of the grille. Our final picture must be of the young genius of a minister, recalled as 'astounding' and high on her list of saints after seventy-five years by one who had known him when she was a teenager, bringing God to many with his insight into the spiritual depths. And of the septuagenarian at the end stumbling at 7.30 am to Mass, offering with the Church 'That only ground of all our hope/That precious, bleeding sacrifice.'

He died on the Feast of the Assumption, 15th August 1975, of emphysema, after a long struggle, though brief at the end. A requiem was held at Daventry, which his cousin, A S Gregory, attended.[11]

Gordon Rupp wrote of him movingly in the *Methodist Recorder* obituary, reminding the readership of the days when T S had adorned the Methodist ministry.

> For a number of young men 'TS' was an inspiration pointing to a depth of spirituality which we did not find outside the Methodist School of Fellowship. Nobody who heard 'TS' preach about the Cross could ever forget or be ungrateful.[12]

Rupp found it poignant to remember how T S Gregory's conversion to Rome had robbed the whole Church of one with great pastoral and preaching gifts. But when Rupp ran into him at the BBC he felt he was in the presence of 'the only human being in a handful of nitpickers.' Most moving of all was Rupp's reminder of how, in the pre-Vatican II era, TS would sometimes stand out in the porch of his local Methodist chapel, simply to hear the hymns of Charles Wesley that never ceased to stir his being to its very depths. Rupp concluded his *Methodist Recorder* obituary by casting his mind back exactly forty years to TS's departure from Methodism – then it was the parting of friends but now it was a re-union.

> The saints make heaven credible for us and now we hail 'TS' with some of those young men, with Alan Kay and Jack Waterhouse and old Uncle Scott Lidgett and all – 'with

shouting each other they greet and triumph o'er trouble and death.'[13]

Perhaps what T S Gregory wrote of Newman's conversion to Rome was a reflection on his own spiritual journey:

> To Newman the Church was a pearl of great price which cost him all that he had, and he sought this goodly pearl since his childhood. Until he found it, nothing else concerned him. When he found it he was a man who had been dead and was alive again.[14]

The Sidcup Retreat – September 1932

The Uniting Conference inaugurating Methodist Union and The Methodist Church was held in London and began on 20th September. Two days later – during the Conference – a 'Retreat' was held at T S Gregory's manse in Sidcup, attended by 'about a dozen friends' including Arthur W Barr stationed in Bristol, Donald R Dugard serving with the SCM, A S Gregory stationed in Sutton, Surrey, T S Gregory, A Kingsley Lloyd stationed in Bedford, Irvonwy Morgan stationed at the Poplar Mission, and (if correctly deciphered) a young minister stationed in Harrow called 'G D Ryder Smith' (who was not *the* Ryder Smith).[15]

A S Gregory drew up a 'Basis for Discussion,' which began with a number of 'general assumptions,' including 'a certain dissatisfaction and uncertainty as regards our own faith and practice ... and the present state and future prospects of Methodism.' Those gathered were seeking 'an agreed course' which took into account that they were not proposing 'to leave the ship' but were not 'content to let things slide.' A S Gregory noted the 'humanistic' tendencies of many Anglicans and Continental Protestants to embrace rather than stand over against prevailing cultures. The counter-cultural forces seemed to be fundamentalism, a Barthian return to Saint Paul, the doctrinal authority lodged in Rome, Anglo-Catholicism and 'Wesley and the Wesleyan tradition.' The trends most feared in contemporary Methodism were illustrated by a current tendency to avoid theology in sermons and the ambiguity newly enshrined in the doctrinal parts of the Methodist *Deed of Union.* In his discussion document A S Gregory clearly feared there was little future in the current 'Evangelise or Perish' movement within Methodism, nor any long-term hope in the approach of the Central Halls. What was needed were 'bellows to fan the spark of the real but scattered residuum of Catholic belief within Methodism.' Evidences of this residuum were the [true] priesthood of all believers, Brevint's sacramental teaching as conveyed through the Wesleys, the 'high Wesleyan' view of the Church as taught by Benjamin Gregory 'the Great,' the Catholic Methodist spirituality such as that of A E Whitham of Bournemouth, the 'vital' hymns in the Methodist hymn-book, the strong churchmanship of Lidgett and Rattenbury. To this list A S Gregory added the far-reaching influence of his cousin, T S Gregory, the spirituality of the Swanwick Methodist School of Fellowship and the quality of work currently undertaken by the Methodist Missionary Society. Could 'some sort of league of disciplined prayer' be raised up to assist younger ministers and students beyond the 'evangelical appeal' to find something 'positive, authoritative, realist and objective,' and to lead them into serious theological study? Those who were called to this 'Sidcup Retreat' were to ask each other nine questions: Do we have serious anxieties about the present state of Methodism? How do we engender 'present faith?' Is the Communion Service we have just celebrated valid? What prevents our abandoning Methodism out of hand? How is the visible unity of the Church to be brought nearer? How does the journey of devotional discipline begin? How do we help one another in serious theological study? Are we prepared to give Methodism, as the home of a genuine Catholic society, a ten year trial? Are we to hold a 'second' retreat?[16]

A Catholic Interpretation of Methodist Doctrine and Duty

In December 1932 Kingsley Lloyd circulated a letter relating the proceedings of the September Sidcup Retreat, explaining that those attending had celebrated Holy Communion, talked together about their own faith and practice as Methodist ministers, pondered the *raison d'être* of modern Methodism as belonging to the Church Catholic, and how the conversation had turned mainly on 'the meaning of the Incarnation and of Holy Communion.' Lloyd reported that the only decision taken was to hold another similar retreat, to which any Methodist minister would be invited 'either holding or desiring to study a Catholic interpretation of Methodist doctrine and duty.'

Enclosed with a copy of Lloyd's December 'Report of the Proceedings' was a 'memorandum' prepared since the Retreat, 'as an indication of the basis upon which we agree to meet.[17] Lloyd indicated that an envisaged 'back to Wesley' movement or society would aim to satisfy the needs of a number of ministers seeking a theological and devotional discipline, and would focus on these needs of the ministry of a united church. The memorandum was properly printed, published and circulated with Lloyd's Report and carried the heading, *Proposed Basis of a Methodist Catholic Society.*[18]

The Proposed Basis of a Methodist Catholic Society (1932)

1. *We accept the historic Creeds of the Church:*

    (a) The Apostles' Creed and the Nicene Creed
    (b) The Athanasian Creed
    NB: What follows is concerned purely with the interpretation of certain articles

2. *The Incarnation*

    We believe that the incarnation is the supernatural act of God, and that he whom we know as Jesus Christ is equal to the Father as touching his Godhead. We hold to be false the belief that Jesus the Christ is any other than the *fullness* of the Godhead bodily; we think it sin to belittle or modify his deity for [our] easier acceptance.

3. The Church

We believe that the Church is the Body of Christ; the continuance of his Incarnation. The Church is inhabited and commanded by the Holy Ghost and therefore cannot in any sense be merely a congregation of individuals, a utilitarian society or anything other than divine.

We accept Augustine's description of the church as:

> That most glorious society and celestial city of God's faithful which is partly seated in the course of these declining times ... and partly in that solid state of eternity.
>
> *(Civ. Dei. 1.1.)*

And the following Declaration by John Wesley:

> I believe that Christ by his apostles gathered unto himself a Church to which he has continually added such as shall be saved; that this catholic, that is universal Church extending to all nations and all ages is holy in all its members, who have fellowship with God the Father, Son and Holy Ghost; that they have fellowship with the holy angels who constantly minister to these heirs of salvation, and with all the living members of Christ on earth, as well as all who are departed in his faith and fear.
>
> *(Letter to a Roman Catholic, 1749)*

4. The Sacraments

We hold in principle the doctrine of Holy Communion, as properly and duly celebrated by the Church, which is set forth in the volume *Hymns on the Lord's Supper* by John and Charles Wesley, 1745.

This doctrine is sufficiently indicated by the following extract from Dr Brevint's treatise published as a Preface to that volume:

> To [us] it is a sacred table, where God's minister is ordered to represent from God his Master the passion of his dear Son, as still fresh and still powerful for their eternal salvation. And to God it is an altar whereon [we] mystically present to him the same sacrifice, as still bleeding and suing for mercy. And

> because it is the High Priest himself, the true anointed of the Lord, who hath set up this table and the altar, for the communication of his body and blood to [us], and for the representation of both to God, it cannot be doubted but that the one is profitable to the penitent sinner, and the other most acceptable to his gracious Father.

5. *The Means of Grace, according to John Wesley, are:*

> Prayer – Searching the Scriptures – The Lord's Supper
> To neglect any of these for any other good work is sin.
> The end and purpose of proclaiming the Gospel is not [our] enlargement, but the Glory of God.

Kingsley Lloyd's circular of [early] December 1932 indicated that a second retreat was to be held on December 27th [sic] with Holy Communion in the new Chapel at Richmond College. Those in receipt of the letter were urged 'to come and take counsel' and in any case to indicate whether they were in sympathy with the *Proposed Basis of a Methodist Catholic Society.*[19]

The Richmond College Retreat – December 1932

In January 1933 Kingsley Lloyd circulated a Report on the *Richmond College Retreat* which, in the end, was held on 29th December. After Holy Communion 'eleven men' met in the common room. Letters received with 'criticisms and suggestions' were responded to, and it was agreed that current humanistic tendencies in contemporary Methodism could best be counteracted by a revival of worship – of 'liturgy' as the work of God. Four resolutions were agreed. Those present pledged themselves to say a Daily Office at 7.30 am and to invite others to do so; that for the present the form should be Prime from the 1928 Prayer Book; that W G Findlay, T S Gregory and Irvonwy Morgan should, 'with any help obtainable,' draw up a liturgy suitable for daily use and for it to be ready for the next retreat; that all present would read Brilioth's recently published book, *Eucharistic Faith and Practice: Evangelical and Catholic.* Those accepting the 'resolutions' and hoping to attend 'future retreats' were to contact Kingsley Lloyd. The December *Report and Invitation* was signed by 'the eleven,' namely T S Gregory, A S Gregory, W Galliers Findlay, Irvonwy Morgan, Donald R Dugard, D Garnett Benson (Headingley College student), John (Jack) Waterhouse (Assistant Tutor, Didsbury College), John R Gibbs, Joseph C Mantripp (ex-Primitive Methodist), David N Francis and A Kingsley Lloyd.[20]

The Epsom Retreat – May 1933

After a service of Holy Communion celebrated by T S Gregory fourteen ministers met at A S Gregory's Epsom manse, namely Henry G Collins, John Crowlesmith, F Ronald Ducker, Donald R Dugard, W G Findlay, A S Gregory, T S Gregory, Edward J Gawne, Hedley Hodkin, A Kingsley Lloyd, David Mace, Joseph C Mantripp, Irvonwy Morgan and Harry Treadgold. A further eleven ministers had written with the intention of staying in touch. The draft Daily Office, which had been drawn up by T S Gregory, W G Findlay and Irvonwy Morgan, was discussed and accepted. Those present stood and 'took the vow in silence' to say the office daily 'where possible before breakfast, otherwise immediately after.'[21] 'Evening Prayer' was said based on the order for 'Compline' in the 1928 Prayer Book. Slight revisions were made to the *Proposed Basis of a Methodist Catholic Society*, including 'the dropping of the heading' without providing any immediate alternative. Instead of 'Athanasian Creed' it was agreed to put 'the doctrine of the Trinity as contained in the *Quicunque Vult.*' The 'Brevint' quote would be replaced by 'our own wording' composed by T S Gregory. It was resolved that Donald Dugard would ask the President of the Conference if a Retreat for Ordinands could take place during the Methodist Conference, to be conducted by J C Mantripp and T S Gregory. 15th July was suggested for 'our next retreat,' provisionally at Richmond College during the Methodist Conference. Representatives from the group would continue to be involved in 'Friends of Reunion' and the Anglican 'Fellowship of the Way.'

The Southport Retreat – February 1934

In January 1934 A S Gregory and John Bishop called 'any brother minister who would like to come' to meet for Holy Communion and to discuss 'the principle of authority in Christianity, particularly as it bears on Methodism today,' and to consider 'any catholic interpretation of the Faith [over] the questions of Women Ministers, South India and the proposed alternative Office of Holy Communion.'[22]

The Manchester Retreat, Oxford Hall – June 1934

A deep and wide-ranging set of topics was raised including 'directed silence' and the teaching of short prayer responses to one another, including 'our young people.' In a careful summary of the proceedings a need was expressed for a school of prayer and for discovering prayer as 'the giving up of ourselves to God.' Morning prayers might begin with 'waking thoughts of Christ,' kneeling down and turning to the hymn-book or *The Imitation of Christ* or *The Practice of the Presence of God.* There should be an adequate measure of Thanksgiving. Evening prayer 'in the light of Christ' naturally contained an element of confession. Use could be made of a crucifix and of Henry Lunn's *The Love of Jesus.* The day could begin with Prime and end with Compline. In the reading of a daily Scripture portion one could imagine oneself being part of the incident or present for the teaching of the Lord. In addition to Henry Lunn's books of devotion, rich sources of devotional help could be derived from Orchard's *The Temple* and *Divine Service* and from [J M Lloyd Thomas'] *Free Church Book of Common Prayer.* There was much to be said for having a devotional corner in one's room, with appropriate images or pictures and a crucifix.

Beyond the renewal of daily devotion a need was expressed for Methodist preachers to see themselves as 'custodians of revelation' rather than 'purveyors of their own ideas.' Methodism has no clear view of priesthood or 'what is conferred upon us at ordination.' There was an undertaking by those present to read round the subject of 'The Incarnation' before the next gathering.[23]

The Horwich Retreat, Victoria Church – September 1934

In the calling paper from Philip Attwater and John Bishop, Holy Communion was to be celebrated at the Horwich Chapel, followed by a paper on 'The Incarnation,' looking at H R Mackintosh's *The Doctrine of the Person of Christ*, an introduction would be given to *The Mystic Way* by Evelyn Underhill and to the incarnation chapter in Oliver Chase Quick's *Christian Sacraments*. There was a reminder that the aim of 'these retreats' was 'to explore the relationship of Methodism to the Catholic Faith, to grasp afresh the original genius and purpose of Methodism, and to deepen our own personal devotional life, so as to be better fitted to minister to our people in their spiritual needs.'[24]

The Fellowship's Name, Nature and Aims – October and November 1934

Hitherto the gatherings and 'retreats' preparatory to the formation of the MSF had been organised by ministers for ministers and although, for a number of years, there would be a ministerial session of the annual MSF weekend, before the arrival of the lay members, T S Gregory decided to involve the gifts and interests of lay men and women, the first of whom was a member of his Sidcup congregation, R C Simmonds. At the time of the Silver Jubilee of the MSF in 1960 R C Simmonds recalled:

> Some 25 years ago, T S Gregory said to me, with characteristic and significant brevity, "How would you like to help me to form a 'Methodist Catholic Fellowship'?" I, who had never thought of such a thing before, said, "Done." He had just come

back from a week-end preaching at Penrhos College, Colwyn Bay, where, in due course, the Fellowship was constituted.[25]

On 27th October 1934 Simmonds replied to a letter from Miss Elsie Wainwright, Principal of Penrhos College, Colwyn Bay, who had offered the school as a venue for the first MSF residential conference. The preferred venue was to be High Leigh in May. In the course of the letter to Elsie Wainwright Simmonds wrote:

> Last night, [T S Gregory] and I were talking to his father [Stephen H Gregory] and he made what at first sight appears to be a very good suggestion namely, that the title should be 'Methodist Sacramental Fellowship.' What do you think?[26]

On the same day Simmonds wrote to A S Gregory, asking him what he thought of the suggested title for the Fellowship. A question had also arisen as to whether the Fellowship should be open only to Methodists who were 'Catholics' and remain a kind of small 'Order,' or whether membership should be extended to Methodists who were pro-Anglican, even if they weren't yet fully committed 'Catholic' Methodists. Apparently T S Gregory preferred the second more open approach.[27]

A tentative booking of High Leigh was made by Simmonds for 5th–8th April 1935 and a duplicated invitation was circulated in November 1934. It was the first document containing the new permanent title of the Fellowship and its aims.

> Methodist Sacramental Fellowship
>
> In the Methodist Church, there is a growing but often silent conviction that we need:
>
> (a) To reaffirm and emphasise the Faith which inspired the Evangelical Revival and the hymns of the Wesleys – the Faith which is formulated in the Nicene Creed;
> (b) To make Holy Communion central in the life of the Church;
> (c) To hasten reunion with the Church of England as the first step towards healing 'our unhappy divisions.'

> These questions intimately concern us all and ought not to be left to Methodist officials. It is proposed to hold a conference at which they shall be carefully and freely considered and some kind of united action initiated. If you are in sympathy with these aims and intend to be present at the conference send your name and address without delay.
>
> *T S Gregory*
> *R C Simmonds* [28]

The Crisis of T S Gregory's Conversion to Rome

Simmonds wrote to A S Gregory on 23rd January 1935 reporting from Sidcup:

> The position here is very difficult. Things are moving quickly and the result must be, I know, immediate resignation. It will happen. I believe, in the next few days. The Chairman of the District [J Scott Lidgett] and the Superintendent [J Cartright Adlard] are acting now to that end and I do not suppose that our friend will either attempt or even desire to oppose them. It is very grievous, as you say – to many of us it is an awful shock though we had cause to fear it.[29]

Simmonds felt the idea of the MSF was too big to be given up despite the apparently 'dreadful setback.' But who was to be the new and right leader without whom 'we cannot go on'? As the only other signatory, apart from T S Gregory, to the circular about the High Leigh Conference, Simmonds felt he would have to communicate, by mid-February, with the thirty or so folk who had signed up to attend. Simmonds and A S Gregory agreed that, even though they thought T S Gregory would still expect to come to High Leigh, he should not be present even if his new 'spiritual authorities' permitted it. Simmonds confessed, 'My word, how difficult it is to write this.' Simmond's Sidcup friends were not sure whether High Leigh should be postponed or cancelled. Between them A S Gregory and Simmonds were suggesting that either A E Whitham or Kingsley Lloyd should be approached to assume the leadership, and they would share their views with their keenest lay colleague in the north, Duncan Coomer of Southport.

Simmonds replied to a further word from A S Gregory on 2nd February, expressing gratitude and relief that Duncan Coomer and A S Gregory were to meet with A E Whitham, with a view to his assuming the leadership of the Fellowship. Simmonds also reported that T S Gregory, who by this time had resigned from the Methodist ministry and was 'under instruction in the *Penny Catechism*,' had already been offered 'some literary jobs of sorts and was about to lead some Catholic tours,' and 'there has been a newspaper placard at Sidcup station today reading 'Sidcup Methodist Minister joins Roman Catholics.' Simmonds was moved that a number of Methodists in Sidcup had been 'amazingly generous in the matter of a private present for the purpose of tiding [TSG] over the crisis.'[30]

The Pre-Inaugural Day Conference at Westminster – April 1935

In mid-February Simmonds cancelled the High Leigh Conference and he and A S Gegory prepared a circular to be sent to all known MSF sympathisers, intimating that 'the resignation of [T S Gregory] from the Methodist ministry and from membership of the Methodist Church has deprived the movement of his help and [the situation regarding the High Leigh Conference] has to be re-considered.' He further wrote, 'those most primarily concerned in the establishing of the Methodist Sacramental Fellowship have decided that it is essential that the Fellowship be formed and developed, that the inaugural Conference be postponed and that a meeting should take place to formulate the contents of the delayed Inaugural Conference.'[31]

Anyone whose name had been supplied to R C Simmonds was invited to a pre-Inaugural Conference consultation at Westminster Central Hall on 27th April. The three published Aims were re-printed on the invitation and a caveat was added:

> In view of the recent secession to ROME of a well-known Methodist Minister, it is thought desirable to state explicitly that the Fellowship as proposed will look no further than reunion with the Church of England and will regard Roman claims as lying beyond its purview. In the reunion of Methodism with the Church of England, the Fellowship would fulfil its whole function in this regard.[32]

The first printed publication of the MSF was *A Report concerning Meetings held at Central Buildings, Westminster, S.W.1 on Saturday, 27th April, 1935.*

The Report said that Rev Alfred E Whitham had presided, with 25 present in the morning and 32 in the afternoon. Those present committed themselves loyally to Methodism, but would work for a re-emphasis of supernatural religion and a cultivation of a disciplined devotional life. Reunion with other Christian traditions must be sought for its own sake. The new movement must be truly catholic and be based on the richness of the Church's creeds, greater than any individual or age can appreciate. The word 'sacramental' was to be retained in the Fellowship's title. At the afternoon session there was unanimous agreement to form the Fellowship and to adopt the title *Methodist Sacramental Fellowship*. The three aims (hitherto published) concerning the Wesleyan legacy and Nicene Faith, the centrality of Holy Communion and the 'hastening' of reunion with the Church of England were adopted, as was a short Daily Office. An inaugural weekend Conference was to be held in August, with extra London and regional day gatherings. An informal Committee was elected consisting of Rev Alfred E Whitham, Rev A Kingsley Lloyd, Rev Harry Treadgold, Rev Edward Gearey, Rev A S Gregory, Mr Duncan Coomer and Miss M Vennell, with R C Simmonds as secretary. Those present urged one another to convene quarterly gatherings centred around celebrations of Holy Communion and mutual support.

A northern MSF group of Manchester and Liverpool sympathisers, seven ministers and five laymen and women, met in Southport on 14th June 1935 and, whilst affirming the recommendations of the Westminster Day Conference, wanted to broaden the third aim (about reunion) to remove specific reference to the Church of England and to affirm a reunion based on the wider concept of 'Catholic' and 'Historic' Christianity.[33]

Alfred E Whitham

Alfred Whitham was an inspired choice to follow T S Gregory as leader of the Fellowship in the turbulent months following the latter's departure to Rome, although R C Simmonds first impression was, 'I thought Whitham was promising.'[34] Whitham was a son of the Primitive Methodist manse but trained for the Wesleyan ministry at Didsbury, Manchester and, after serving in four London circuits, he had three profoundly influential ministries, first at Leeds, Brunswick (1918 to 1925), then at Edinburgh, Nicolson Square (1925 to 1931) and then, from 1931 until his premature and much lamented death in 1938, at Punshon Memorial Church, Bournemouth, where he was also Circuit Superintendent and District Chairman. It was reputedly reported that the Roman Catholic clergy of Leeds told their flocks that they were perfectly welcome to attend Mr Whitham's weekday devotional services at Brunswick Chapel because 'they would hear nothing contrary to the faith.' Whitham's obituary in the *Minutes of Methodist Conference* said, 'his preaching revealed unusual gifts of rapid and brilliant thinking, incisive speech, dramatic gesture, a passionate love for his Lord and his Church, and an overmastering concern for the souls of his people and that as a man he was a great friend, quick, sensitive and deeply affectionate and only those who belonged to his congregations could truly relate how he brought God to them.'[35] Gordon Wakefield thought it was probably Henry Lunn who wrote of Whitham: 'There was much about him of the troubadour and more than a little of the Franciscan. There was in him a beautiful blend of goodness and gaiety. He was one of the gayest and most seriously religious persons I have ever met, and how he yearned to enter more deeply into the secret of the saints.'[36]

Looking back over his life Whitham testified, 'I had [but one enemy] the Roman Catholic Church, which for me included High Church and Eastern Church ... I must, as far as I could, get right with my enemy ... and I have extended my fellowship and enriched my mind and heart with their immense contributions to the Church of Christ.'[37] It was to Samuel Chadwick that Whitham went for guidance in catholic theology and devotion. 'Few people,' wrote Whitham, 'knew how wide a reader that stout apostle of Protestantism was, or how heartily he loved Catholic devotional manuals. He once confessed to me he always had a Catholic book of devotion in constant use on his table.'[38] Gordon Wakefield said Whitham was widely appreciated for 'his eloquent journalism, inspired by the conviction that the life of man is the vision of God.'[39]

The MSF Pledge – the Re-drafting of the Third Aim

Sometime during the summer of 1935 Kingsley Lloyd produced the First Draft of the MSF Pledge:

> I, desiring to join the Methodist Sacramental Fellowship, solemnly pledge myself in the presence of God and in his strength to keep the following vow:
>
> 1 to say the Daily Office of prayer as adopted by the Fellowship.
> 2 to receive Holy Communion at least once a month, after duly preparing myself.
> 3 to submit my mind humbly to the Faith of the Church as expressed in the Apostles' Creed and the Nicene Creed.
> 4 to support with all loyalty the Methodist Church as a part of the Catholic and Apostolic Church of Christ.

Lloyd felt the usefulness of the vow depended on the regularity and loyalty with which it was kept, by each and all. He was of the opinion that failure through personal fault to carry out the vow should be regarded as sin, and that the Pledge should be regarded as a minimum and did not cover, by any means, one's whole duty in relation to prayer and service. He noted that R C Simmonds had an addition to the fourth pledge:

> 4 to support with all loyalty the Methodist Church as a part of the Catholic and Apostolic Church of Christ *and to pray and work for the reunion of the Church Militant into the body of Christ on earth.*

Duncan Coomer of Southport was emerging as one of the leading lay thinkers in the embryonic Fellowship and on 4th August 1935 he reported to A E Whitham, Edward Gearey and R C Simmonds the results of 'a talk' that he had shared with A S Gregory and C R B Shapland, a former United Methodist ordinand. The three of them proposed that 'every presumed member of the Fellowship' be circulated ahead of the forthcoming Inaugural Conference at Colwyn Bay and be offered a slight revision of the Lloyd-Simmonds version of The Pledge, namely:

1. To say *daily such Office of Prayer* as may be adopted by the Fellowship.
2. To receive Holy Communion at least once a month after duly preparing myself.
3. To submit my mind humbly to the Faith of the church *as expressed in the Apostles' and Nicene Creeds.*
4. To support with all loyalty the Methodist Church; and to help forward, as I can, both by prayer and service, the corporate re-union of all believers.

A S Gregory, Shapland and Coomer also put forward an alternative version of the earlier draft of the Third Aim, changing from:

> 3 To hasten reunion with the Church of England as the first step towards healing 'our unhappy divisions.'

to:

> 3 Adhering to the principles of the Reformation, yet believing in God's purpose that His Church on earth shall be one, the Fellowship works and prays for corporate re-union.[40]

The Inaugural Weekend Conference at Penrhos College – August 1935

In June 1935 R C Simmonds, 'the Honorary Secretary, pro. tem.,' called for 'as representative an attendance as possible' to attend the Inaugural Weekend Conference at Penrhos College, Colwyn Bay from Thursday 22nd to Sunday 25th August, under the presidency of A E Whitham. Expenses were to be pooled and any case of need would be met confidentially by the honorary secretary through the equally confidential generosity of others attending.[41]

An eleven-sided Agenda document was circulated by post to the 33 people attending the Conference. After Thursday dinner the Principal of Penrhos College, Elsie Wainwright, offered an MSF update, 'Things as they are.' A E Whitham presided at the Friday pre-breakfast Holy Communion. The first morning session looked at the Daily Office, with draft copies of an MSF version of *Prime* and *Compline* printed out for the participants. The second Friday session looked at Re-union and the Friday evening sessions looked at The Faith. Saturday was given over to The Sacraments, to the MSF Constitution, its Aims, the Pledge and the election of Committees.

The Aims of the Fellowship were agreed in a slightly amended version of the ones brought to the Conference, and now read:

(a) To re-affirm and emphasise the Faith that inspired the Evangelical Revival and the hymns of the Wesleys – the Faith that is formulated in the Apostles' and Nicene Creeds

(b) To make Holy Communion central in the life of the Methodist Church

(c) Re-union. Adhering to the principles of the Reformation, yet being convinced that the divisions of the Church militant are becoming ever more clearly contrary to the will of God, the Fellowship works and prays for corporate re-union of all believers.[42]

The Pledge was agreed at Colwyn Bay more or less in the Lloyd-Simmons version:

> I, desiring to join the Methodist Sacramental Fellowship, solemnly pledge myself in the presence of God and in his strength to keep the following vow:
>
> 1 To say the Daily Office of prayer as adopted by the Fellowship.
> 2 To receive Holy Communion at least once a month, after duly preparing myself.
> 3 To submit my mind humbly to the Faith of the Church as *contained in Holy Scripture* and expressed in the Apostles' Creed and the Nicene Creed.
> 4 To support with all loyalty the Methodist Church and to help forward, as I can, both by prayer and service, the corporate reunion of all believers.

After the early Sunday morning Holy Communion time was devoted to outreach and MSF Publications, a *Bulletin* and future gatherings. Each day concluded with evening prayers. The principal Sunday morning service was at St John's Methodist Church, Colwyn Bay. A E Whitham gave the closing address of the Conference.[43]

The Prayer of the Fellowship

As part of the Inaugural Conference session on the *Daily Office* a first draft of what was to become a memorable collect, *A Prayer for the Methodist Sacramental Fellowship*, was printed in the Agenda:

> O Almighty God, who didst raise up Thy servants John and Charles Wesley to recall Thy church to the work of saving the lost, and didst gather Thy people together in the fellowship of the Methodist church; Be with us their children, and revive Thy work in our midst, that with the faith that inspired the Methodist Revival, and the hope of the final reunion of all Thy people, and the love of Jesus in the most holy sacrament Thy Kingdom may be extended, and Thy glory manifested in the salvation of souls; through Jesus Christ our Lord. Amen.[44]

It was agreed in its 'classic' though not its final form in an amended version proposed by K Vaughan Jones:

> O Almighty God, Who didst raise up Thy servants John and Charles Wesley to recall Thy Church to the work of redemption, be with us their children, and revive Thy work among us that inspired by the same Faith and upheld by the same Grace of Thy holy sacrament, we and all Thy children may, in obedience to Thy command, be made one in the unity of Thy Church on earth, even as in heaven we are made one in Thee; through Jesus Christ our Lord. Amen.[45]

3

Organised Opposition

The September Circular of 1935

In September 1935 a single-side printed sheet was circulated which bore the newly adopted logo of the MSF – a fairly richly decorated Cross, whose design was based on the one in Penrhos College Chapel where the Fellowship had first met to pray and celebrate Holy Communion – a logo that continued with modifications into the nineties, when it was replaced by the current 'Chalice and the World' logo. The officers of the Fellowship consisted of Rev A E Whitham as President, Mr Duncan Coomer as Treasurer, Mr R C Simmonds as Secretary, Rev K Vaughan Jones as Editor and seven other committee members, namely Rev E Gearey, Rev S H Bosward, Rev A S Gregory, Rev A Kingsley Lloyd, Miss E Wainwright, Miss M Vennell and Miss Olive Jones.

Membership was open to Methodists and non-Methodists willing to undertake the pledge of Membership. The 'first' General Conference of the Fellowship would be held in the April of 1936.[1]

An October article about the Inaugural Conference appeared in the *Methodist Recorder*, lifted, more or less without comment, from the MSF September Circular, but by the beginning of December 1935 there had been three weeks of criticism and response about the MSF in the correspondence columns of the *Methodist Times and Leader* and six weeks of correspondence in the *Methodist Recorder*.

The Selly Oak Conference – April 1936

In the broadsheet advertising 'the first meeting of members' people were informed that the whole policy of the Fellowship was to be open to discussion. Membership stood at 187 and was spread over all parts of England, and was represented in

Scotland, Wales, Ireland, India, the West Indies and Australia. It included ex-Wesleyans, ex-Primitives, ex-United and 'Continuing Wesleyan' [sic].

Fifty-four people came to Kingsmead College, Selly Oak, Birmingham for the 'First General Conference.' A E Whitham began the programme by speaking on 'The Devout Life.' W F Howard shared 'in the friendliest possible way' certain difficulties in the path of the Fellowship under the heading 'Criticisms of the MSF.' J E Rattenbury introduced his favourite topic of 'Evangelism and Sacramentalism.' S H Bosward urged the conference to turn its future efforts to 'Young People and Spirituality.' Edward Leach looked at Christian doctrine from the perspective of a Birmingham Anglo-Catholic priest who had contended with Bishop Barnes. A S Gregory raised issues concerning Re-union, including the need to shy away from a Free Church re-union and to embrace a re-union that spanned the Catholic-Protestant divide. Each full day began with Holy Communion and the final act of worship was 'The full Office of Communion' with five Charles Wesley hymns!

The First Kensitite Broadside

In 1936 the *Protestant Truth Society* published a 16-page booklet devoted entirely to the MSF.[2] The Preface criticised the *Methodist Recorder* for keeping readers in the dark about the rising controversy surrounding the MSF, but praised the *Methodist Times and Leader* for opening its correspondence columns on the matter, and was even more delighted that a third Methodist publication, *Joyful News*, had 'dealt faithfully and fairly with the retrograde Movement.' The PTS believed it was time 'to reveal a new movement perilously akin to Dr Orchard's *Society of Free Catholics*.' Exception was taken to the Fellowship's referring to 'The Holy Sacrament' and its advocacy of frequent communion. There were three sections to the PTS booklet. The first dealt in incredibly well-informed detail with the proceedings of the Selly Oak conference and was clearly based on insider information. Indeed W F Howard, in referring to the *Churchman's Magazine* as a 'strident organ,' believed that its account of his contribution to the Selly Oak Conference had been 'violently twisted out of recognition by some "spy" who was present at a private meeting.'[3] In the *Churchman's Magazine* Howard had in fact received praise for breathing 'the most evangelical spirit of the whole conference,' whereas Bosward was censured for saying that he went to Thomas à Kempis next to his Bible, Rattenbury for supporting Orchard's view that 'the Mass preached the gospel,' Simmonds for wanting to preserve the Fellowship's aims and objects inviolate, A S Gregory for wanting to draw near to other traditions that had a sacramental faith, Whitham for conducting a communion service in cassock and surplice accompanied by candles on the altar, Vaughan Jones for preaching in 'a very pronounced Roman type cassock' and 'crossing himself as he spoke in the name of the Father etc.,' and finally the whole assembly was censured for reciting the closing Evening Office before a candle-lit altar.

The second section of the PTS booklet was a list of the seventy-five ministerial members of the MSF re-printed from the *MSF Bulletin*. The third section of the PTS booklet was a transcript of a dozen or so pieces of correspondence, from the press and from private exchanges, which had passed between J A Kensit and various Methodist defenders or critics of the MSF. Copies of the PTS 'red pamphlet' were freely distributed outside the 1936 Methodist Conference as it assembled.[4]

The First Memorial about the MSF to the Methodist Conference

Although 1937 was to be the year when there was a concerted move for circuit after circuit to memorialize the Methodist Conference about the existence and dangers of the MSF there was a lone memorial in 1936 from the Hereford Circuit:

> According to reports received from reliable sources, the practices of the Methodist Sacramental Fellowship have a definite Roman tendency, and are in our opinion contrary to Methodist belief and usage. We view with alarm the existence

in Methodism of such a Fellowship, and beg to memorialize Conference (1) To disown the Fellowship; (2) to call for its discontinuance; (3) to allow the use of the name of Methodism only to such Societies as have the sanction of Conference.

Speaking on behalf of the Memorials Committee, A W Harrison was of the opinion that the report referred to by the Hereford Circuit about what was said at the Selly Oak MSF Conference was inaccurate. He had letters from both Dr Rattenbury and Dr Howard assuring him that most of the anxiety about that meeting was based 'on a good deal of misinformation.' The Conference concurred with the proposal of the Memorials Committee that no action be taken. A further move in the same Conference to prohibit societies using the name 'Methodist' without express sanction of the Conference was not voted on.

The MSF Manifesto – September 1936

At the beginning of the Connexional Year, in the *Methodist Recorder*, the *Methodist Times and Leader* and in *Joyful News*, the MSF published *A Manifesto by the Committee*, setting out 'a duty [we] owe to the Methodist public.' The Manifesto, drafted by Duncan Coomer, claimed the MSF was firmly based on New Testament preaching and teaching and therefore proclaimed the doctrinal and historical facts concerning Christ, believed in the necessity of repentance and Christian ethical instruction. The current trend in Methodism was to present the call to follow Christ without any real understanding of Christ's incarnation, atoning death, resurrection or ascension. The invitation by the MSF to Methodism to make Holy Communion central in its life and worship was wholly in accord with the teaching and practice of the Wesley brothers. In advocating Re-union the MSF believed that the genius of Methodism was to be 'primitive and catholic' as well as Protestant in its churchmanship. Readers of the Manifesto were reminded that the Methodist Conference had declared a statement it had received about the Fellowship to be absolutely untrue. At no MSF gathering were eucharistic 'vestments' ever worn, and candles and the sign of the cross, being 'insignificant' in the life of the Fellowship, had never been discussed in the life of the Fellowship.

In thanking A S Gregory for a copy of the Manifesto, the editor of *Joyful News*, W H Heap, said he would print it as it stood but 'followed by a few comments of my own.' He still thought about seven or eight MSF members had 'real Romish longings and tendencies.'

Scott Lidgett, in thanking Simmonds for his copy of the Manifesto as well as the MSF publication of *Hymns on the Lord's Supper*, believed:

> the Manifesto should clear away much misconception [and] with the aims set forth I am in entire accord, and should have said so in the Conference had an important debate on the subject arisen – [you] have suffered from unbalanced statements ... the essential need is to set forth the practice of the Wesleys in regard to the Sacrament and also to promote a truly Catholic not sectarian spirit with a view to closer union between all those who hold to the head ... trusting that the movement may be wisely and Divinely guided to these ends.[5]

Russell Maltby, friend of both the Gregorys, and a fellow contributor to the Swanwick School of Fellowship, was not at all supportive. He thought the Manifesto concealed more than it revealed and that Whitham was far from being as simple minded as the arguments put forward. Maltby, the brilliantly minded liberal, believed the Creeds had their limitations and that Holy Communion was not central either to the New Testament or to Wesley. There was too much superstition in the MSF about the consecration of the elements. The Fellowship had got its Re-union policy back to front. Re-union should first be with the Free Churches with whom there was 'no fundamental difference regarding the truth,' then possibly with the Church of England and then finally, perhaps, with Rome, where for the present there is 'much untruth – even about God.' Some, like himself, had watched the road taken by those they knew personally such as Orchard and 'TS,' and it was only out of the love he bore 'TS' and Whitham that he had 'refrained with some difficulty' from any public references to the MSF.[6]

In late November 1936 W F Howard wrote a long letter to A S Gregory from Handsworth College. He had gone to the Selly Oak MSF conference with great reluctance. He regarded the formation of the Fellowship as 'the most unwise thing that could be done if we are to raise the general standard of worship and sacramental observance in reunited Methodism.' Howard reported, 'No one will ever know what distress I suffered over the Kensitite misrepresentations regarding Selly Oak' and the trouble inside and beyond the colleges over the supposed influence of the MSF on students in training for ordination. He feared that, had he spoken his mind in the Methodist Conference about the MSF, he would have provided a spark bringing the greatest blaze and explosion since Methodist union. He confided that Bond, the Secretary of the Methodist Conference, feared a 'passionate and useless debate' following his having been deluged with letters critical of the MSF from all over the country. Howard told Gregory how much he regretted the high profile buffoonery – within and beyond the Methodist Conference – of the most eccentric of MSF members, E J B Kirtlan, whom he described as 'that uncertified lunatic.' Rattenbury had himself written to Howard lamenting the ritualistic eccentricities of one or more of the extreme brethren in the MSF.[7]

By the autumn of 1936 more than 50 new members had joined the MSF and three members – all ministers – had resigned. By April 1937 another 35 members had joined and seven had resigned, and by the end of 1937 another 42 members had joined and another two had resigned. The membership was now over 300.

The MSF Annual Conference – April 1937

The programme, the worship and the AGM passed without incident, and the pledge with regard to the Daily office was amended to include the daily undertaking of 'some other discipline of prayer,' which has remained in the pledge up to thc present.

There was, however, a memorable 'blot' on the Low Sunday Conference of 1937 when, during its course, suspicions began to develop that there was a strangely unsympathetic individual who had booked himself into the weekend! Eventually A E Whitham challenged one A W Martin, who was then rumbled as an agent of the Protestant Truth Society.[8]

An Appeal to Disband

On 25th May 1937 Robert Bond, Secretary of the Methodist Conference, wrote to the MSF President, A E Whitham, 'as an outcome of the interview' that he had had with Witham and R C Simmonds. He gave the utmost credit to the MSF members in their desire to promote every reverence in regard to 'the Holy Sacrament' and deprecated the methods of the Kensitites. However, the Secretary felt that post-Union Methodism was still hovering between the clear decline of the old sectional loyalties and the creation of a new single loyalty to a United Church. The Secretary's one regret about the Fellowship was its potential to create division. He had already heard of some form of counter Fellowship being mooted. Though the Secretary would himself continue to uphold what he believed to be constitutional regard and reverence for the Sacrament, he truly regretted the existence of the Fellowship. The sacrament of unity was in danger of being a sacrament of division. Though he believed there were 'large numbers' in Methodism who totally followed the sincerities of the Fellowship he reluctantly concluded:

> I trust while sacrificing nothing of the desire for reverence and the pure spirit of devotion, you may be willing for the sake of the whole Church, and with a view to unity in the Sacrament of our Lord, to cease the Organised Fellowship.
>
> I trust you will not read into this letter any spirit of carping criticism, for that is the last thing in my mind, but

you will give me the credit for sincere sympathy and an earnest desire for the best interests of the Church of God.[9]

The Methodist Conference – July 1937

In the May of 1937 the Fellowship sent a pamphlet to every District Chairman and Synod Secretary, setting out in detail the history, aims and methods of the Fellowship, showing how these were 'in strict harmony with Methodist tradition.' The hope was that between them the Chairman and Secretary of each synod would 'be able to correct any misconception of our purpose.'[10]

On 15th June R C Simmonds circulated the Fellowship with a private and confidential memorandum, attaching the letter from the Secretary of Conference and containing the proposed response of the MSF to Dr Bond. The memorandum suggested that the Fellowship took the view that its aims 'were not sectional or controversial or unimportant, but were catholic, positive and vital.' The vocation of the MSF was to emphasise the significance of the Faith, of the Sacrament and of Re-union, which had now been embraced by a growing number who had placed their trust in the Fellowship. The promotion of opposition and objection to the Fellowship did not mean that its aims and conduct had been incompatible with the standards of Methodism. Until the contrary was established the Fellowship intended to continue.

Included in the circular was an extract from Dr Rattenbury's letter to the President of the Fellowship, indicating that he would sternly resist any challenge to the Fellowship that might emerge in the forthcoming Methodist Conference:

> I am all for fighting this matter vigorously. I am not prepared to be deprived by ignorant prejudice of my heritage. I shall fight on this question, partly because I think the Kensit propaganda is one of the chief obstacles in the way of a reasonable Protestant defence against the forward march of Rome.[11]

When the Methodist Conference of 1937 assembled in Bradford, with Robert Bond as both President and Secretary, there were no less than 15 Memorials about the MSF. The Chester and Warrington Synod requested Conference to clarify whether the Fellowship's beliefs, objects and practices were in agreement with the doctrine, polity and usages of the Methodist Church. Nine circuits requested a definite ruling of the Conference as to whether the declared principles of the MSF contravened the doctrine of the Deed of Union. The Birmingham Sparkhill Circuit wanted the Conference to direct the MSF to remove the word 'Methodist' because the Fellowship was open to other Christian traditions and because it was not representative of Methodist teaching and practice. The Runcorn Circuit urged the Conference to subject the Fellowship's teaching and practice 'to an immediate and searching examination' and to publish the results of its investigation. The Buxton Circuit, with only 30 for, 16 against and 36 neutral, called upon the Conference 'to put an end to the activities of this organisation.'[12]

The Memorials Committee recommended that the memorials should be remitted to the Doctrinal Committee of Appeal. W H Heap, editor of the *Joyful News*, then gave notice of his intention to ask the Conference formally to request the MSF voluntarily to disband. However, seeing the undesirability of a debate there and then on the floor of Conference, W H Heap moved that the memorials should go to a special committee of ministers and laymen for consideration, and report back to the next Conference. A E Whitham seconded the proposal and it was adopted by the Conference. The President of the Conference hoped that, in view of this procedure, 'both sides' would refrain from public discussion of the issues involved. Of the 25 members of the 'Special Committee' twelve were lay, including David Foot Nash and Christopher L Wiseman, and thirteen were ministers, including Henry Bett, W H Heap, Scott Lidgett, Richard Pyke and A E Whitham, with Walter J Morgan as convener. A E Whitham was the only MSF representative on the committee. In the weeks that followed, through the pages of the *Methodist Times* and the *Methodist Recorder*, Richard Pyke, the former Bible Christian and United Methodist statesmen, and W F Howard urged all concerned to refrain from propaganda and hoped that, while the matter was *sub judice*, 'agitators would cease from their work of disturbance.'

The Conference Daily Communion Services

What has become a permanent Conference practice was first mooted by the MSF at the 1937 Methodist Conference, with the suggestion 'that the Conference authorities at Hull next year might be asked to [provide] early Communion services in various churches, and that MSF members might offer useful service in conducting these as convenient.'[13]

By 1939 this practice had been adopted by the Conference arrangements committee and the MSF printed and provided *Holy Communion: The Methodist Order as used at Daily Services during the Sessions of the Methodist Conference.* In addition to the Communion Order there were eight Wesley hymns from *Hymns on the Lord's Supper*, a 'Collect for the Conference' and a 'Collect for Unity,' which was the Prayer of the MSF now revised and appearing in what was to be its most familiar form:

> Almighty God, who didst raise up thy servants, John and Charles Wesley, to proclaim anew the gift of redemption and the life of holiness: be with us their children and revive thy work among us; that, inspired by the same faith and upheld by the same grace in Word and Sacrament, we and all thy people may be made one in the unity of thy Church on earth, even as in heaven we are made one in thee; through Jesus Christ our Lord.

4
Second Spring

The Death of A E Whitham

1938 was the most significant year in the entire life of the Fellowship. In January the Fellowship was devastated by the sudden death of its first President, A E Whitham. He had graced some of Methodism's leading pulpits with his ministry, and crossed Catholic-Protestant boundaries as his deep spirituality revealed the One whom he called 'The Catholic Christ.' He had reluctantly assumed the Presidency of the embryonic MSF as it endured the trauma of T S Gregory's departure to Rome. Whitham had deftly seen the hostile action against the Fellowship expertly removed from the floor of the Methodist Conference and into the safer arms of a competent Committee of Enquiry.

The Appointment of J E Rattenbury

In February the Fellowship was informed that J E Rattenbury had accepted the invitation of the Committee to be the MSF President. Four regional gatherings of the Fellowship were reported in the April 1938 edition of the *Bulletin.* The largest of these had been held at the end of March in Brunswick Chapel, Leeds. 50 members and friends attended with the Vicar of Leeds as the speaker and W E Sangster in the chair! A further 55 members joined the Fellowship in 1938 and there were 10 resignations. The Fourth Annual Conference of the Fellowship met over Low Sunday Weekend at Digswell Park, Welwyn, attended by 60 members. No member of the Methodist Conference Committee of Enquiry accepted the invitation to attend.

The Meeting of the Conference Committee of Enquiry

On 2nd June, at the request of the Methodist Conference Committee of Enquiry into the Fellowship, Dr Rattenbury, as the Fellowship's new President, made a statement on behalf of the MSF. Dr Rattenbury said that he strove only for the peace of the Church and therefore sought to remove any misunderstandings which underlay current criticism. He was willing to make any reasonable concessions asked for. He also begged for a statement from the Enquiry to the Methodist Conference to be framed in a spirit of mutual tolerance. He reminded the Committee that the MSF was a private 'Devotional Society' that had never looked for official sanction. It sought only Methodism's re-affirmation of the evangelical faith in the Nicene Creed, the centrality of Holy Communion and corporate Re-union. The life of the Fellowship was built on three of Wesley's means of grace: daily Prayer, daily Scripture reading and constant Communion. He regretted that no member of the Committee of Enquiry had accepted the invitation to attend the Low Sunday Weekend Conference of the Fellowship.

The Fellowship was surely acting for the whole Church in its emphasis on Creed and Sacrament as counter balances to the current fashions of liberal humanism. A further balance laid on the conscience of the Fellowship was to remind Methodism that its vocation to Re-union must look as much to the Church of England as to the Free Churches.

The key part of Dr Rattenbury's presentation revolved around the possible ambiguity of the Fellowship's aim 'to make Holy Communion *central* in the life of the Church.' He had the sanction of the MSF Committee to concede that this phrase should be re-examined by the Fellowship. Those Methodists who thought the Fellowship's intention was to replace the centrality of Christ with the centrality of the Sacrament were obviously mistaken. Those who thought the MSF placed Quakers and Salvationists outside the mercies of God were equally mistaken. But those who thought it improper that some Methodists should defend the key place

Wesley gave to the Lord's Supper were being less than just. So, despite the fact that Charles Wesley sang, 'this eucharistic feast our every want supplies,' the MSF was willing to look again at the wording of its commitment to the significance of Holy Communion.

Dr Rattenbury took the opportunity to speak of those in the connexion who were not strictly Methodist at all but were never challenged, such as those who believed 'every gathering of the faithful was Holy Communion,' those who were really memorialists, those who omitted the words of institution, and one well-known Connexional figure who had recently advanced the view that Jesus had founded the Lord's Supper 'on a sudden impulse.'[1]

It was then necessary for Dr Rattenbury to address the suggested expediency of the Fellowship's voluntary dissolution for the sake of the unity and peace of a recently re-united Methodism. He was of the opinion that the Conference could dissolve the MSF only by excommunicating all the Methodist members who belonged to the Fellowship – which was unlikely! He then argued that the real difficulty was that Methodism was not excited by the Fellowship's defence of the Nicene Creed, nor by questions of Re-union, nor by its approach to the means of grace. What really disturbed the Connexion was 'our alleged Romanising.' The blame for this panic had to be laid at the door of the *Churchman's Magazine* and the slanderous Kensitite publication on the MSF. The Conference Committee of Enquiry had a duty towards the ministers maligned by the Protestant Truth Society. Once the hounds of the 'Protestant Underworld' had dug their teeth into the Fellowship they 'never will unloose their hold.' The Committee surely had a duty to tell Methodism that the reports of the Protestant Truth Society were untrue. Each of the four most shocking Romanising practices of which MSF ministers were accused Dr Rattenbury personally knew to be the practice of at least four former Presidents of the Conference – and he intended to cite these at the ensuing Methodist Conference! Finally, Dr Rattenbury personally undertook to ask for the resignation from the Fellowship of any minister whose behaviour at MSF events could legitimately be objected to on Methodist grounds. While he remained President of the MSF the Fellowship would do nothing inconsistent with the principles of the Protestant Reformation or with the Standards or Constitution of the Methodist Church.[2]

The Report of the Conference Committee of Enquiry

On Monday 18th July the Conference Committee of Enquiry into the MSF presented its printed report to the Methodist Conference. The Committee said 'it understood' that one of the primary objects of the Fellowship was the pledge to a disciplined life. The report reprinted the three aims of the Fellowship, relating to the faith of the evangelical revival that inspired the Wesleys and which was formulated in the Nicene Creed, to the making of Holy Communion central in the life of the Methodist Church and to the corporate re-union of all believers. The Committee said:

> ... it shares with the Fellowship and with multitudes of Methodists a sincere concern for discipline in the Christian life and for faithfulness to the doctrines of the Evangelical Revival, the regular observance of the Sacrament of the Lord's Supper and the Re-union of the Churches.[3]

With regard to the Fellowship's first aim, the Committee could not discover in the Connexion convincing evidence of any widespread departure from the fundamental beliefs of the Christian Church or its own Evangelical standards. Nor could the Committee find in the programme and methods of the MSF 'the promise of any recovery of the fullness of Evangelical truth that cannot be found in the usual ministrations and teachings of our Church ... and we cannot agree to the assumptions of the Sacramental Fellowship that there is widespread indifference to these.'

With regard to 'making Holy Communion central in the life of the Methodist Church,' the Committee was at one with the

Fellowship in believing that in every church there should be 'a regular observance' of the Sacrament of the Lord's Supper and it admitted that 'frequently this means of grace has been too slightly or casually observed.' However, the use of the word 'central' by the Fellowship had probably been responsible for much of the uneasiness and alarm among the Connexion. The Lord's Supper was regarded by Wesley as neither 'central nor primary' but a chief means of grace, alongside prayer and searching the Scriptures. Methodism would best fulfil its mission by placing 'an equal emphasis' on prayer, fellowship, scripture and 'the reverent and frequent observance of the Sacrament of the Lord's Supper.'

> In our judgement the Sacramental Fellowship has isolated the Lord's Supper from other means of grace, and has given to this Sacrament a position which is not in harmony with the teaching and practice of the Methodist Church.[4]

With regard to the Fellowship's working and praying for the corporate Re-union of all believers, the Committee believed Methodism was committed by its recent Union to this aim. It was committed to inter-church Life and Work, to Faith and Order and to the promotion of union in South India. Not all members of the MSF had demonstrated their commitment to union with the other Free Churches. The Committee refrained from mentioning the Church of England by name. The Report concluded with a vague recommendation that the Fellowship should forgo its identity and be absorbed into the general life of the Methodist Church.

> We are convinced, however, by the evidence placed before us, that the members of the Methodist Sacramental Fellowship would do much to restore confidence and peace, by uniting freely with the whole body of their fellow Methodists in emphasizing the great truths and practices for which the Methodist Church stands.[5]

The Rattenbury Reply in the Methodist Conference

Dr Rattenbury thanked the Chairman and Convener of the Committee for the kind manner in which they had introduced their Report and he noted how mild had been their condemnation and exhortation. But owing to everyone's reckoning with 'an External Body' [the Kensitites] statements in the Report must be met with before they are exploited. Those who had submitted Memorials and the MSF had all asked for the Report and, moreover, that it should be representative. In fact, Dr Rattenbury noted, there were no MSF members remaining on the Committee after the death of A E Whitham and no member of the MSF was present when the Report was drafted. He drew attention to the fact that the criticisms, though mild, were still criticisms. The Committee had searched for the vulnerable points in the Fellowship rather than understanding its essential character. The comments on the Fellowship's approach to re-union were trivial and did not take into account that its new President was a recent ex-President of the National Free Church Federal Council.

As far as its comments on making Holy Communion central in the life of the Methodist Church were concerned, Dr Rattenbury had freely admitted in his submission to the Committee that the MSF phrasing was ambiguous. He had also given an undertaking that this would be addressed. Why then was there no Committee reference to the admission of the ambiguity or the likelihood that the Fellowship would revise the wording? The Committee had available to them all the Fellowship's literature which made abundantly clear that *daily* prayer and *daily* Scripture and a *monthly* communion were part of the MSF pledge. The Committee's reference to Wesley's teaching on the importance of all the means of grace carefully avoided Wesley's specific emphasis on the Lord's Supper in his sermon on *The Duty of Constant Communion,* his own practice of communicating on average every four days of his ministry, and his rubric in the *Sunday Service of the Methodists* for the Lord's Supper to be celebrated every Lord's

Day. Dr Rattenbury wondered if Ensor Walters, the chairman of the Committee, had forgotten that, two years previously in the Conference, he had extolled Hugh Price Hughes for making Holy Communion 'central' to all his work in the West London Mission. The Conference had but recently adopted the Report of the World Conference on Faith and Order, in which 'The Lord's Supper was held to be a supreme moment of prayer.' Would the Conference and the Committee be happy if the Fellowship removed the word 'central' and spoke of restoring the Sacrament to the place it had in the practice and preaching of the great founders of Methodism? The MSF certainly wants it to become impossible for Methodists to celebrate the Lord's Supper 'as a tag-end of a Sunday evening service when everyone is tired out.'

The one accusation that had been levelled at the Fellowship was that it was 'out of harmony' with the Methodist theological position. Dr Rattenbury was of the view that they were not out of harmony with the Wesleys, or Adam Clarke, or W B Pope, Methodism's greatest theologian, or with Hugh Price Hughes, Methodism's greatest evangelist, or John Scott Lidgett, Methodism's greatest living Free Churchman. What the Committee surely meant was that the MSF was out of harmony with *modern* Methodist teaching and practice. The Committee spoke of the means of grace being casually observed. The Fellowship was out of harmony with that practice. What of the omission of the words of institution? The Fellowship was out of harmony with that practice. What of the view that Jesus instituted the Lord's Supper only on a sudden impulse? The Fellowship was out of harmony with that practice. The *British Weekly* recently reported that Methodist teaching about the real presence at the Lord's Supper was memorialist. The Fellowship was out of harmony with that practice. If there were MSF individuals who had been ritualistically extravagant they would be reined in so as not to provide fuel for external agitators. The Committee had been assured of that.

Dr Rattenbury made a final appeal to the Conference to do nothing to discourage the Fellowship. He believed it to be the work of God, therefore God would see that it either flourished or perished. Did the Conference realise the depth of the devotional life of the MSF? This would have been obvious to any member of the Committee if they had taken up the invitation to attend the Fellowship's annual gathering. If there had been such a Fellowship for him to join at the outset of his ministry Dr Rattenbury would have been a better minister and a better man. He had felt God's call to the Presidency of the MSF. His own reason for stressing the Lord's Supper was that there he had met Jesus Christ at his own Table, there he had found pardoning love and a new zeal for evangelism. When the pulpit had sounded an uncertain note, eating the bread and drinking the cup had proclaimed the Lord's death. In this way both he and the MSF proclaimed the Lord's death until he comes.[6]

The Methodist Conference declines to adopt the Report

The Convener and Chairman of the Committee moved that the Report of the Committee of Enquiry should be *received and adopted.* Charles Ryder Smith, an ex-President of the Wesleyan Conference, immediately after Dr Rattenbury's speech proposed that, to avoid discussion and amendments, the Report 'be *received* and not *adopted.*' Almost unanimously the Conference agreed. This had the effect of the Conference refusing to express an opinion on even the mildest rebuke and recommendations of the Committee.[7]

A S Gregory noted, in his copy of the *Daily Record* of the Conference, 'This marked the end of the attacks and controversy begun in 1936.'[8]

MSF responds to 'the making of Holy Communion central in the life of the Methodist Church'

On 27th August the MSF Committee and 'Local Representatives' met at the Charing Cross Hotel, London and responded to what Duncan Coomer called 'the outstanding importance and influence of Dr Rattenbury's [Conference] speech' by having it published by the Fellowship forthwith. The Committee also proposed a revision of the third aim of the Fellowship in order to remove 'The making of the Holy Communion *central* in the life of the Methodist Church,' as promised by Dr Rattenbury to the Committee of Enquiry and the Conference. The revision was later accepted by the Annual Meeting of the Fellowship without amendment.

> To restore in Methodism the Sacramental Worship of the Universal Church, as set forth in the lifelong practice and teaching of the Wesleys.[9]

MSF Invitation from the Archbishop of York, 1938

As a result of a conversation between an MSF member, Rev James Sheen, stationed in Bridlington, and the Bishop of Hull, James Sheen was invited to meet with Archbishop William Temple at Bishopthorpe. Following a general discussion on Re-union the question arose in Temple's mind of an Anglican fellowship working in 'confessedly sympathetic association' with the MSF. A further informal conversation took place between the Archbishop and three MSF members (Sheen, Coomer and Simmonds) on 2nd April. The Archbishop raised the issues of lay celebration of Holy Communion in Methodism and of the level of support for the Aims of the MSF in Methodism at large. Dr Temple was seeking, among other things, to build on the possibility of Anglican bishops authorizing the admission of baptized Methodists to communion at Anglican altars. The Archbishop suggested a further overnight meeting with six MSF members and six Anglicans (2 lay and 4 ordained from each tradition).

The gathering would meet at Bishopthorpe and Dr Temple would inform the Archbishop of Canterbury of the proceedings. During the summer, at the suggestion of Dr Temple, two of the MSF representatives met with Nathaniel Micklem at Mansfield College, Oxford, where there was a helpful conversation about a similar group of Congregationalists working in 'confessedly sympathetic association' with the MSF and an equivalent group of Anglicans.

The meeting at Bishopthorpe was held on 9th and 10th December. The MSF representatives were J E Rattenbury, A S Gregory, H Vavasor Griffths, James Sheen, Duncan Coomer and R C Simmonds. The proceedings of the Bishopthorpe gathering were never revealed, but reminiscing almost fifty years later, A S Gregory recalled, 'Anglican bishops and twentieth-century followers of John Wesley opened their hearts in conference and celebrated the Eucharist together.'[10]

The MSF visit to Bishopthorpe took place against the background of a protracted invitation from Anglicans in general and the Church of England in particular for the Free Churches to adopt the historic episcopate as a basis for Christian Re-union. The 1920 Lambeth Conference launched its famous appeal to all Christian people, including the invitation:

> ... we who send forth this appeal would say that if the authorities of other Communions should so desire, we are persuaded that, terms of union having been otherwise satisfactorily adjusted, bishops and clergy of our Communion would willingly accept from these authorities a form of commission or recognition which would commend our ministry to their congregations, as having its place in the one family life. It is not in our power to know how far this suggestion may be acceptable to those to whom we offer it. We can only say that we offer it in all sincerity as a token of our longing that all ministries of grace, theirs and ours, shall be available for the service of our Lord in a united church ... [11]

Out of the appeal and many consultations there emerged the 1938 *Outline of a Reunion Scheme for the Church of England and the Evangelical Free Churches of England*. 'The Joint Conference' that prepared the scheme had been convened by William Temple and the Congregationalist, A E Garvie. The Anglican contingent consisted of eleven diocesan bishops, an overseas bishop, one dean and two ordained professors of divinity! Of the eighteen Free Church representatives all were ordained except Sir Henry Lunn! The other Methodists in addition to Henry Lunn were Benjamin Gregory, Scott Lidgett and W F Lofthouse. By 1941 the Free Churches, including Methodism, had found too many obstacles in the scheme for it to prosper. The Church of England sent the scheme 'for further study.'

5
Eucharistic Faith

Five Wesley Reprints

In 1936–37 the MSF re-published five Wesley devotional classics which had been at the heart of eighteenth-century Methodist faith and practice. The first reprint was *A Selection of Hymns on the Lord's Supper with a Preface extracted from Dr Brevint*, the second and third, Wesley's sermons on *The Means of Grace* and *The New Birth*, the fourth *A Companion for the Altar – extracted from Thomas à Kempis*, and the last in the first series of reprints, Wesley's discourse on *The Duty of Constant Communion.*

'Hymns on the Lord's Supper'

The approach of the Wesleys to the nature and design of the eucharist owed a great deal to the significant devotional writing of Daniel Brevint (1616–95), who was Dean of Lincoln from 1682. In 1673, for the French Protestant wife of the Vicomte de Turenne, Brevint published *The Christian Sacrament and Sacrifice; by way of Discourse, Meditation, and Prayer, upon the Nature, Parts, and Blessings of the Holy Communion.* In August 1732 Wesley bought a copy for four shillings. In July 1734 he began to produce an 'extract' of Brevint and took either the full version or his 'extract' to Georgia. There is a manuscript amendment to a copy of the Minutes of the first Methodist Conference held in 1744 recommending Brevint as a study text for the Assistants.[1]

By September 1744, if not earlier, Charles Wesley became fully conversant with probably the full 1673 text of Brevint and also with his brother's extract. After what must have been a fairly brief consultation between the brothers, Charles set out to compose and compile, as a joint publication, what became the *166 Hymns on the Lord's Supper.* In his extract from *The Christian Sacrament and Sacrifice* John had kept the original eight chapters of Brevint but shortened the chapter titles. In his versifying of selected passages from Brevint Charles reduced the eight sections to the celebrated six headings. To create the 166 hymns Charles wrote, paraphrased or included from elsewhere the hymns that made up his six sections. There were 27 hymns on *The Lord's Supper – As it is a Memorial of the Sufferings and Death of Christ*; 65 hymns on *The Lord's Supper – As it is a Sign and Means of Grace*; 23 hymns on *The Sacrament a Pledge of Heaven*; 12 hymns on *The Holy Eucharist as it implies a Sacrifice*; 30 hymns *Concerning the Sacrifice of our Persons* and 9 hymns for use *After the Sacrament.*

Two of the hymns are John's adaptations from George Herbert and a third is John's translation of Zinzendorf. Six of the hymns were transferred 'in a cluster' from *Hymns and Sacred Poems of 1739* and two were based on liturgical material from the *Book of Common Prayer.* A significant number of the eucharistic hymns – but by no means all – are inspired by Brevint's prose text 'down to their precise wording.'[2]

> [However] it must be recognized that there are substantial blocks, [and indeed a total of 75 hymns out of the 166] in the Wesleyan collection which owe little very directly to Brevint and one must wonder whether some other recent [seventeenth century?] sources were being massively exploited, apart from well-known elements from traditional liturgies [namely the 1549 and 1662 Prayer Books and the Apostolic Constitutions].[3]

The collection was never allowed to go out of print during John Wesley's life-time, with a total of nine editions up to 1790, justifying W F Flemington's observation that *Hymns on the Lord's Supper* was 'the most popular hymn book that Wesley ever produced.'[4]

The 1745 collection also appeared in the 1773 William Pine edition of *Wesley's Works.* There were two further separate Wesleyan editions, one in 1794 and another when the

Methodist Conference chose to commend the hymns for congregational and devotional use in 1825. Their only other Wesleyan appearance was in the third of the thirteen volumes of *The Poetical Works of John and Charles Wesley*, collected by George Osborn and published by the Wesleyan-Methodist Conference Office in 1869. In 1871 William E Dutton edited an Anglo-Catholic publication, *The Eucharistic Manuals of John and Charles Wesley*, which reprinted John Wesley's *A Companion for the Altar – extracted from Thomas à Kempis* and the 1794 10th edition of *Hymns on the Lord's Supper* with Wesley's extract from Dean Brevint. The Anglican church historian and liturgist, Darwell Stone, made use of the eucharistic hymns in the second volume of *A History of The Doctrine of the Holy Eucharist* in 1909.

The MSF Edition of the Eucharistic Hymns

As a collection accessible to the Methodist public, the 166 *Hymns on the Lord's Supper* of 1745 had more or less lain dormant in Methodism since 1825. After a gap of more than a century it was the MSF that put 53 of the eucharistic hymns, with their Wesley extract from Brevint, back into orbit. As first in the field of the renaissance of the eucharistic hymns the MSF anticipated the long-term scholarly awakening and an unabated liturgical, devotional and theological interest in the original *Hymns on the Lord's Supper.*

Gordon Rupp

In 1947 Gordon Rupp, an MSF member in its earliest years, wrote about the Methodist eucharistic tradition in the final essay of *The Holy Communion – A Symposium*, edited by Hugh Martin for the SCM Press. He introduced the section on *Hymns on the Lord's Supper* saying that the great theme of Brevint and the Wesleys was 'the eternal Priesthood of Christ, made new and present for the believer in the sacrament.'

With solemn faith we offer up,
And spread before thy glorious eyes,
That only ground of all our hope,
That precious, bleeding sacrifice,
Which brings thy grace on sinners down,
And perfects all our souls in one.[5]

Rupp noted that Wesley followed Brevint in refusing to define the mode and manner of Christ's presence:

Sure and real is the Grace.
The manner be unknown.
Only meet us in Thy ways
And perfect us in one.[6]

At the heart of the sacrament for the Wesleys was the solemn remembrance of the availing sacrifice:

Victim divine, thy grace we claim,
While thus thy precious death we show;
Once offered up, a spotless lamb,
In thy great temple here below,
Thou didst for all mankind atone,
And standest now before the throne.

We need not now go up to heaven,
To bring the long-sought Saviour down;
Thou art to all already given,
Thou dost ev'n now thy banquet crown:
To every faithful soul appear,
And show thy real presence here![7]

With the Wesleys, the epiclesis or patristic invocation of the Spirit, only faintly discernible in Cranmer, was restored to English worship:

Come, Holy Ghost, thine influence shed,
And realize the sign;
Thy life infuse into the bread,
Thy power into the wine.

Effectual let the tokens prove,
And made, by heavenly art,
Fit channels to convey thy love
To every faithful heart.[8]

Towards the end of his essay Rupp contrasted the paucity of Methodist eucharistic faith and practice among his contemporaries with that of the Wesleys:

> 'Well, we've had a nice little service,' chirruped a modern Methodist to the minister at the close of a great Easter celebration. Nice! Little! That is a vast distance from Charles Wesley's
>
> The altar streams with sacred blood
> And all the temple flames with God.[9]

J E Rattenbury

Although J E Rattenbury devoted some key passages to *Hymns on the Lord's Supper* in his 1928 *Wesley's Legacy to the World* and in his 1945 *The Evangelical Doctrines of Charles Wesley's Hymns*, it was his *magnum opus* of 1948, *The Eucharistic Hymns of John and Charles Wesley to which is appended Wesley's Preface extracted from Brevint's 'Christian Sacrament and Sacrifice' together with 'Hymns on the Lord's Supper*,' that was to hold the field on the Wesley eucharistic hymns – unchallenged for sixty years. Rattenbury dedicated the work 'To the Members of the Methodist Sacramental Fellowship,' over whose life he had presided for ten years and amongst whom he had shared the eucharistic hymnody of the Wesleys. Nobody who wrote subsequently on *the Hymns on the Lord's Supper* failed to acknowledge a debt to Rattenbury.

His exposition of the eucharistic hymns was grounded in the submission that the 'real presence' and the 'eucharistic sacrifice' of the Wesleys could not be equated with the Roman mass, nor with certain Anglo-catholic theologies, nor with classic Protestant memorialism – but, being faithful to Brevint, it stood on its own ground. 'The Christian Sacrament' was at once crucifix, symbol, instrument and realized eschatology. The once for all 'Christian Sacrifice' was offered by the priesthood of the whole church in union with the one eternal sacrifice and the one eternal altar of the New Covenant. Calvary was once and for all, but in the eucharist it was set forth and experienced as for ever new. Only the corporate priesthood of the whole Church could confer 'valid' apostolic ministry on its ministers. The most moving passage in Rattenbury's classic revolves around his personal testimony:

> A man writing as I am, in his seventy-seventh year, brought up in an Evangelical household, cannot but realize the immense change that an altered Christian teaching has made to our approach to the Atonement and the Atoning Lord. As I look back on a childhood nearly seventy years ago, the difference of the modern Methodist approach from my early days is amazing ... I have memories of children's hymns learned, possibly at [my] mother's knee ... and yet ... there is one hymn which I was never taught, but often heard sung, which ... expresses more perfectly than any of the Eucharistic hymns what all of them together teach ... the central verse has been in my mind all my life:
>
> Five bleeding wounds he bears,
> Received on Calvary;
> They pour effectual prayers,
> They strongly speak for me:
> Forgive him, O forgive! they cry,
> Nor let that ransomed sinner die![10]

Because the MSF publication of 1936 contained only 53 of the original 166 *Hymns on the Lord's Supper* one of the glories of Rattenbury's book was that, as well as containing the extract from Brevint, it contained all 166 of the *Hymns on the Lord's Supper*. For those without access to Osborn's scarce *Poetical Works* or Dutton's equally scarce *Eucharistic Manual of John and Charles Wesley* it was Rattenbury's appendix around which most of the subsequent study and scholarship relating to the hymns was to gather.

John Bowmer

John Bowmer, a member of the MSF from his pre-collegiate days, devoted a whole chapter of his seminal work, *The Sacrament of the Lord's Supper in Early Methodism*, to the eucharistic hymns. He concluded that, when Charles Wesley follows Brevint most closely, 'he is at his most pedantic, but when he passes Brevint through the fires of his own evangelical experience, he is most inspired.'[11]

At the close of his chapter on the Wesleys' eucharistic doctrine there is a fine summary of their teaching on the Lord's Supper concluding with the memorable lines:

> As the Cross is timeless, so is the eucharist. Time and space lose their significance as believers take their place amid those who crucified the Lord of Glory. Yet in the light of his forgiveness there bestowed, they rise with a foretaste of eternal bliss in their heart. In the Eucharist, the Church, as a corporate body of worshipping Christians, re-presents the sacrifice so that its effects become a present reality. It is his Body offering His body.[12]

Raymond George

Over a period of fifty years Raymond George spoke at a number of local and national MSF gatherings. On each occasion – having imitably tucked his hand inside his waistcoat – he would begin, 'Whilst I am not a member of this Fellowship I am in complete sympathy with its aims.' At the 1964 World Methodist symposium he gave the most significant of his papers on *Hymns on the Lord's Supper.* He was the first scholar to speak of the ecumenical dimension of the Wesleys' eucharistic theology. The Wesleys clearly anticipated the recovery of *anamnesis* as a dynamic re-calling of Calvary. They re-introduced *epiclesis* into English liturgical theology. Their hymns on 'The Pledge of Heaven' were now echoed in the contemporary emphasis on 'realized eschatology.' Raymond George devoted the central part of his essay to the teaching of the Wesleys on eucharistic sacrifice. Whilst the atoning sacrifice of Calvary was unique for the Wesleys it could not be separated from Christ's continuing intercession in heaven. *The Hymns on the Lord's Supper* celebrated Cyprian's 'commemorative sacrifice,' in which we plead the eternal and timeless offering of Calvary and offer our own self-oblation to be joined to that of Christ. Raymond George saw a final ecumenical dimension to the Wesley's eucharistic hymns in their teaching on the real presence. Theirs was a theology of real presence which transcended time. The eucharist for the Wesleys made present in time the once-for-all sacrifice of Christ.[13]

Franz Hildebrandt

In 1967 Franz Hildebrandt held up Brevint, Wesley and Rattenbury to fresh scrutiny in his detailed exegesis, *I offered Christ: A Protestant Study of the Mass.* Brevint and Wesley were mistaken in attempting to join the two oblations, Christ's sacrifice and ours. Zinzendorf's 'flirtations' with the wounds of Christ got the Wesleys off to a bad start and these trends were not helped by the 'aberrations' of Brevint.[14] Hildebrandt also contended that, in the final section of *Hymns on the Lord's Supper* – 'Concerning the Sacrifice of Ourselves,' there was a great deal which, relying as it did on Brevint, was 'scripturally and experientially untenable.'[15]

Ole Borgen

Hildebrandt was roundly answered throughout a long and thorough study of the sacramental teaching of the Wesleys and of the eucharistic hymns in Ole Borgen's 1967 study, *John Wesley on the Sacraments.*

> Without a recovery ... of the substance of Wesley's theology of the sacraments and the means of grace, the future of the Methodist Church as the living body of Christ is rather

> doubtful ... the distinction between 'evangelicalism' and 'sacramentalism' must never be applied to Wesley. For him these two aspects were one, and later Methodism has paid dearly for tearing apart what God has united.[16]

Geoffrey Wainwright

The most scholarly and thorough use of *Hymns on the Lord's Supper* came with Geoffrey Wainwright's significant work, *Eucharist and Eschatology*. Published in 1971 it was a response to a challenge from the 1964 World Council of Churches on Faith and Order 'to provide a study of the eucharist in the eschatological perspective.' Throughout his study the work is heavily illustrated by the eschatological verses of Charles Wesley, no more so than when the theses of the book converge with the third major section of *Hymns on the Lord's Supper*, namely *The Sacrament a Pledge of Heaven.*

> It was not until the Wesley's *Hymns on the Lord's Supper* (1745) that the Western church achieved again a rich appreciation of the eucharist as the sign of the future banquet of the heavenly kingdom. The supper is there called 'the type of the heavenly marriage feast' but the Wesley's favourite expressions are *pledge*, *earnest* and the *taste* of the fullness . .
>
> By faith and hope already there,
> Even now the marriage-feast we share,
> Even now we by the Lamb are fed ...[17]

Gordon Wakefield

Gordon Wakefield was editor of the *MSF Bulletin* from 1954 to 1956, a frequent contributor to its regional meetings and Low Sunday Weekend Conferences, and President of the Fellowship from 1978 until his death in 2000. In retirement two of his contributions to symposia relied on *Hymns on the Lord's Supper.* The first was given at Keble College, Oxford in a series of lectures to celebrate the bi-centenary of the birth of John Keble. Only Gordon Wakefield could say that it might be possible to view the Wesley brothers 'in the crepuscular light of historical scepticism refracted by the social sciences,' which mercifully he did not then himself undertake! What he did go on to do was to compare the brothers' shared conversion crisis, shared mission and shared eucharistic theology.[18]

In an essay in tribute to Donald Gray, a long-time colleague on the Joint Liturgical Group, Wakefield wrote a chapter on *Hymns on the Lord's Supper*. Wakefield took the view that, for the Wesleys as for Brevint, the eucharist was 'the means of grace, supreme above all others.'

> The prayer, the fast, the word conveys,
> When mix'd with faith, thy life to me:
> In all the channels of thy grace
> I still have fellowship with thee:
> But chiefly here my soul is fed
> With fullness of immortal bread.

The means by which Christ comes in the eucharist is a mystery:

> Who shall say how bread and wine
> God into man conveys! ...
> Sure and real is the grace,
> The manner be unknown ...[19]

Of the Wesleyan view of 'the rending of the veil' at the eucharist Wakefield wrote:

> The Orthodox believe that the Eucharist, the Liturgy, is our entrance into heaven. Brevint and Wesley rather suggest that because Christ's sacrifice rends the veil which separates earth and heaven, its representation brings heaven to us and we are joined with it without doing any more than obeying Christ's command. There is a distinction without a difference.[20]

Christopher Cocksworth

A comparatively recent and succinct British summary of the teaching of the *Hymns on the Lord's Supper* has been provided by Christopher Cocksworth who in 2010, as the Bishop of Coventry, gave the 75th MSF Anniversary Commemorative Lecture on *Evangelical and Catholic in the Twenty-First Century*. At the outset of his paper he paid tribute to J E Rattenbury who had 'an abiding influence on [his] faith and life' by opening up for him the spirituality of Charles Wesley eucharistic hymns derived from John's 'inspired reworking' of Dean Brevint.[21]

In 1993 Christopher Cocksworth had published his study, *Evangelical Eucharistic Thought in the Church of England*. In his chapter on the received evangelical tradition Cocksworth said that the Wesleys proclaimed the sole sufficiency of Christ's atoning work in the sacrifice once offered but which, in the *anamnesis* of the eucharist, was encountered again.

For the Wesleys:

> Behind the possibility of a converting-faith encounter in the Eucharist lies a complex matrix of relationships between the Cross, the ascended Christ, the Church and the individual. The sacrifice is past and complete but the death is ever new. It subsists in the eternal Lamb. The sacrifice is eternal through the eternal presence of the Victim-Priest who permanently prays to the Father ... the eucharist sets the scene for an ever closer union with Christ.[22]

Arnold Cooper

A moving and contemporary response to *Hymns on the Lord's Supper* came late in his life from Arnold Cooper. Cooper was a distinguished Methodist minister who, with his family, had sustained the death of a grandson of twenty. Faced with the question as to whether there was a hope of eternal salvation for those who, like his grandson Robert, had no formal commitment to Christ, Cooper turned to the eucharistic theology of *Hymns on the Lord's Supper*. Is the Christ of the eucharistic hymns forever interceding for absolutely everyone? Does Wesley teach that, in the end, we can sustain the deep conviction that everyone is held in the all-embracing and healing mercy of Christ until they are saved? Or does the ascended Christ only pray for justified saints? Not only is Cooper driven back on most of the eighty pages of the book into the text of the eucharistic hymns, but he finds himself quoting from T S Gregory's *According to Your Faith*:

> We make our home in those deep wounds the centurion never saw, in the hunger of God for man, in the divine patience of the divine creation.[23]

In *Hymns on the Lord's Supper* Cooper found Charles Wesley profoundly dependent on Christ's universal intercession:

> Look as when thy closing eye
> Saw the thief beside the cross;
> Thou art now gone up on high,
> Undertake my desperate cause,
> In thy heavenly kingdom thou
> Be the friend of sinners now.

Cooper argues that it is dangerous to say that, because God loves everyone, he will exclude no one and in the end all will be saved.

> I am arguing that the intercession of the ascended Lord, his continuing passion in glory, his praying with strong crying and tears in which the church is privileged to share, is God's costly way of bringing all to salvation.[24]

Daniel Stevick

In 2004 an American Episcopalian, Daniel B Stevick, published a 250 page study, *The Altar's Fire: Charles Wesley's 'Hymns on the Lord's Supper' 1745 Introduction and Comment.* For all its thoroughness it is a disappointing alternative to Rattenbury.[25] More than any other writer Stevick provides some clear and precise instances of Charles Wesley's departure from Brevint. However, without providing significant evidence, he takes the view that *Hymns on the*

Lord's Supper 'followed' the original text of Brevint, rather than John's 'extract.' It is a great pity that Stevick did not follow Rattenbury in printing the text of all 166 hymns as an appendix. We still await a detailed text providing posterity with the relevant sections of Brevint and other known sources in parallel with the appropriate sacramental hymns. We should then know where to begin the search for the unknown source or sources behind the remaining hymns.

Collections of the Sacramental Hymns

Over the years a number of writers and groups have shared the MSF tradition by publishing selections from *Hymns on the Lord's Supper*, largely to supplement the dozen or so found in previous or current Methodist hymn books. In 1911 Henry Lunn published eighteen in the first book of his devotional trilogy, *The Love of Jesus.* The MSF 1936 selection of 53 hymns was re-issued in 1951. Thirteen are found in *Devotions to the Passion* by Geoffrey Parrinder (1947 and 1960). Francis Westbrook printed thirteen in *The Holy Communion Service: Explanatory Notes* (1959). The West London Mission reproduced seventeen in their *Selection* (c 1965). The Epworth Press included nine in *Hymns for Holy Communion Services* (also c 1965). H A Hodges and A M Allchin made use of twenty-two in *A Rapture of Praise*, which they edited in 1966. Frank Whaling's *Classics of Western Spirituality: John and Charles Wesley* contained twenty-five. Jack Burton's *The Richest Legacy* (1981) contained the huge number of 122 of the original 166.

In 1995 the Charles Wesley Society published *Hymns on the Lord's Supper by John and Charles Wesley, A Facsimile of the First edition*, edited by S T Kimbrough Jr and Charles A Green, with an introduction by Geoffrey Wainwright. Donald Rogers provided an introduction to a new MSF *A Selection of John and Charles Wesley's Hymns on the Lord's Supper*, published in 1995 to celebrate the 250th anniversary of the Wesleys' first edition. It contained sixty-six of the hymns in whole or in part, and also contained suggested tunes for each of the hymns.

Henry Lunn, Geoffrey Parrinder and Francis Westbrook were members of the MSF almost from its beginning. Donald Allchin spoke at a number of MSF events and Donald Rogers has, for his entire ministry, been a stalwart member of the MSF, serving in several key capacities, including that of Chairman.

6

Constant Communion

The Means of Grace

The second of the 1936 MSF reprints was Wesley's sermon on *The Means of Grace.* Written in 1739 it was issued to consolidate Methodist opposition to the Moravian, Philip Molther, and other quietists who challenged the necessity of the ordinances.

Wesley's text was, *Ye are gone away from mine ordinances, and have not kept them,* from Malachi 3.7. By means of grace Wesley understood outward signs, words, or actions, ordained by God, and appointed to be the ordinary channels of conveying preventing, justifying, or sanctifying grace. Wesley said his own Church taught that a sacrament was 'an outward sign of inward grace, and a means whereby we receive the same.' The chief means of grace were prayer, searching the Scriptures; and receiving the Lord's Supper.

Though there is no inherent power in the words that are spoken in prayer, or in the letter of Scripture or in the bread and wine received in the Lord's Supper, yet God can as well work through them all as without them. The great Christian tradition is that all who desire the grace of God are to wait for it in the means which God has ordained, using them and not laying them aside. Christ has given the direction, 'This do in remembrance of me,' and the Apostle has taught, 'For as often as ye eat this bread, and drink this cup, ye do show forth the Lord's death till he comes.'

All must examine themselves as to whether they understand the nature and design of the sacrament. The eating of the bread and the drinking of the cup are the outward and visible means whereby God conveys into our souls all the spiritual grace, righteousness, peace, and joy in the Holy Spirit. This God provides in the body of Christ once broken and the blood of Christ once shed.

What of those who advise leaving off the means of grace for a short time, to see whether they have over trusted them? Are we to disobey God, in order to know whether we trusted and obeyed him? Some say, 'Stand still, and see the salvation of God.' But the Israelites entered into God's salvation not by standing still but by marching forward with all their might! It is true the *opus operatum,* the mere work done, profits nothing. The sacrament has indeed no power of itself to save, but in God's chosen ordinance the Spirit of God conveys grace to the soul that trusts in him. We use the ordained means of grace not for their own sake, but for the renewal of the soul in righteousness and true holiness.

'A Companion for the Altar'

The fourth of the 1936 MSF reprints, following on from a sermon on *The New Birth,* was Wesley's extract from Thomas à Kempis, *A Companion for the Altar.*

After the Bible *The Imitation of Christ* is reckoned to be the most printed book in the world. First published in the Netherlands in 1420 it was first translated into English in 1470. By 1640 there were forty-six English editions. Along with Jeremy Taylor's *Holy Living* and *Holy Dying* it was the *Imitation* that awakened Wesley's devotional life and, in 1725, became the turning-point of his life. In that year Betty Kirkham encouraged Wesley to read the *Imitation.* Initially he was not sure about it, but was persuaded by his mother to persevere until he believed. He testified, 'the religion of the heart now appeared to me in a stronger light than ever it had done before.'[1]

Wesley's first acquaintance with the *Imitation* was in the version by Dean George Stanhope, *The Christian's Pattern,* printed in 1632, but in July 1732 Wesley bought a 1677 edition by John Worthington entitled *Christian Pattern.* Worthington's was a more dignified and more accurate version of the *Imitation.*[2]

In his journal for New Year's Eve 1734 John Byrom noted that Charles Rivington, the printer, was bringing out a 'new edition' of Thomas à Kempis and that Wesley was one of those who undertook 'to overlook it.' In 1735, having procured several Latin versions of the *Imitation*, Wesley took Worthington's text and used it as the basis of his own edition of à Kempis – a beautifully produced 350 page volume, with a title page in black and red:

> *The Christian's Pattern or a Treatise of the Imitation of Christ written originally in Latin by Thomas à Kempis with a Preface containing an Account of the Usefulness of this Treatise, Directions for Reading it with Advantage and likewise an account of this Edition, Compared with the Original, and corrected throughout by John Wesley, M.A. Fellow of Lincoln College, Oxon.*

In 1735 Wesley also published a much cheaper pocket edition of his à Kempis with a shortened preface. In 1741 Wesley authorized an even more popular book, *An Extract of the Christian's Pattern*. This was the version which Wesley urged upon his preachers at the 1746 Methodist Conference. A further abridgement went into the 1771-74 edition of *Wesley's Works*.

In 1742 Wesley published an extract from Book Four of the *Imitation* on the Holy Communion. This he entitled:

A COMPANION for the ALTAR,
extracted from Thomas à Kempis
by JOHN WESLEY M.A., Fellow of Lincoln College, Oxon

Between 1742 and Wesley's death in 1791 there were eight editions of *A Companion for the Altar*. After the tenth edition of 1792 there were no other editions until, in 1871, it appeared in Dutton's Anglo-Catholic publication, *The Eucharistic Manuals of John and Charles Wesley*.[3]

Apart from its inclusion in Henry Lunn's manual of devotion, *The Love of Jesus*, in 1911, there was no separate Methodist publication of *A Companion for the Altar* between 1792 and the MSF reprint of 1936 – that is from the death of Wesley until four years after Methodist Union – a gap of 144 years! (There is every indication from the lay out and printer's blocks that even the MSF edition of *A Companion for the Altar* – as indeed the MSF edition of *Hymns on the Lord's Supper* – had been designed and printed for the MSF with a copy of Dutton's 1871 edition in the hands of their Southport printer.)

How strange it was then and how uncomfortable it is still to find Wesley – in a pamphlet of forty pages – urging the Blessed Sacrament on the Methodist people, both as a gift to the faithful communicant and as a blessing to the devout celebrant.

Highlights from 'A Companion for the Altar, extracted from Thomas à Kempis by John Wesley'

Chapter I

With how great Reverence Christ ought to be received

... Thou commandest me to come confidently unto Thee, if I will have part with Thee; to receive the food of immortality, if I desire to obtain everlasting glory. O the admirable and hidden grace of this Sacrament, which such as will be slaves unto sin cannot experience! In this Sacrament spiritual grace is given, the strength which was lost is restored in the soul ...

Chapter II

That the great Goodness and Love of God is exhibited to Man in this Sacrament

... In confidence of Thy goodness, I come, O Lord, a sick [soul] unto my Saviour, hungry and thirsty to the fountain of life, needy to the king of heaven, a servant unto my Lord, a creature to my Creator: disconsolate to Thee my merciful Comforter ... O most gracious Jesus, how great reverence and thanks, together with perpetual praise, are due unto Thee for the receiving of Thy sacred Body, whose preciousness none is able to express!

Chapter III

That it is profitable to communicate often

... I desire to receive Thee now with devotion and reverence. I long to bring Thee into my house, that with Zaccheus I may be blessed by Thee, and numbered amongst the children of Abraham. My soul thirsteth to receive Thy Body and Blood, my heart desireth to be united with Thee. Let heaven and earth, and all the hosts of them, be silent in Thy presence ...

Chapter IV

That many Gifts are bestowed upon them that communicate devoutly

... My Lord God, prevent Thy servant with the blessings of Thy goodness, that I may approach devoutly to Thy glorious Sacrament ... Enlighten also my eyes to behold so great a mystery, and strengthen me to believe it with steady faith ... What therefore shall I, unworthy sinner, dust and ashes, be able to comprehend of so high and sacred a mystery ... hereby my vices are cured, my passions bridled, temptations overcome, grace infused, holiness increased, faith confirmed, hope strengthened, and love inflamed ...

Chapter V

Of the examining our Conscience, and giving up ourselves to God

... Above all things, thou oughtest to receive this Sacrament with great humility of heart, and lowly reverence ... And, if thou hast time, confess unto God in the secret of thine heart all the miseries of thy disordered passions ... So unwatchful over thy outward senses, so often entangled with vain imaginations ... So negligent and cold in prayer, so un-devout in celebrating, so dry in receiving ...

Chapter VI

That we ought to offer up ourselves, and all that is ours, unto God, and to pray for all

... Thine, O Lord, are all things that are in heaven and in earth. I desire to offer up myself unto Thee, as a free oblation, and to remain always Thine. O Lord, in the simplicity of my heart I offer myself unto Thee this day, for a sacrifice of perpetual praise, to be Thy servant for ever ... Consume and burn them all with the fire of Thy love ...

Chapter VII

That the Body of Christ, and the Holy Scripture, are most necessary unto a faithful Soul

... it would be a sweet thing unto me to pour out tears from the very bottom of my heart in Thy presence: and with holy Magdalene to wash Thy feet with my tears. But where is this devotion? Surely in the sight of Thee and Thy holy angels my whole heart should be inflamed, and even weep for joy! For I enjoy Thee in the Sacrament truly present, though hidden under another representation ... O how great and honourable is the office of God's ministers, to whom it is given with sacred words to consecrate the Sacrament to the Lord of glory, with their lips to bless, with their hands to hold, with their mouth to receive, and also to administer it to others ... Nothing but what is holy, no word but good and profitable, ought to proceed from his mouth who so often receiveth the Sacrament of Christ.

Chapter VIII

How he who is to communicate ought to prepare

Christ speaks

... Make ready and adorn for Me the great chamber, and I will keep with thee the Passover among My disciples ... and think of nothing else. Thou art of mere grace and favour suffered to come to My table.

Chapter IX

That we ought to desire with our whole heart to be united unto Christ in the Sacrament

... O unspeakable grace! O admirable condescension! O infinite love singularly bestowed ... But what shall I give unto the Lord in return of His grace, for so eminent an expression of love? ... Be merciful unto me, good Jesus, sweet and gracious Lord, and grant me thy poor needy creature, to feel sometimes at least, in this Holy Communion, somewhat of Thy tender cordial affection ...

Chapter X

How the Grace of Devotion is obtained

Thou oughtest to humble thyself, when thou feelest little or no devotion; and yet not to be too much dejected, nor to grieve inordinately. God often giveth in a moment that which He hath a long time denied ...

Chapter XI

That we ought to lay open our necessities to Christ, and crave His Grace

... Behold, I stand before Thee poor and naked, calling for grace, and craving mercy. Refresh Thy hungry beggar, inflame my coldness with the fire of Thy love; enlighten my blindness with the brightness of Thy presence ... For Thou only art my meat and drink, my love and my joy, my sweetness and all my good.

Chapter XII

Of vehement Desire to receive Christ

... My Lord God, my Creator and Redeemer! I desire to receive Thee this day, with such affection, reverence, praise, and honour, with such gratitude, worthiness, and love, with such faith, hope and purity as Thy most holy mother, the Virgin Mary, received Thee when she humbly answered the angel. Behold the handmaid of the Lord, let it be done unto me according to Thy word ... And let all that reverently celebrate Thy most high Sacrament find grace and mercy at Thy hands.

The Fellowship was to return to the *Imitation* in 2006, when Robert Jeffrey gave the MSF Annual Lecture at the Edinburgh

Methodist Conference on *Imitating Christ: Wesley's 'Christian Pattern' and Spirituality for Today*, which the lecturer dedicated to Gordon Wakefield.

'The Duty of Constant Communion'

The last of the 1936–37 MSF 'Wesley Reprints' was Wesley's sermon, *The Duty of Constant Communion*, which was re-published by the Fellowship in the 1960s. The sermon invariably has Wesley's note at its head.

> The following Discourse was written above fifty-and-five years ago, for use of my pupils at Oxford. I have added very little, but retrenched much; as I then used more words than I do now. But, I thank God, I have not yet seen cause to alter my sentiments in any point which is therein delivered. 1788 J.W.[4]

Wesley first 'published' the 'discourse' in the *Arminian Magazine* for 1787, with an annotation that it had been 'written' in Oxford, on 19 February 1731/2. The Wesley scholar, Albert Outler, advanced the theory that Wesley had based his Oxford 'discourse' on a published exhortation by his father, Samuel Wesley, about 'frequent communion.'[5]

In the 1970s Ole Borgen studied a copy of Wesley's original hand-written script. He confirmed that, like a number of his key sacramental tracts, Wesley's Oxford discourse was not primarily his own work, but the source was not his father. As much as a fifth of Wesley's Oxford discourse was either paraphrased or verbatim quotes from the work of the non-Juror, Robert Nelson, *The Great Duty of Frequenting the Christian Sacrifice and the Nature of the Preparation Required, with Suitable Devotions* (1706). Other material was taken from William Beveridge's *The Great Necessity and Advantage of Frequent Communion* (1710), and to some of his own material Wesley added phrases from the Book of Common Prayer.[6]

Richard Heitzenrater established that Wesley's first version of the Oxford discourse was entitled *The Duty of Receiving the Lord's Supper* and only subsequently did he settle on the title *The Duty of Constant Communion.* The shift of emphasis from

Nelson's 'frequenting the Christian sacrifice' to Wesley's 'constant communion' may have been suggested by Arthur Bury's tract of 1681, *The Constant Communicant*. Bury was Rector of Exeter College, Oxford, and his tract was also read by the Oxford Methodists.[7]

In his discourse Wesley argued that the duty of 'constant communion' was a response to Christ's command. In the sacrament Christ offers forgiveness, strength and refreshment. At the Lord's Table we are one with the first Christians who frequented the sacrament every Lord's Day. Faithful to the gospels and to St. Paul we recall the institution of the outward signs of the inward grace of the body and blood of Christ. Christians do not communicate with measured frequency but constantly, that is, as often as they can.

The time to obey Christ's command to 'Do this' is now. The sacrament is a means to holiness on earth and to everlasting glory in heaven. The wise seek the mercy of Christ at every opportunity. If you are 'unworthy' to receive *this* mercy you are unworthy to receive *any* mercy, but no one through unworthiness ever draws back from God's mercy. The only unworthiness that is dangerous at the sacrament is not discerning the Lord's body and blood.

Where does the Bible teach us to atone for the breaking of one commandment – our sinning – by breaking another – refusing to come to the Table? Lack of preparation is no cause for neglecting the sacrament. The only requirement is repentance. To be worthy of the sacrament is impossible. Our great reverence for the sacrament is a reason for receiving it, not abstaining from it. Receiving the sacrament is not about how we feel at the time but that we have been obedient. When the Prayer Book bids us communicate at least three times a year it is a minimum and not a guide or restriction. Finally, Wesley wrote that the Prayer Book enjoined the Communion Service every Sunday and holy day of the year. Any who have neglected the sacrament should by the grace of God come to a better mind.[8]

7

Vital Elements

Rattenbury's Manifesto

In 1936 J Ernest Rattenbury published his 180-page book, *Vital Elements of Public Worship*, which the Epworth Press kept in print until 1954. In many ways it stood as the manifesto of the MSF. It was dedicated to J Scott Lidgett, 'A great Protestant and Free Churchman who always cherished and affirmed our Catholic heritage.' The thrust of the book was a need for Methodism to rediscover its continuity with the early church, the requirement for objectivity in worship, the restoration of a balance between word and sacrament and a return to the theology that had driven the Eucharistic faith and practice of the Wesleys. The book concluded with a devotional commentary on the Prayer Book communion office.

With almost thirty years of retirement ahead of him Dr Rattenbury was to provide huge encouragement to the MSF, and to assist in consolidating the advantages he had won for the Fellowship in the courts of the connexion. Under his leadership and his colleagueship with K Vaughan Jones, the MSF editor, the Fellowship formed a theological committee to build up its publishing programme. Rattenbury encouraged an informal gathering during the Methodist Conference, helped to draw seventy members to the Weekend Conference of 1939, and assisted in the push that increased the membership by 1939 to 320. He welcomed a representative of Archbishop Temple to the Low Sunday Weekend Conference of that year, and fittingly marked the death of one of the Fellowship's great icons and one of his own heroes, the Anglican-Methodist Sir Henry Lunn.[1]

The Fellowship welcomed the publication by Oxford University Press of the magisterial collection of essays by the 'High Genevans' on *Christian Worship*. Edited by Nathaniel Micklem, it proved to be the manifesto of scholarly catholic

Presbyterians and Congregationalists of the calibre of Wheeler Robinson, T W Manson, C H Dodd, James Moffatt, C J Cadoux, J S Whale, E R Micklem, A G Matthews and Nathaniel Micklem himself.[2]

The Liverpool Methodist Conference of 1939 came to be regarded by the Fellowship as something of a landmark, since they had persuaded the Conference Arrangements Committee to permit the MSF to hold services of Holy Communion on seven mornings of Conference. Though attendances were small the Fellowship rejoiced that, in the following year, Conference decided to follow the precedent of a daily celebration. The Fellowship hoped that 'the disorderly Communion service in the Conference Hall' had gone for ever.

Anglicans and Orthodox

By the beginning of 1940 it was obvious that the Low Sunday Weekend Conference would need to be cancelled, though Dr Rattenbury recalled, from the previous World War, that conflict would drive more people towards Holy Communion! 1940 also marked the beginning of support for the Fellowship from the Orthodox scholar and ecumenist, Nicholas Zernov, who spoke at the MSF Northern Meeting in Bradford and was eager to maintain contact between the MSF and the Anglican-Orthodox Fellowship of St Alban and St Sergius. It was also the year a young man from Crewe, by the name of Gordon Wakefield, joined the Fellowship. Dr Rattenbury now retreated to rural Cumberland to avoid the London bombing. 'Dr. Rattenbury is at present in Cumberland, and though his interest in the MSF is as keen as ever he is unable to face the strain of travel *and discussion.*' An instruction was given to members coming to hear Eric Mascall at the Residential Conference of 1942 that 'owing to special war conditions they will bring their own butter, sugar and breakfast bacon.' One member reported on Eric Mascall's papers, 'He was not academic, but neither did he refuse any theological fences. He was fundamental. He was absorbingly interesting and he was at home.'[3]

Surviving in War-time

The MSF Conference of April 1943, scheduled for Sunbury-on-Thames, was cancelled, but the recruitment of new members continued with the addition of two figures who were to make a significant contribution to the Fellowship, Leslie Orchard and Arthur Saunders. The seventh MSF Annual Conference of 1943 was re-scheduled for October at Central Hall, Westminster with sleeping accommodation in the Hall shelter! Ministerial members met for the first hour on their own! At the MSF Committee Meeting held at Wesley's Chapel, City Road there was approval for the proposal 'that all ministers belonging to the MSF should maintain a full Communion Service once a month, with Creed, as the main Morning Service' and that 'Re-union schemes for members of the MSF must include the Church of England.' The MSF Annual Conference for 1944, scheduled for April at the Central Hall, Westminster, was postponed.

Is the Fellowship to continue?

In November 1945, after Dr Rattenbury's return to London, the Committee met again. There was a wry lament from the MSF stalwart, C R B Shapland, 'Today if we are remembered at all in Methodism, it is as a rather quaint people with a fondness for Holy Communion and an addiction to ecclesiastical trimmings.' Francis Westbrook commented, 'Since Wesley's death Methodism has been growing from a movement into a Church.'[4] This was in slight contrast to the oft repeated remark of A S Gregory, 'Methodism has always been strong as a society and weak as a church.'

For over thirty years, from March 1946 until Kingsway Hall was closed in the late 1970s, the MSF began to support and then supply celebrants for a mid-week Communion Service. Norman Beasley and other MSF London secretaries rendered sterling service for many years in drawing up a quarterly rota. There was a report of the decision from the London MSF meeting: 'From Friday 1st March 1946 there will be a weekly celebration of Holy Communion in the Little Chapel at Kingsway Hall at 12.30 pm at which Dr Rattenbury will officiate and give a short address. MSF members are urged to give this service their support and to find in it a strengthening of their own Fellowship.'[5]

The Fellowship had not held a national gathering in the years 1944 and 1945, but in October 1946 the Fellowship met at Kingsway Hall for its Eighth Conference and took a number of decisions. Eighty members had indicated their intention to come to Kingsway Hall for the Conference. Thirty members crowded into the Little Chapel for the Friday noon Communion. Dr Rattenbury presided at a ministers' meeting in the afternoon. Fifty members attended the Fellowship's Annual Meeting on the Friday evening. W H Gunton made a formal proposal that the Fellowship should continue and this was agreed unanimously. The Saturday morning Committee met at Wesley's Chapel and authorised a fifth printing of the popular leaflet, *What is the MSF?* The Weekend Conference concluded with Holy Communion at Hinde Street at which Dr Rattenbury was the preacher.[6]

From 1947 the Fellowship decided that, in addition to the President of MSF, the Committee needed its own chairman. The first to occupy this position was H Vavasor Griffiths, who had already been a principal and guiding light alongside Dr Rattenbury, A S Gregory and R C Simmonds. The need for the whole Fellowship to have a Chair as well as a President came much later, in the late 1960s.

Dom Gregory Dix

Although Dom Gregory Dix's magisterial work, *The Shape of the Liturgy*, was published in 1945 Dr Rattenbury's review of its 750 pages went to press only in the late autumn of 1946. He gave Dix's *magnum opus* a good review, at the end of which he couldn't resist putting the question, 'Would not Gregory Dix agree with Charles Wesley when he wrote:

Ask the Father's Wisdom how!
Him that did the means ordain!
Angels round our altars bow,
To search it out in vain.[7]

It was a great delight for the Fellowship to read, in Gregory Dix's *Introduction*, about 'a number of movements for the deepening of the Christian idea and practice of worship [including] ... the *Wesleyan* [sic] *Sacramental Fellowship*.'[8]

The Church of South India

September 1947 saw the inauguration of the Church of South India, bringing together over a million Christians – Anglicans, Methodists, Congregationalists and Presbyterians – in a united church embracing the threefold ministry of bishop, presbyter and deacon. Its new bishops were drawn from all four traditions and ordained in the historic succession. Bishop Lesslie Newbigin warned that if, after forty years, the parent churches had not entered into organic union themselves then in many ways the CSI would have failed! Marcus Ward, a founding father of the MSF, was on the CSI negotiating committee and would go on to be a member of the Anglican Methodist Conversations. In January 1947 he contributed an article on the CSI negotiations to the *MSF Bulletin*.[9]

A Cumbrian Outpost

Those joining the Fellowship in 1947 included Stella Buckley, senior mistress at Penrith Grammar School from 1942 to 1965. Newly appointed to Cumbria she formed a friendship with A S Gregory who, by 1946, was stationed in Kendal, and with Dr Rattenbury who had spent the war years in the nearby Kirkoswald Circuit with Colonel and Mrs Cecil Thompson of Nunwick Hall. (It was to the Thompsons, in 1956, that Dr Rattenbury dedicated the last of his books on the Christian Year, *Festivals and Saints Days*.)[10]

Every year Dr Rattenbury returned to Wordsworth Street Chapel, Penrith to preach on the successive Sundays of August while the town ministers took their holidays, moved circuit or preached in the country chapels. In the 1950s Frank Ward, a stalwart ex PM minister and the Circuit Superintendent, would pass the George Hotel in Penrith and, seeing Stella Buckley and Dr Rattenbury sharing coffee in the window seat, would remark, 'There's Stella dining with the Pope!' When he was nine or ten and in the Wordsworth Street Sunday School the present author remembers being taken to shake hands with the ancient Dr Rattenbury, little knowing what a long shadow the venerable patriarch would cast on his life. Later, as a pupil and sixth-former at Penrith Grammar School, the author came under the spell of Stella Buckley's Cambridge scholarship and high church Methodism. This, coupled with journeys to meet A S Gregory in Kendal, drew him into the MSF in 1964. Stella Buckley later became a valued member of the MSF Committee and, in the 1960s, organized MSF day conferences in York. But, like many others in retirement, her experience of rural Methodism (by this time in the Yorkshire dales) drove her to the life and comparatively decent liturgy of the Church of England, where she was twice elected to the General Synod.

Publicity and Advance

The Committee held at the High Leigh Residential Conference in 1947 resolved to convene regional meetings in Birmingham, Bristol, Leeds, Manchester, Newcastle and Plymouth. Dr Rattenbury offered to write a short 4-page pamphlet about the MSF to be circulated to all ministers. 5000 copies were to be printed.[11] In the 1948 Fifth Edition of *What is the MSF*? A S Gregory introduced a significant footnote about the Fellowship's usage at Holy Communion:

> The Fellowship desires no innovations whatever, either in the Methodist Service of Holy Communion or in the Methodist interpretation of it. The order of Holy Communion in our own

> Book of Offices has always been used: and the Committee has made it perfectly clear, both privately to its members and in the Methodist press, that the Fellowship lends no countenance to any departures from Methodist usage. The manual acts in the Prayer of Consecration, though little used, have of course been part of the Methodist tradition from the first, and up to 1881 were directed in the Wesleyan Book of Offices.

At the same Annual Weekend Conference the 'Ministerial Session' resolved that, when MSF ministers were asked to guide those about to begin celebrating the Lord's Supper for the first time, 'instruction given to those beginning to preside at Holy Communion should be based on the two authorized orders.'[12] Annual Conference speakers included Eric Baker, Fr Gabriel Hebert and W J E Jeffrey. Eric Baker noted, 'For thirteen years John Wesley was engaged in the pursuit of holiness. At Aldersgate Street he discovered how to attain it – entire sanctification meant the sanctification of everything including work.'[13] Fr Hebert said he believed that the re-union of the churches required the re-discovery of the totality of Scriptural witness and revelation.[14] W J E Jeffrey, one of Dr Orchard's successors at the King's Weigh House Church, London, spoke about the *Society of Free Catholics* and the Evangelical Catholic Communion. The Annual Meeting heard that, in less than a year, Dr Rattenbury's pamphlet, *The Witness of the MSF*, had obtained forty new members for the Fellowship! At the Bristol Methodist Conference of 1948 the Lord's Supper was celebrated daily at the New Room, and one morning the Conference opening devotion included the MSF Prayer.[15]

Not everything reported by the MSF in 1948 was good. The issue of the ordination of women was 'talked down' in the Bristol Conference, especially by Daniel T Niles, and the *Bulletin* Editorial took the view that the negative response of the Conference 'cannot but be welcome by the MSF.'[16]

Studies on the Eucharist

In the same *Bulletin* of 1948 John Bowmer asked for help in certain aspects of his thesis, *The Sacrament of the Lord's Supper in Early Methodism*, which in due course Dacre Press published in 1951. After sixty years this is still a much sought-after work. In January 1949 the Epworth Press published Dr Rattenbury's seminal study on *The Eucharistic Hymns of John and Charles Wesley*. The book was dedicated to the Fellowship and, in April, it was given a four page review in the *Bulletin* by Duncan Coomer, who ended his piece, 'the Methodist Sacramental Fellowship are proud of our association with the author of the greatest book on the Eucharist ever written by a Methodist.'[17]

The Annual Conference of that year was held at Swanwick with Dom Gregory Dix, Gordon Rupp and the President's brother, Harold B Rattenbury, as the speakers. The *Bulletin* report said: 'we shall not forget Dom Gregory's daring conception of the Orthodox Liturgy as that of an air-raid with the congregation in the shelter, occasionally visited by the Deacon, the Air-Raid Warden, to give the All Clear.'

The Old Guard

In the Annual Business Meeting Dr Rattenbury intimated that he felt it necessary soon to relinquish the active duties of his Presidency of the Fellowship.[18] One by one the first runners were handing on the baton. R C Simmonds also tendered his resignation from the Secretariat. He had been an organiser of the MSF before its inception and had been its Secretary from the Fellowship's foundation in 1935. H Vavasor Griffiths was also relinquishing the chair of the MSF Committee, which he had exercised as the first in that post and filled the office for seven years, from 1942 to 1949.

The New Brooms

Donald Soper was to spend the greater part of his ministry as the figure-head of three Methodist movements: the *Order of*

Christian Witness, which he had founded in 1946, the *Methodist Peace Fellowship*, of which he became President in 1951, and the *Methodist Sacramental Fellowship*, which he actually joined only when he became President of the Fellowship, in succession to J E Rattenbury, in 1950!

Already in 1949 Donald Soper had written an article on *The Holy Communion and the Order of Christian Witness* in which he set out his stall.

> I know nothing that can compare in clarity, precision and economy with the order of Holy Communion (competently explained) as the presentation in word and deed of the Christian religion. The Sacrament of the Lord's Supper is Christianity brought into practical and contemporary focus. Holy Communion is the Church in action. It provides the authentic and actual means whereby decision can be expressed and discipleship begun in the Christian Life.[19]

At the Annual Conference of 1950 at High Leigh Donald Soper was formally elected to the Presidency of the Fellowship. Tribute was paid to Dr Rattenbury for his twelve years of leadership of the Fellowship, and for his role as its saviour and defender. He was then elected President Emeritus. For the first time four Vice-Presidents were elected, namely Revd F Ronald Ducker, Revd A S Gregory, Dr Duncan Coomer and Mr R C Simmonds. David Sharp was elected as General Secretary and John Bishop as Editor of the *Bulletin*.

On 29th March 1951 Donald Soper and David Sharp had a letter published in the *Methodist Recorder* which included the paragraph:

> It is of the utmost importance that our place in the Catholic tradition be recovered, while our place in the Protestant succession continues to be stressed. Proper and essential to both these roles is the sacramental nature of the Christian Church and its worship, the treasuring of its historic creeds, the maintenance of its liturgical glories – in short, a zealous care for those characteristics of the Catholic Church which still offer the only sure foundation upon which to build this United Church of Christ which is to be. With this spirit and

temper our people must join forces with all movements towards one united Body of Christ.

The Penrhos Cross

At the Annual Weekend Conference of 1951 R C Simmonds gave an historical survey of the MSF, pointing out that, when first mooted in 1934, the original name was Methodist Catholic Fellowship. The first Conference at Penrhos College, Colwyn Bay in August 1935 had been attended by fifteen ministers and eighteen lay people. The MSF Cross was based on the cross on Penrhos School chapel communion table at the time of the Fellowship's first meeting.[20]

Eric Milner-White

In the January *Bulletin* of 1952 Gordon Wakefield reviewed and commended Eric Milner-White's *A Procession of Passion Prayers*. For much of his ministry the reviewer treasured the Dean of Kings and of York by keeping a photo of him in his study. Eric Milner-White was to feature again in 2012, when the present author devoted a whole MSF Quiet Morning to his liturgies, prayers and poetry.

Dr Duncan Coomer

In the April *Bulletin* of 1952 Dr Rattenbury paid tribute to Dr Duncan Coomer, a Vice-President of MSF and a pioneer and early benefactor of the Fellowship, who had served its needs from the beginning as a banker, a published church historian and as a book-binder.

The First Elevation

The *Bulletin* of September 1952 carried heartiest congratulations to Donald Soper on his being designated as President of the Conference of 1953. In December he told the Fellowship:

> During my Presidential year I am asking local churches to arrange the afternoon meeting as a full communion with hymns and sermon. I am so much hoping that by this means many of our fellow Methodists will find their Churchmanship deepened and the great central truths of our faith reinforced.[21]

The *Bulletin* of September 1952 also reported that between three and four hundred had attended the first official MSF Public Meeting at St Anne's-on-Sea during the Methodist Conference, Donald Soper being one of the speakers.[22]

Kindred and Affinity

MSF kindred spirits were welcomed at the Annual Residential Conferences in 1952 and 1953. Dr Percy Scott willingly acknowledged the place of the Fellowship in the current scheme of things:

> In the last twenty years theology has been reborn. The bread of life offered in the liberal era was found to consist of empty husks. My generation was seeking positive content. Many found their chief sustenance in the Holy Communion. I do not think the primary interest of the MSF was ritual but the catholic faith. Part of the revival of the apostolic faith is seen in the growing emphasis on the sacraments. As to evangelicalism and sacramentalism I like either but will have them both.[23]

Gordon Wakefield wrote in the *Bulletin* that Taizé, the recently formed monastic community of the French Reformed Church consisting of twelve professing brothers, could meet and restore the kind of situation which the MSF was raised to remedy. Geoffrey Parrinder, writing from University College, Ibadan, Nigeria, felt it was time to address the issue of the consumption of the elements. There was an urgent need in Methodism at home and abroad to revive the ancient practice of eating the remainder of the bread and wine at the end of the Communion Service. He suggested the consumption of the bread and wine remaining should take place before the blessing, the remaining wine to be poured in a common cup and consumed.[24]

The April *Bulletin* of 1953 recorded a welcome to Eric Thacker as he joined the Fellowship. He was to give faithful years of service to the MSF, especially to the Northern Meetings in Manchester. He was probably the only member to maintain his membership of the MSF as he journeyed, as a married man, from the Methodist ministry via Anglican ordination to the Roman Catholic priesthood.

The principal speaker at the Low Sunday Weekend Conference of 1953 was George MacLeod of the Iona Community. It was also the first occasion in nearly twenty years that the Sunday morning Eucharist included a collection![25] Among new members were Ronald Gibbins and Eric Wright. The Methodist Conference Public Meeting of 1953 in Birmingham was addressed by Kingsley Lloyd, George Thompson Brake, and Donald Soper as both President of the Fellowship and President of Conference. The President told a gathering of five-hundred, 'If union is to come it must come at a High Church level.'[26]

In September Mr J Munsey Turner of Wolverhampton joined the Fellowship and Dr Irvonwy Morgan rejoined. In the December *Bulletin* the President published a four-monthly itinerary of his Presidential visits, reporting on his Presidential Communion Services since the Conference, where he had experienced very large crowds, with nearly everybody communicating and 'evidence of the pouring out of evangelical power.'[27]

St Peter's Hall, Oxford

The Low Sunday Weekend Conference of 1954 met at St Peter's Hall, Oxford and was considered the best attended since the War. The programme included a joining rubric which, in more or less the same form, was to survive for the best part of the next 50 years – *Please bring soap and towel, Methodist Hymn Book and Methodist Book of Offices*! On the Friday evening fifty members assembled for dinner, after which Revd A Raymond George spoke on *The Shape of Methodist Worship*. He argued for a new Methodist Communion rite:

> A hymn including the little entrance with the Bible should be followed by the seasonal prayer of invocation, penitence and then Kyrie, Gloria and collect. Three lessons should be followed by the sermon and a hymn. Intercessions should precede the offertory of money, bread and wine. The Great Prayer should be followed by the Lord's Prayer, the Fraction, Humble Access, Communion, Post Communion Prayer, hymn and Blessing. The essence of liturgical theology is the four-fold understanding of the sacrifice we offer, namely we offer and present the sacrifice of Christ, we offer the gifts, we offer ourselves and we offer praise and thanksgiving.[28]

The Annual Meeting recorded an increase for the year of forty new members, including Mr Colin Wilson of Wharfedale, The Revd Philip Blackburn serving with the Methodist Missionary Society, Mr A Guthrie Burgess, Mr John Newton of Boston, Lincolnshire and Francis B James, all of whom were to make a distinctive contribution to the life of the Fellowship. Gordon Wakefield became editor of the *Bulletin*.

The Return of the Kensitites

The Kensitites had a further stab at the Fellowship in 1954. *The Churchman's Magazine* for September of that year noted:

> The drift in Methodism away from the simplicity of that Gospel which called Methodism into being continues. It is not however a flood-tide and for that Evangelicals must be thankful. It is, however, far more serious than the mere figures of membership of the Methodist Sacramental Fellowship would indicate. We are told in its latest Bulletin that it now numbers in its ranks 324 members. The whole movement should now earnestly be looked into [again] by the higher authorities of the Methodist body.[29]

Having been appalled at the Fellowship allowing Dom Gregory Dix to speak at its Annual Conference, the magazine took Stewart Denyer to task for speaking on the theme *Methodism must be Catholic or Perish*, and suggesting that Free Church members could be Catholics and remain in their own traditions. This, the magazine feared, was exactly the dangerous view advocated by W E Orchard and the Free Catholics of the 1930s. The magazine was also critical of Raymond George's remarks on Methodist worship.

> Mr George noted with satisfaction that among Anglicans there is a general turning back to 1549 from 1552 and 1662. This is precisely what all true lovers of the English Church are endeavouring to resist, for the 1549 book was only halfway out of Rome. There was a suggestion in this paper for the [Methodist] service to begin with a hymn, and then the minister to enter in procession carrying a Bible. After following largely the Prayer Book for the Communion Service, Mr George added that after the Sermon non-communicants should depart, though those who wish to pray and watch ought to be encouraged to do so. This Methodist made the cardinal mistake of the sacerdotalist that Christ is now High Priest at the heavenly altar. We invite Mr George to think again on this point, for Christ does not stand before any altar, but is seated at the right hand of the Father.[30]

The magazine then reproduced the whole of the MSF membership with addresses, presumably with a view to discouraging Methodist circuits from inviting any of the 130 ministers whose names appeared in the list. In 1958 the article and the membership list were published as a separate 16-page Protestant Truth Society pamphlet, *The Methodist Sacramental Fellowship.*

Rupp and Rattenbury

At the MSF Annual Conference at High Leigh in April 1955 there was still a 'Ministerial Session' on the Friday afternoon before Tea! In the main sessions Gordon Rupp, newly awarded his Cambridge Doctor of Divinity, spoke on the *Protestant Martyrs* based on Foxe's *Book of Martyrs*, typically remarking 'for the most part all three hundred of them were very ordinary men who exercised that consecrated cussedness – the mark of the true Protestant throughout the ages.'[31]

In 1955 the Fellowship recorded fifty-four new members and re-published Dr Rattenbury's pamphlet, *The Witness of the MSF*, with a new introduction:

> As President Emeritus I agreed to write this pamphlet in the hope that others may share our experience. Absurd prejudices and misrepresentations have given to many Methodists a false conception of the principles and practices of our Fellowship. Probably we have been more severely criticised than any contemporary Methodist organisation. We have been attacked from within Methodism and very maliciously and ignorantly from without on account of our falsely alleged Roman Catholic tendencies. However, we have survived, unhurt by our critics.
>
> I have no apologies to make, but in order to prevent further misunderstanding I assert that our Society is evangelical in spirit, while both evangelical and sacramental in practice. Our actions and teachings are fully justified by the teachings and practices of John and Charles Wesley in their *post conversion careers.*
>
> [The MSF is] not a large body, nor do we aim to be. Gideon's army is our model. Our Fellowship is grounded on daily disciplined personal devotions. We do not seek members amongst those who merely sympathise with our sacramental views and practices although we are grateful for their sympathy as we are also gratified by many signs of increasing Eucharistic worship in our Church, the development of which, though no doubt there are other factors, has not we think been uninfluenced by our witness. Primarily our Fellowship is based on personal devotional practices which are obligatory and even selective.[32]

Corpus Christi

In his last *MSF Bulletin* as Editor, Gordon Wakefield reproduced Eric Abbott's BBC Broadcast, *A Meditation for Corpus Christi*, including Evelyn Underhill's lines from her own *Corpus Christi*:

> Come, dear Heart!
> The fields are white to harvest: come and see
> As in a glass the timeless mystery
> Of love, whereby we feed
> On God, our bread indeed.
> Torn by the sickles, see him share the smart
> Of travailing Creation: maimed, despised,
> Yet by his lovers the more dearly prized
> Because for us he lays his beauty down—
> Last toll paid by Perfection for our loss!
> Trace on these fields his everlasting Cross,
> And o'er the stricken sheaves the Immortal Victim's crown.
>
> From far horizons came a Voice that said,
> 'Lo! from the hand of Death take thou thy daily bread.'
> Then I, awakening, saw
> A splendour burning in the heart of things:
> The flame of living love which lights the law
> Of mystic death that works the mystic birth.
> I knew the patient passion of the earth,
> Maternal, everlasting, whence there springs
> The Bread of Angels and the life of man.
>
> Now in each blade
> I, blind no longer, see
> The glory of God's growth: know it to be
> An earnest of the Immemorial Plan.
> Yea, I have understood
> How all things are one great oblation made:
> He on our altars, we on the world's rood.
> Even as this corn,
> Earth-born,

We are snatched from the sod;
Reaped, ground to grist,
Crushed and tormented in the Mills of God,
And offered at Life's hands, a living Eucharist.[33]

The Centrality of the Eucharist

When Ronald Gibbins presided over the congregation that returned to Wesley's Chapel in 1978 after its restoration he instituted a weekly Eucharist as the principal morning service. That was at least the second time in his ministry that he had such an achievement to his credit. He reported that, in 1952, on the Thorntree Estate, Middlesbrough, where he was the minister, they began a weekly Methodist 'Parish Communion' attended by thirty-five out of a membership of eighty adults, and that they used the 1936 Full Communion Order with Sermon. This included Parade Sundays! 'The Scouts and Guides [were] by now experts in their knowledge of the liturgy!'[34]

In November 1955 Irvonwy Morgan spoke at the MSF London Meeting at Kingsway Hall under the title *Methodism and the Lord's Supper*, and reminded his audience that, in July 1740, John Wesley set down four propositions on the Sacrament:

> The Lord's Supper was ordained of God as a means of conveying preventing or justifying or sanctifying grace. It was ordained to show us that our sins are forgiven and that our souls can be renewed in the image of God. It was ordained that we might receive whatever Christ chooses to give us. It was ordained that our sinfulness and our helplessness might be the only fitness required of those receiving the sacrament.[35]

Having already sent to the *Bulletin* a suggestion about consumption of the elements remaining after the Eucharist, Geoffrey Parrinder now wrote with a further suggestion:

> ... that in our new Methodist Churches, and in re-planning old ones, architects and builders should be prevailed upon to

> leave enough room for the altar to be situated away from the east wall to enable the minister to preside from behind the table facing the people.[36]

Record Membership

At the Annual Conference of 1956, with an increase for the year of twenty-one, the membership of the Fellowship was reported as three hundred and ninety-four – the highest so far recorded! Dr Rattenbury, now eighty-six, was unable to be present for Low Sunday Weekend 'owing to his increasing infirmity.' The weekend was held at St Peter's Hall, Oxford with Erik Routley, Hugh Ashdown, Philip Watson and Colin Morris as speakers. Donald Lee led the Sunday morning communion at Wesley Memorial Church and Donald Soper preached the sermon.

The Anglican-Methodist Conversations begin

In 1955 the Anglican-Methodist *Conversations* began. On behalf of the MSF David Sharp, the Secretary, wrote to Leslie Weatherhead, the President of Conference, expressing regret that none of the Fellowship's officials had been asked to serve on the Methodist panel in the forthcoming talks with the Anglican Church. Leslie Weatherhead replied:

> ... in consultation I have had to choose the members of the panel very carefully, and I think you need not fear the point of view to which you refer will be overlooked in our conversations ...[37]

Indeed of the twelve original members Harold Roberts, Eric Baker and Gordon Rupp had all spoken at MSF gatherings. Gordon Rupp would later tell his Cambridge students, 'When I use the word Protestant I mean by it what most people mean by the word Catholic.' In the later stages of the Conversations two founder members of the MSF did become part of the process, namely Marcus Ward and Kingsley Lloyd.

'All His Grace'

The Methodist Lent Book of 1957 was Donald Soper's *All His Grace*, which was re-printed within the first year. It was said that the first chapter, *Single-mindedness*, could only have been written by a Protestant and the last full chapter, *Four Acts of Offering*, could only have been written by a Catholic!

He told his Methodist readers, 'I will presume some acquaintance on the reader's part with the Order of Holy Communion and the Roman Catholic Mass, and with the Eastern liturgies.' At the heart of the final chapter Soper wrote of the Eucharist, 'This offering up of Christ, and of ourselves in Christ, is the absolutely necessary condition upon which depends the reality of the act which follows it. Unless we are first crucified with Christ we cannot rise with him.'[38]

At the 1957 MSF Conference, held at Woodbrooke College, Selly Oak, Nicholas Zernov, Lecturer in Eastern Orthodox Culture at Oxford, identified five characteristics of the general spiritual atmosphere of the contemporary western churches – a return to orthodoxy, a recovery of confidence in freedom, a sense of the universality of the gospel, the ecumenical movement and a new emphasis on the Eucharist.[39] The Annual Meeting reported thirty-six new members for the year with a membership of four hundred and twenty-three. At the Fellowship's Sunday morning communion Marcus Ward celebrated the liturgy of the Church of South India.

In the *Bulletin* editorial for 1958 Stewart Denyer reflected on the Anglican-Methodist Conversations, *An Interim Statement*.

> The statement by representatives of both traditions notes that the Christian Body is throughout in a state of schism. A most definite gain is the clear statement that nothing less than the visible unity of the whole Church of Christ is the goal. The heart of the matter is clear – the historic episcopate ought to be accepted not as a price of unity but only as a gift of God to his Church despite all its faults and distortions down the ages. The Methodist section of the last chapter is calling

Methodism to find in episcopacy an enrichment of its own inheritance.[40]

In 1958 Epworth Press published what proved to be Dr Rattenbury's last book, *Thoughts on Holy Communion.* A S Gregory welcomed it as 'a simple, short and readable account of the history and meaning of Holy Communion in which clear light is thrown on the real presence, the priesthood of all believers, corporate and individual oblation, the true altar, the church triumphant, the manual acts and the declaratory absolution.'[41] Forty-seven members attended the Annual meeting at which the membership was recorded at four hundred and fifty.

One Lord, One Faith, One Baptism

During a late night discussion at the 1959 Annual conference it emerged that a member of the Fellowship, though a frequent communicant, had not been baptised. The next day, during the liturgical round of services, he was baptised by Donald Soper, the President! At the Sunday morning Eucharist among those remembered was James Raim, who had served the Fellowship both as Publicity Secretary and as Treasurer. He had long acted as chapel steward for the Low Sunday Conferences and was proud of the fact that he was an Anglican as well as a Methodist. John Newton was the main speaker on the words from the MSF Prayer, 'The same Grace in Word and Sacrament.'[42]

The other speaker was T S Gregory who, for the only occasion since the formation of the Fellowship, addressed the Low Sunday Conference. In his address on *The Church in History* he noted first the necessity of the secularizing of the church under Constantine for its very survival. Secondly he noted that, although the Church of England had preserved the monastic life, it had lost the sacrifice of the Mass. Thirdly the Christian Person, so visible in the writings of Saint Augustine, was supremely seen in Charles Wesley. Fourthly the scientific revolution was forcing the Church to abandon a closed system view of creation. Finally the Church must continue in its commitment to such absolutes as God, the world, humanity and sin. In a second, impromptu address TS spoke on the meaning of Wesley's conversion and the nature of his churchmanship.[43]

A decision was taken to print, with the next *Bulletin*, the *Orders for the Morning and Evening Offices* in a slightly revised form, and with versions that could be used on both private and public occasions. At the AGM the membership of the MSF peaked at four hundred and sixty-three members, comprising 266 lay men and women and 197 ministers, with 69 of these members living abroad. David Sharp was thanked for his ten year stint as Secretary of the Fellowship. The Fellowship welcomed a new book for church membership preparation by one of its stalwarts, Francis Westbrook.[44]

In November 1959 Kingsley Lloyd spoke at the London MSF meeting at Kingsway Hall on the Anglican-Methodist Conversations, saying that, if Methodism had gone down the Free Church unity route, any hope of re-union with the Church of England would never have come within our sights nor would the Church of South India have come into existence. The vocation of the MSF was to lead Methodism towards re-union with the Church of England.[45]

At the end of 1959 Lawrie Ginn wrote an open letter in the *Bulletin*, putting forward a three-fold strategy for MSF members to adopt. First that each minister make a pledge to celebrate Holy Communion weekly in one of the congregations in his pastoral charge. Second, that both ministers and local preachers in the MSF set forth the Fellowship's aims in their preaching. Thirdly, he proposed that all MSF members eligible for the ordained ministry or for accreditation as local preachers consider whether they have a vocation to these callings.[46]

8

Ecumenical Odyssey

The MSF Silver Jubilee

In 1960 the Fellowship celebrated its Silver Jubilee. The President Emeritus, J Ernest Rattenbury, wrote:

> I am glad that my life has been spared long enough – and I have now entered my *ninetieth year* – to congratulate the MSF ... While I was not an originator of the Fellowship, and indeed, knew nothing of its existence for some little time after it was organised, I joined it immediately and became an active member, and was surprised and much honoured, after the resignation (sic) of A E Whitham, to be elected President ... In our early years we passed through troubled waters, partly through what I still think the unfortunate conversion of several of its leading members to Roman Catholicism, and partly from the violent attacks of the *Joyful News* in our own denomination and from unscrupulous fanaticism of a journal of another denomination ... the Report on the MSF to the 1937 Methodist Conference was much misinformed and highly condemnatory and it will be remembered by not a few that I was able to persuade the Conference that though we were strong sacramentalists we were essentially an evangelical organisation ... It is a great gratification to me that the Fellowship has never been more flourishing ...
>
> But out of all the Lord
> Hath brought us by His love;
> And still He doth his help afford,
> And hides our life above.[1]

Ronald Ducker, a Vice-President of the Fellowship wrote:

> Those of us who have been associated with the MSF from the beginning are quite sure it was raised up of God to bear a very necessary witness ... the inevitable adjustments and compromises involved in Methodist Union had temporarily

> blurred the picture of a worshipping church and the Fellowship helped many of us to retain and often rediscover our faith in the essential catholicity of Methodism **...** the Fellowship can only be properly understood within the context of the whole sacramental, liturgical and ecumenical movement ...[2]

A S Gregory, a founding father and senior Vice-President of the Fellowship, wrote:

> I remember that in the course of the pre-1935 talks that brought a Methodist Catholic Fellowship to birth someone advocated a five-year plan ... the task was presumptuous but among present-day issues such as the meaning of church membership, of Baptism, of the ministerial office, of social problems, of industry, of rural issues and of our relationship with the Church of England ... none are solvable except on a catholic basis ...[3]

R C Simmonds, who was T S Gregory's circuit steward and co-worker in the formation of the Fellowship and who picked up the reigns of administration when T S went over to Rome, wrote:

> Some 25 years ago, T S Gregory said to me, with characteristic and significant brevity, "How would you like to help me to form a 'Methodist Catholic Fellowship'?" I, who had never thought of such a thing before, said, "Done." He had just come back from a week-end preaching at Penrhos College, Colwyn Bay, where, in due course, the Fellowship was constituted, its three Aims were formulated and its Morning and Evening Offices framed, in a conference attended by some 30 persons, with the Rev A E Whitham as President.
> Mr Gregory, meanwhile, had become a member of the Roman Catholic Church, but it must be remembered with deep gratitude that not only was the original impulse his, but also much of the preliminary work was done, and could only be done by him.
>
> The actual name of the Fellowship was suggested before the Penrhos Conference by Mr Gregory's father during one of the early talks at Sidcup.[4]

The Fellowship celebrated its twenty-fifth birthday at the Annual Conference of 1960 at the Beechwood Court Hotel, Harrogate over Low Sunday Weekend. Forty members and friends attended and the Sunday morning Communion Service was held at Trinity Church, Harrogate on The Stray.

During the Conference A S Gregory said that the significant Methodist opposition they were then enduring to the Anglican-Methodist Conversations was indicative of the lip service that the Connexion had given to Re-union and that the MSF had huge work to do in this regard.[5]

David Paton, Secretary of the Church of England Council for Ecumenical Co-operation, spoke at the Conference on plans to promote the Anglican-Methodist *Interim Statement* at a national conference involving the Parish and People movement, the MSF and similar groups in the other Free Churches.[6]

Roger Ducker, working with the SCM, spoke of the rediscovery of the Christian Year among the Free Churches and in Methodism in particular. It was time for the MSF to look beyond '1662' to the wider liturgical revival which was going on throughout the Churches.[7]

Marcus Ward had spoken to forty members at the London MSF Meeting earlier in the year on the Church of South India, emphasising that organic union was the only model of the church present in the New Testament and, although there was a new experience of organic union within the CSI, it was still far from the full vision of the organic union of the one Catholic Church.[8]

The Ordination of Women to the Methodist Ministry

Responding to the recent Methodist Conference Report on the Ordination of Women to the Methodist ministry, Stewart Denyer wrote the first of his articles on the subject and teased out Biblical arguments, all of which he said were against it![9]

In the second of his articles he wrote arguing the essential maleness of God the Father, of Christ as the Bridegroom and of this maleness being representatively present in the male presbyter and bishop! Future ecumenical relations with Anglicans, Roman Catholics and Orthodox would be further impaired if Methodism decided to ordain women ministers. From somewhere he had dragged up the thesis that 'When the ministers of religion are female, there is a tendency towards eroticism of one kind or another.'[10]

'Studia Liturgica'

The Annual Low Sunday Weekend Conference of 1962 was cancelled owing to a smallpox outbreak in South Wales, not far from the intended venue of the Conference.[11] The *Bulletin* welcomed the first issue of *Studia Liturgica*, in which there were contributions by W D Maxwell of the Church of Scotland, the Anglican Fr Mark Gifford, the Orthodox liturgical theologian, Boris Bobrinskoy, and by the great Anglican friend of the MSF, Fr Donald Allchin. In due time a number of MSF members were to join the international *Societas Liturgica* and make regular contributions to *Studia Liturgica.*[12]

The Renewal Group

Guthrie Burgess, one of the treasurers of the Fellowship, was ordained at the Methodist Conference of 1962 and moved from London into circuit in Bolton. He and his wife Kathleen had a chauffeur, 'Ben,' by whom they were usually driven to their various appointments.[13]

At the end of 1962 Guthrie Burgess wrote about the launch of the Methodist Renewal Group, which had been founded by fourteen ministers and one layman with 'a common concern about the deadness of much Church life, and its irrelevance to the world; the lack of radical thought or action to deal with this; the failure to learn from the great movements of the world Church today.'

The Group's aim was 'To work together for the renewal of the Mission, Worship and Structure of the Church.' Their commitment included a theological study of the nature of the

Church of Christ; a deepening of ministry through a common discipline of prayer, training and study and seeking new types of ministry for the present age; the study of and the experimenting with patterns of worship and expressions of Church architecture; the developing of training in Churchmanship, discipleship and relevant witness; the finding of ways of Christian action in social, economic and political life; the reviewing of the theory and practice of methods of evangelism and the working, wherever possible, with members of other communions towards ultimate Christian unity.

The Renewal group's intention was to avoid a party line but to discern what God was saying through the three great movements of Biblical Theology, Ecumenism and Liturgical Renewal. In the first year there were sixty members. Some significant overlap with the aims of the MSF was clear. Attendance at the annual Whitsuntide conference was to be regarded as obligatory. The membership was, on the whole, young and of the post-war generation. At the first gathering ministers outnumbered the laity ten to one! One involvement and manifestation of the group already was the Notting Hill team ministry.[14]

The Death of Dr Rattenbury

Dr Rattenbury died on 19th January 1963 'in the ninety-third year of his age and in the seventieth year of his ministry.' There were two obituaries for him in the *Bulletin*, but they were prefixed by one from Keith Beck, the editor of the *Bulletin*, on Pope John XXIII!

The first of the Rattenbury obituaries was from Donald Soper, who spoke of his long-term colleague and predecessor as possessing 'unusual and quite moving oratory' and as one willing to proclaim 'the true catholicity of his faith.' Donald Soper felt that those who spoke of the great West London Mission days of Hugh Price Hughes and Mark Guy Pearce needed to recall 'that equally splendid reign of Ernest Rattenbury.' However, Soper knew from experience that, as well as acknowledging the innumerable company whom Rattenbury had brought to Christ, 'it was idle to pretend that he possessed any cocktail graces. He found it difficult to suffer fools at all, let alone to suffer them gladly! But how generous were his judgments. His connexional career was not consummated in the election to the Presidential chair, and we all know why! There are not a few who now see in the current Anglican-Methodist proposals the perceptiveness of his judgments in 1932!'[15]

In the second tribute A S Gregory noted that *The Times* obituary had mentioned the MSF and he wrote, 'without Rattenbury's heartfelt advocacy the MSF could hardly have survived the storm of ill-informed criticism of those early days ... I met him on the pavement after the 1938 Hull Conference session and remember the deep feeling with which he told me what he had just done.' Worship for him was the *Ter Sanctus* and 'the sight that veils the seraph's face.' Gregory was one of those who vividly recalled the MSF Conference of 1949 with its thrill of Rattenbury's exchanges with Dom Gregory Dix![16]

Merbecke

The Low Sunday Weekend Conference of 1963 was the first to hold a choir practice under Francis Westbrook to rehearse Charles Cleall's realization of Merbecke's setting of the Communion Office, with Cleall himself as the organist! This was the first Choral Eucharist at the Annual Conference.[17]

The Anglican-Methodist Conversations Report of 1963

In the Trinity *Bulletin* of 1963 Stewart Denyer surveyed the Anglican-Methodist Conversations Report of 1963. Clearly its contents and proposals were music to the ears of the Fellowship and this despite the reaction of some 'spiky' Anglo-Catholics, some evangelical Anglicans and most notoriously by the four leading Methodist dissentients, Tom Meadley, Kingsley Barrett, Norman Snaith and T E Jessop, and their supporters. But who in the MSF could not rejoice in the

Report's statements on the nature of the ordained ministry, on its clarity over the priesthood of all believers, in its section on episcopacy, in its presentation on baptismal regeneration and on the Eucharistic presence? Denyer drew attention to the dissentients and some of their 'unscholarly and sweeping remarks about tradition and succession.'[18]

Hopes and fears issuing from the Anglican-Methodist Conversations Report were highlighted in the editorial of the next *Bulletin.* Members of the Fellowship were urged to put their weight behind the informal ginger group supporting the Scheme, *Towards Anglican-Methodist Unity*, of which an MSF leading light, Kingsley Lloyd, was a prime mover.[19]

The MSF Annual Meeting of 1964 sent a letter to the President and Secretary of the Conference and sought their permission to publish it in the Press.

> The members of the Methodist Sacramental Fellowship, meeting in their Annual Conference, send their sincere and cordial greetings to the President and Secretary of the Methodist Conference and assure them of our loyalty to the Methodist Conference. We are grateful for the courtesy and care which have been exercised in the matter of the Anglican-Methodist Report during the recent difficult times. We have given considerable study to the Report and find the proposals generally acceptable. We are, therefore, commending them to our members with the request that exhaustive study and discussion should be devoted to them, thus enabling an informed decision to be reached.[20]

Bright spots in the quest for unity included a report to the Fellowship on steps to found the Ecumenical Centre for Prayer and Unity, to be inaugurated at Farncombe, Surrey under the inspiration of Sister Carol Graham of the Church of South India, with a ruling from the Bishop of Guildford that, from the outset, the altar would be open to everyone staying in the house.[21]

Two liturgical ecumenical landmarks were also reported to the Fellowship. The first was the formation of the Joint Liturgical Group of Britain and Ireland with Anglican and Free

Church representatives from England, Scotland and Wales. Raymond George and Rupert Davies were the first Methodist representatives. Since Rupert Davies' retirement from the Group all his successors have been members of the MSF! The second liturgical ecumenical event was the publication of the Church of South India *Book of Common Worship*, destined to have a far reaching effect on the liturgical revision of its constituent churches.[22]

'New Directions'

As a result of a decision at the Low Sunday Weekend Annual Conference of 1964 it was agreed that the *Bulletin* would be subsumed in the Renewal Group's publication, *New Directions*, which had similar views to those of the Fellowship and would reach a wider readership. The MSF would be represented on the editorial board and space would be given to MSF news and issues.[23]

At the London MSF meeting at Kingsway Hall in November the Jesuit, Fr Tom Corbishley of Farm Street, spoke on *The Sacrifice of the Mass.* He pointed out that it was not the physical death of Christ that was acceptable to God the Father, but the free will that offered 'the invisible sacrifice of inner obedience.' At the Mass we are present at the eternal sacrifice because God has broken through time and space, and though he is independent of both, he penetrates them in 'the Lamb slain before the foundation of the world.'[24]

The Office of MSF Chair

In October 1964 the MSF Committee wrote inviting Stewart Denyer to consider accepting the new post of Deputy President of the Fellowship. Chairing and pro-active leadership of the Fellowship was clearly no longer being offered by Donald Soper or by the aging Vice-Presidents. Following on from this conversation, the Annual Meeting of 1965 created the permanent office of Chair of the MSF, establishing a clear role of leadership in the Fellowship, first fulfilled by Stewart Denyer himself, and subsequently by Donald Rogers, Philip Blackburn, Norman Wallwork and, in two terms of office, by Pat Billsborrow. Leslie Orchard, a prime mover in this development and a former civil servant, commented, 'the Fellowship already has a head of state in its President and now with a Chairman we have a head of government.' Scent of another elevation for Donald Soper came during the Annual Weekend in a veiled but not understood reference which he made to Downing Street and the Prime Minister. Donald Soper was about to be given a Life Peerage!

The 'Vote' and the Letter that was never sent

The MSF Annual Meeting of 1965 was taxed over the future of the Fellowship if the Church of England voted in favour of the Anglican-Methodist Unity Proposals and the Methodist Conference voted against. If this proved to be the case then a letter was to be sent to every member of the MSF inviting them to consider corporate reception of the MSF into the Church of England, with the implication that they would leave the Methodist Church.

The following letter was prepared but never sent because the voting of the two governing bodies was the other way round!

> 5 July 1965
> Dear Member,
>
> It was resolved at the MSF Conference at Easter that, should the Methodist Conference this year give an insufficiently positive lead towards implementing the Report on Anglican-Methodist union, a letter should be sent to all our members, asking them if they desire the officers of the Fellowship to take action.
>
> In view of the decision of the Methodist Conference today, we now write to you to ask if you would support an approach to the Archbishop of Canterbury.

We should ask the Archbishop if it is possible for those members of the MSF, who are so minded and guided, to be received into the Church of England as a body.

We recognize that such a decision, for us Methodists and for the Church of England, would be much more far-reaching and serious in its consequences for ministers than for the laity. We cannot assume that the Church of England would be able or willing to receive a large number of ministers into the priesthood easily.

Yet we believe that our Lord's declared will for the oneness of his Church is being decisively rejected by the Methodist Church, and that unilateral action of this drastic kind is called for by those who are dedicated to the Body of Christ in its unity.

If you agree with this proposal, will you kindly sign the statement at the foot of this letter and return it to us not later than the 31st of July?

We will immediately inform you of the result of this inquiry, if you sign and send us the slip.

Reply

I support an approach to the Archbishop of Canterbury for Corporate Reception of Members of the MSF into the Church of England. (*Signature, Date, Address, Ordained or Lay requested*).[25]

The main speaker at the 1965 Low Sunday Weekend was Donald Allchin on The Orthodox Church. The Saturday Eucharist was according to the Church of South India Rite. At the Sunday Choral Eucharist, for the first time, stoles were worn over cassock, gown and bands by the celebrant, Keith Beck, and by his assistant, Vivian Harvey!

The 'Bulletin' returns

It was resolved that, after September 1966, the Fellowship would resume the publication of its own *Bulletin* and that thereafter the Fellowship would not be part of *New Directions*. After an absence of three years the *Bulletin* resumed publication at Pentecost 1967. Members of the Fellowship had not found the partnership with *New Directions* amenable. MSF issues had not been well covered, duplicated house news had not been satisfactory and the 'radical' stance of *New Directions* had meant that the Catholic emphasis of the Fellowship was not duly represented.[26]

The Crèche Incident!

It was at the 1966 Annual Conference that the first Low Sunday Weekend crèche appeared. Those running it in the room next to the main lounge took it in turns with other parents to be 'in' or 'out.' Those involved insisted on a change-over in the crèche during Donald Soper's address. Those about to enter quietly enquired about the speaker's topic. Those leaving exchanged a quick opinion. Unfortunately the entire Conference, including the speaker, heard the news relayed a little too clearly as Eric Wright reported, 'Brenda says it's all a load of waffle!'

Margaret Wallwork

New members in June 1966 included Sister Margaret Buttling of the Wesley Deaconess Order, who subsequently became Mrs Margaret Wallwork and a key member of the Fellowship's secretariat and publishing concerns, with an almost unbroken record of forty-five years of executive service to the Fellowship from 1969 to the present.

Another Kensit Tract

In January 1967 the Protestant Truth Society published a broadsheet, *Whither Methodism?* It carried a 1964 photograph of the snow-clad notice-board of Putney Methodist Church bearing the announcement:

> Week of Prayer for Christian Unity – Sunday Evening – This Church will Close – The Congregation is invited to attend

Mass at the Church of our Lady of Pity – Limited Seating – Overflow Service at the Baptist Church

The tract declared Methodism to be in grave danger from within and from without. The first danger was *ecumenism*, which had taken the President of the Methodist Conference to see the Pope and the Apostolic Delegate had recently preached in St Aidan's Methodist Church in Eastbourne! The second danger came from *the MSF* whose founder, T S Gregory, had gone over to Rome. The Jesuit organ, *The Month*, had rejoiced in the existence of the MSF, as it would reveal to many Methodists the unknown God they worshipped! The third danger was the *Anglican-Methodist unity scheme* which, if it was accepted, would turn Methodist presbyters into sacrificing priests.[27]

Domestic Arrangements

In 1967 Clifford and Mary Padgett retired from the Secretariat. Donald Rogers became Secretary and Brenda Rogers Treasurer. The post of Overseas Secretary became Ecumenical Secretary, with the job going to Vivian Harvey. Colin Penna was appointed to the Committee. At the Annual meeting the Publications Fund was launched.

The Saturday visit was to the Birmingham Oratory, where members gazed upon the original score of *The Dream of Gerontius* and the enthralled Francis Westbrook almost fainted with ecstasy! The midnight sessions centred round the challenge of what it was to be truly 'Catholic.' Then enter far right Philip Blackburn, recently returned from serving Methodism in the Caribbean – the beginning of a new era for the Fellowship! Francis Westbrook presided over the rehearsals for Merbecke. He also famously fell asleep on to the open keyboard of the grand piano during the Sunday morning Eucharist! Leonard Schiff spoke on the Liturgical Movement and Anglican Liturgical Revision. In the weekend workshops copies were available of the new Methodist Eucharistic rite which was compared with the new Anglican Rite and the CSI Liturgy.

The Bulletin of Pentecost 1967 carried an advertisement for: 'Brenda Rogers, Church Needlework, Pulpit Falls, Communion Table Runners, Ministers' Scarves and Stoles and Communion Linen.' The Fellowship now had its own Wippells!

The Epiphany *Bulletin* of 1968 reported that four MSF members who were Local Preachers in the north of England had been confirmed by their local bishop and were communicating at their parish church as well as leading Methodist services.[28]

Major Revisions

At the Northern Group Meeting of 1968, held at Headingley Methodist Church, Raymond George presided and preached at a Communion Service, saying that the similarities between the order being used and that newly prepared by and soon to be made available from the Connexional Faith and Order Committee were purely co-incidental!

At the Annual Meeting of 1968 in Sheffield the list of new members included Francis Henman and Neil Dixon. Philip Blackburn was appointed to the new post of Conference Secretary, and the present author offered to run the first of many bookstalls for the Annual Conference!

Leslie Orchard presented a paper to the Low Sunday Weekend Conference with his proposed revision of the three aims of the fellowship, with an eye on what he called 'the eventual restoration of communion with the Apostolic See of Rome.'

1. To re-affirm the Catholic Faith, formulated in essentials in the Nicene Creed, taught by the undivided Church and professed down the ages.
2. To restore in Methodism the sacramental worship of the universal church.

3. Paying due regard to our Methodist origins, to work and pray for the restoration of Catholic unity in the one Church Militant. [29]

The Epiphany *Bulletin* of 1969 reported among the new members Dorothy Aston, who was to give many years of service to the Fellowship as treasurer and membership secretary. Another somewhat 'colonial' returning missionary from the Bahamas and Jamaica was Bill Armstrong, who became Ecumenical Secretary in place of Vivian Harvey.

R C Simmonds

R C Simmonds died in 1969 and in his tribute A S Gregory wrote:

> The MSF owes its formation and survival in a very special sense to the assiduous devotion and competence of two laymen, R C Simmonds and Duncan Coomer. To focus and express in an organised Fellowship the catholic affinities of British Methodism in the thirties was a venture which needed not only the leadership of men like Whitham and Rattenbury but also the practical wisdom and professional expertise of a very high order and this R C Simmonds was outstandingly fitted to provide ... I had ample cause to love the man and admire his gifts.[30]

T S Gregory himself wrote to A S Gregory, his cousin:

> Simmonds was a great lover of old England – Shaftesbury, Blandford and Chichester. These ancient unchanging places delighted him. His attitude to the English Church was like T S Eliot's. They both thought of it as home, a home full of sane and venerable, sober and pre-eminently Christian humanities. But Simmonds was never an Anglo-Catholic like Eliot. The village parish church and the Book of Common Prayer were all he needed. He was the mainstay of the little prayer-meeting I had in the manse at Sidcup. He was a completely loyal person. I never met anyone in whom loyalty was so outstanding, so exacting a commandment ... How he managed to carry such private sorrows with such a brave face is a marvel to me. He

> had a very swift, buoyant sort of mind. He was moreover singularly humble. He had no self-importance at all. His generosity was always on the principle of never, never letting his left hand know what his right hand was doing. He was very loveable – so spontaneous and sincere and at the same time clear-headed ... he was a good man.[31]

It was only those who attended his funeral who discovered that 'R C' Simmonds was Reginald Claud. He had a magnificent requiem at the Guild Church of St Mary Woolnoth. As an architect and surveyor Simmonds was a member of the Worshipful Company of Paviours, who had originally supplied paving for the City of London. Their Livery Company dated from 1276. Their motto, 'God Can Raise to Abraham Children of Stone,' seemed wholly appropriate for the one man who, almost single-handedly, had rescued the fragile and fledgling MSF from the threatening storm caused by T S Gregory's departure for Rome. The singing at the service was led by the Choir of the Chapel Royal within Her Majesty's Royal Palace and Fortress, more commonly known as the Tower of London. Before the service the Master of the Music played Bach's Choral Prelude, *Deck Thyself.* The Prayer Book Sentences were sung to Croft. The prayers of commendation concluded with the singing of the Russian Kontakion of the Departed and, after Wesley's 'Rejoice, the Lord is King' and the Blessing, the choir sang Walford Davies' setting of 'God be in my head.' The congregation left to the strains of *Rhosymedre* by Vaughan Williams.

At the Annual Meeting of 1969 Leslie Orchard was elected a Vice-President of the Fellowship in place of R C Simmonds, and Norman and Margaret Wallwork were appointed editors of the *Bulletin.*

Special Announcement

For a long time a number of MSF members had realized that a decision on the subject of Anglican-Methodist Union, one way or the other, was bound to make a difference to the Fellowship.

If, in the Summer of 1969, the two Churches decided to proceed with Anglican-Methodist union the Fellowship would need to review its role in the new situation. If it was decided to reject the current proposals the Fellowship would need to offer guidance to its members about individual or corporate action in such circumstances. The Annual General meeting passed a resolution:

> A Special General meeting of the Fellowship shall be held after the Methodist Conference Public Meeting of the MSF. This meeting will not have power to take any far-reaching action. It will have the power to convene another meeting (by giving notice in writing to all members of the fellowship) and *this second meeting will have power to take any action considered necessary.*[32]

Yet again it was the Methodist Conference that affirmed the unity proposals and the new General Synod that rejected them! On behalf of the Fellowship the General Secretary of the MSF, Donald Rogers, wrote to Michael Ramsey at Lambeth Palace, expressing the deep regret of the Fellowship at the outcome but thanking the Archbishop for his positive leadership in favour of the proposals. He received the following reply:

> Lambeth Palace
> 15th July, 1969.
> My dear Mr Rogers,
>
> Thank you for your letter which I greatly appreciate. I know a little of the Methodist Sacramental Fellowship and how ardently it has worked for unity. Last week's episode is very saddening, but now that the Methodists have given a courageous lead I do not think it can be long before the Church of England follows it.
>
> With best wishes,
> Yours sincerely,
> Michael Cantuar [33]

In the wake of a 'Yes' vote on the Anglican-Methodist Unity Scheme from the Methodist Conference (78%) and a 'No' vote from the Church of England Church Assembly (69%) Stewart Denyer, the MSF Chairman, wrote:

> We must continue local and national efforts towards the reconciliation of our two churches. Many of us can do no other because of our love for the Church of England as the mother church of all English Christians and our love, gratitude and faithfulness to the people called Methodists as a part of that Church.[34]

The One Church

At the request of the new editors of the *Bulletin* T S Gregory wrote his first and only contribution to an *MSF Bulletin.* In his article on *The One Church* he wrote:

> Wonderful as Wesley's preaching was it was not more wonderful than the fact that even ignorant Englishmen knew what he was talking about ... he lived, prayed, worked and preached within an organic structure and tradition which the Christian Church had been making through the centuries. It was the Church who made John Wesley, not Wesley the Church ...
>
> This was the whole power of Wesleyan preaching – Jesus himself to be with us all our days – the Event which happens here and now, the Event of Christ which is what the Catholic means by the Blessed Sacrament. Every Eucharist rolls up the distances of space, time, number and brings us home to the Cross, as near as his Mother and his beloved disciple ... there is no repetition of the Event of Calvary in The Mass – it *is* the Event itself ... we do not ask whether the Sacrament is valid, full of grace, but simply – Is it *this*? Here is the real unity of the Church.[35]

The one who had laid the foundations for the MSF forty years before and had then disappeared from its life now made this brief but prophetic reappearance in the life of the Fellowship. This was the moment when the Fellowship was moving, under the vision and influence of Leslie Orchard and others, from being what Donald Soper called 'high chapel' to being inwardly and outwardly seriously Catholic in liturgy, life and devotion. A Fellowship that had wisely eschewed the name 'Methodist Catholic Society' at the beginning was now about to experience what it meant to be just that.

9

Catholic Society

Towards Catholic Revision

In 1970 Leslie Orchard brought a formal suggestion to the Annual General Meeting that the Aims of the Fellowship were ripe for revision along the lines he had proposed at a Northern Meeting in Headingley Chapel, Leeds two years previously.

1. To re-affirm the Catholic Faith, formulated in essentials in the Nicene Creed, taught by the undivided Church and professed down the ages.
2. To restore in Methodism the sacramental worship of the universal church.
3. Paying due regard to our Methodist origins, to work and pray for the restoration of Catholic unity in the one Church Militant.[1]

In the autumn Marcus Ward, a member of the MSF and of the sub-committee of the Connexional Faith and Order Committee revising the *Covenant Service* for the new *Methodist Service Book*, wrote of the process to date. The service would be set *within* the Eucharist rather than being the first part of it and therefore there would be 'thanksgiving' only at the time of the Great Prayer. In a slightly frivolous vein he noted that one response to the provisional 'You' version of the revision had been, 'This is the first time we have enjoyed this service!' Dr Ward doubted if one submission of a revised Covenant Prayer would see the light of day!

You have taken me over.
Now it is for you to choose my job and my workmates.
Whether I am employed or redundant,
On the Board or the shop-floor,
Have a fat salary or a thin wage-packet,

It is all one to me.
After all, it's Your firm![2]

In the following year Neil Dixon reviewed *Hymns and Songs*, the new supplement to the *Methodist Hymn Book*, noting its friendliness to Methodists of a catholic persuasion. On the Eucharist he welcomed 'Let all mortal flesh keep silence' and 'Sing, my tongue, the Saviour's glory,' Charles Wesley's 'O Thou who this mysterious Bread,' Briggs' 'Come risen Lord and deign to be our guest,' Fred Kaan's 'Now let us from this table rise' and Doddridge's 'My God and is thy table spread.'

In welcoming Newman's 'Firmly I believe and truly' Neil Dixon suggested that, had MSF members promoted this hymn at the time of their foundation, they would surely have been pilloried!

And I hold in veneration,
For the love of him alone,
Holy Church as his creation,
And her teachings as his own.[3]

The Order of the Holy Family

In 1971 the *Bulletin* printed Brenda Rogers' account of the launch of the Order of the Holy Family. For the years of its faithful existence it ran in fellowship with and close proximity to the MSF itself. The Order was committed to disciplined prayer, Bible study, the regular observance of Holy Communion, stewardship of time and money, hospitality especially to missionaries.

Donald and Brenda Rogers took their vows on the Ninth Sunday before Christmas 1969. The founding of the Order had been preceded by eight years of planning and commitment. Before breakfast the family shared in a version of the *MSF Daily Office*, following the revised Anglican *Daily Lectionary* and the Overseas *Prayer Manual*. The children, aged eight, six and three, chose the hymns and led the Saturday Office. The *MSF Evening Office* was used at the close of the day. There was a celebration of Holy Communion on all Sundays and Holy Days, except when there was an early celebration with one of Donald's congregations. One room in the manse served as a chapel. At the Daily Office Donald and Brenda and the children wore the dark blue habit of their Order. At the Eucharist Donald wore full Eucharistic vestments and, on festivals, a cope for the Office.

A journal was kept of income and expenditure and of the use of time and talents. Two significant donations were made to the hungry at Christmas and on Good Friday. Guests were invited to the Office and the Eucharist. Donald and Brenda renewed their vows annually. Others were invited to consider joining the Order.[4]

In a second article on the Order of the Holy Family in 1972 Brenda hoped that it might be possible for a trust to begin to set up a Methodist Retreat house and that two or three families would live in community and run such a centre.[5]

Faithful Members

Among the new members in 1971 were Cedric Hallam and Kenneth Warburton, both outstanding in their secular occupations – the one an international banker and the other a Cambridge schoolmaster. Both were to render to the Fellowship gracious and invaluable years of faithful service.

There was no residential Low Sunday Weekend Conference of the Fellowship in 1971 due to a prolonged national postal strike. When the Annual Conference met in the autumn for one day only at Lidgett Park, Leeds the venerable, scholarly and aging Stanley Lamming was elected as a Vice-President of the Fellowship in place of Ronald Ducker who applied to retire. Stanley Lamming had attended national and regional gatherings without fail each year since his enforced return from China in the 1930s, during the military advances of Chiang Kai-shek. Deep in the memory of the Annual Conference was the famous occasion when, in all innocence, Stanley Lamming invited those at Morning Prayer to sing – unaccompanied and from memory – Jackson's *Te Deum* (1052 in the *Primitive Methodist Hymnal* of 1889!). As Stanley Lamming was the only one present who knew the setting, after a hopeless attempt huge embarrassment (and suppressed mirth) ensued all round. For years one simply had to ask, 'Do you remember Jackson's *Te Deum*?' and the company would dissolve into fits of laughter![6]

Catholic Conversations

It was reported to the Annual meeting that two hundred and nine members had paid a subscription in 1965 or since. One hundred and seventy members had paid up to 1968 and one hundred and thirty-five up to 1970 or 1971. New members included David Butler, who was to place ecumenical studies in his debt with his significant study, *Methodists and Papists: John Wesley and the Catholic Church in the Eighteenth Century*, published in 1995.

In reviewing the *Anglican-Roman Catholic Statement on Eucharistic Doctrine* in the Lent *Bulletin* of 1972, Gordon Rupp thought the statement was much to be welcomed, but he wondered if it was really in accord with official Roman teaching and felt it was perhaps *behind* rather than *ahead* of the statements published by the Anglican-Methodist Unity Scheme![7]

In the Pentecost issue of the *Bulletin* for 1972 the Chairman of the Fellowship, Stewart Denyer, lamented that, like the earlier General Assembly, the new Anglican General Synod failed to reach the required majority for the Anglican-Methodist Unity Scheme to go forward. He feared the ground gained for Catholic Methodists in the Anglican-Methodist Unity Scheme over the historic episcopate, ministerial priesthood, the eucharistic sacrifice and baptismal regeneration would now be lost for the foreseeable future.[8]

The Annual Meeting of 1972 reported the membership as one-hundred and ninety-five. New members included Sister Mary Holliday, who was to play a key role in the Farncombe Community, in the Methodist Retreat Movement, and at the spirituality desk during and after the inauguration of

Churches Together in Britain and Ireland. Margaret Wallwork became General Secretary, Arthur Saunders became Conference Secretary and Philip Blackburn became Overseas Secretary.[9]

The United Reformed Church

In the 1972 All Saints issue of the *Bulletin* John Huxtable (he of the 'High Genevans') wrote an article marking the inauguration of the United Reformed Church, the coming together of the Presbyterian Church of England and the Congregational Church in England and Wales, which had been inaugurated in the October as the result of nine years' work by a Joint Committee set up in 1963. The attempt had been made to produce a Church which was both Catholic and Reformed and at the same time sufficiently open ended to encourage other communions to think it desirable and possible to envisage a wider union. The URC represented the first coming together in these islands across trans-denominational barriers. It was hoped that the Churches of Christ would soon ask for negotiations to be opened with the URC, thus bridging the 'Baptist' issue.

At its first General Assembly the URC sent an invitation to the governing bodies of five major denominations in England and Wales: 'On what terms, or within what limitations, would our churches be prepared to enter into multilateral conversations towards a scheme for the organic union of our churches?' (Stewart Denyer, the MSF Chairman commented, 'I am glad that the slightly soiled words *conversations, scheme* and *organic union* are boldly used for we cannot get anywhere without them!)[10]

The Ordination of Women to the Methodist Ministry

As the Methodist Church in Britain prepared for the admission and ordination of women to the ministry Daphne Hull, a minister in the URC, wrote in the *Bulletin* on *The Ordination of Women*, reminding readers that Phyllis Guthardt had been ordained by the Methodist Conference of New Zealand in 1959![11]

The *Bulletin* Editorial hoped that, whatever previous views MSF members had held concerning the ordination of women ministers, the promise of the MSF to support the Methodist Conference 'with all loyalty' would now override previously held opinions and govern future attitudes. Some members of MSF had pleaded for loyalty to the Conference over other controversial matters. It was now time for some members of the Fellowship to swallow their own medicine![12]

'The Catholic Faith' included in the Revised Aims of the Fellowship

The Chairman reported that the 1973 AGM of the Fellowship had accepted a revised version of the MSF Aims based on a careful re-working of those proposed by Leslie Orchard.

1. To reaffirm the Catholic Faith based on the apostolic testimony of Holy Scripture, witnessed to in the Nicene Creed, and professed by the Church down the ages.
2. To restore to Methodism the sacramental worship of the Universal Church and in particular the centrality of the Eucharist - as set forth in the lifelong practice and teaching of the Wesleys.
3. To work and pray for the restoration of Catholic unity in Christ's Church.[13]

The Methodist Retreat Group

Mary Holliday reported in the *Bulletin* that, following the 1969 opening up of the Association for Promoting Retreats to non-Anglicans and previous interest in Connexional and District retreats, a Methodist Retreat Group had been formed, partly with the hope of having a Methodist Retreat Centre, but also encouraging local and regional Methodist and ecumenical retreats.[14] Donald and Brenda Rogers had prepared and published a booklet on *A Methodist Community and Retreat House*.[15]

Among the new members in 1973 was Michael Blades, who was to render diligent service to the Fellowship as chapel steward at a considerable number of Low Sunday Weekend Conferences and as Secretary of the London Districts. In 1974 W Jardine Grisbrooke, the distinguished Orthodox liturgist and church historian, joined the Fellowship and later spoke at a Low Sunday Weekend Conference. As the leading authority on the Non-jurors he became the literary executor for Frederick Hunter, who wrote on Wesley and the Non-jurors in *John Wesley and the Coming Comprehensive Church*, the Wesley Historical Society lecture for 1968.

The Resignation of Stewart Denyer

In 1974 the Chairman of the Fellowship, Revd Stewart Denyer, resigned from the Methodist ministry, intending to seek ordination in the Church of England. As he also resigned as the Chairman of the Fellowship, the President, Officers and Committee of the Fellowship appointed Donald Rogers as Acting Chairman until the following Annual General Meeting.[16]

In the autumn Stewart Denyer published an *Apologia* in the *Bulletin*, about his journey from the Methodist ministry into Anglican orders. After forty years serving overseas and in British Methodism he had been led forward by three experiences. The first, that he had been half-Anglican and a lover of the Church of England from childhood; the second, that he had endured the optimism and then the reality of the twenty-year journey of the Anglican Methodist Re-Union scheme; the third, that his Methodist people in Exeter had not renewed his initial invitation and, for the first time, he felt his own style of pastoral, sacramental and liturgical ministry was unacceptable to the majority of his congregation. The time between his resignation and his ordination as a deacon included much support and welcome from the Exeter Diocese. He had been a member of the MSF almost from the beginning and hoped to remain part of its life and fellowship.[17]

The Fellowship's Own Bishop!

New members in 1974 included Bishop Norman Carr Sargant who, after the Leys School and ministerial training at Handsworth College, Birmingham, served in Mysore from 1931, becoming Bishop in Mysore in the Church of South India from 1951 till 1972. Upon his return to Britain he was an honorary and residentiary Canon of Bristol Cathedral from 1974 until 1981. He attended MSF Low Sunday Weekend Conferences regularly. The officiant at MSF offices and Eucharists would often pause for him to give the absolution or the blessing. He would preside at MSF liturgies in his purple cassock, rochet and the saffron cuff-bands and stole of a CSI bishop. He gave the members of the Fellowship a decade in which they at least could enjoy a true Methodist *episcopos*, even when the rest of the Connexion dithered endlessly over the historic episcopate. Bishop Sargant convened several Western Districts regional gatherings of the Fellowship. As a boy at the Leys School in the 1920s he had heard J Ernest Rattenbury preach on the opening verse of Hebrews chapter twelve, with memorable gesticulations and much repeating to the boys (and by the boys) of his three points, 'Strip! Look! Run!'[18]

The Wesleyan Succession

In the All Saints *Bulletin* of 1974 Francis Westbrook wrote on *The Wesleyan Succession*, revealing a lineal succession in British Methodist ordinations. Thomas Coke (who had been ordained as bishop/superintendent by Wesley in 1784) had ordained Thomas Squance on 19th November 1813. On Wednesday 31st July 1861 Squance among others (with John Rattenbury as President) had ordained Charles H Kelly. On Thursday 1st August 1889, at the Sheffield Conference, Charles Kelly, who was President that year, ordained among others Herbert B Workman. On Tuesday 29th July 1930, when he was President of the Conference, H B Workman ordained among others Maldwyn Edwards, Kingsley Lloyd and

Francis Westbrook. Both Maldwyn Edwards and Kingsley Lloyd were themselves to become Presidents of the Conference.[19]

The Cellarer

New members in 1975 included John Fisher, who went on to be the Conference Secretary of the Fellowship and a conscientious Northern Districts Secretary. For many years he placed the annual Low Sunday Weekend gatherings for ever in his debt by acting as Cellarer. In the days before retreat and conference centres had their own bars this was a great boon! ('If they is low church they eats a lot – if they is high church they drinks a lot'!) John Fisher was one of the first Methodists to engage in serious studies on devotion to the Virgin Mary.

Also in 1975 Stanley Morrow succeeded W H Gunton as a Vice-President of the Fellowship and Brian Pickett became Conference Secretary.[20]

W H Gunton

In the Pentecost *Bulletin* of 1975 Leslie Orchard paid tribute to W H Gunton. 'WH' died in his eighties and belonged to a generation that eschewed Christian names outside the family circle! After the Leys School he trained as an architect, with the design of some significant national buildings to his credit. He had joined the MSF in 1939 and watched over its finances as treasurer for many years with 'prudence, sagacity and imperturbability.'[21] Guthrie Burgess once told Donald Rogers that if you shook Gunton's overcoat you could pay off the national debt with what fell out of the pockets! It was also in 1975 that Donald Rogers was formally elected as Chairman of the Fellowship.[22]

The Little Red Booklet

There was, in the 1975 Pentecost *Bulletin*, an unqualified welcome for the final form of *The Sunday Service* booklet. This despite its pages being numbered with 'Birmingham postcodes' so that it corresponded to the complete *Methodist Service Book* where the pages of each section had a different letter, and thereby instituted the celebrant's immortal phrase, 'We begin on page B5!' British Methodists now had a liturgy corresponding to the new Roman Rite and to Anglican Series 3, but with the acknowledgement that the Preaching Service was the Liturgy of the Word, that the Collect of the Day belonged with the first group of prayers, and the Liturgy of the Faithful began with the Peace and the Creed. What could match the succinct and eschatological post-communion prayer from the pen of Geoffrey Wainwright?[23]

T S Gregory and Francis Westbrook

T S Gregory died on 11th August 1975. A tribute by Marcus Ward appeared in the *Bulletin*, as did one from A S Gregory to Francis Westbrook, who had died on 19th September.

Francis Westbrook was present at Penrhos College for the first meeting of the MSF in 1935. Though his greatest gift was in music, as a composer, conductor, professor of harmony and counterpoint and an organist, he also wrote a fine devotional commentary on the Cranmer-Wesleyan Communion Office. He also taught the Annual Conference of the Fellowship to sing Merbecke each year at the Sunday morning Eucharist. He was a fine preacher, something of a raconteur and had a great capacity for friendship. As far as Methodism was concerned, he was the greatest exponent of music in the service of the church that it had had since the Wesley family. In his diary for 17th June 1953 he had written:

> Scott Lidgett has gone at last. It happened on Tuesday June 17th – Wesley's birthday. He had hoped to live to a hundred and preach on Wesley's birthday then. Though that has been denied him, he has had a wonderful innings. His is a story of much endeavour, favourable positions, and great fulfilment. Lidgett was the sole survivor of the old school. He was

distinguished in every way. One thing, however, he lacked! He had no music in him![24]

'Forms for the Divine Office'

In Gordon Wakefield's predictably favourable review of the new MSF daily prayers, *Forms for the Divine Office*, he hoped they would sooner, rather than later, move from classic 'AV English' into the 'you' language of most current worship texts such as the latest Roman, Anglican and Methodist liturgies.[25]

The Book Men

Keith Burrow was ordained in the 1980s and brought with him into the Fellowship his artistic and publishing skills, which he put to good effect in designing the pamphlets of MSF and, for some years, as Editor of the *Bulletin*.

Laurie Gage became a familiar figure at the MSF Annual Conference and at London MSF events. He was a dealer in antiquarian and second hand books and specialized in Methodism, theology and church history. He had a phenomenal knowledge of Methodist authors and connexional literature, and year by year brought Methodist treasures to the Low Sunday Weekend Conference, including, on one occasion, a copy of Wesley's 1735 version of *The Imitation of Christ*, which only one lay member of the Fellowship finally decided he could afford![26]

New members in 1976 included Robert Davies of Culcheth, Warrington who, in addition to his circuit ministry, developed a publishing concern which survived the demise of the Methodist Publishing House and the Epworth Press, and published books for several MSF members including the writings of Gordon Wakefield and indeed this very book!

Bill Armstrong

The Lent *Bulletin* of 1976 reported the death of Bill Armstrong who had died the previous October. Leaving school at fifteen,

Bill worked in a newsagent's, trained as a librarian and then entered the Primitive Methodist ministry in 1931. He served for seventeen years in the Bahamas before becoming Deputy Chairman of Panama, Canal Zone and Costa Rica. For ten years he was Caribbean Secretary of the Bible Society, covering a vast area. He was a popular preacher and *raconteur extraordinaire* with a phenomenal memory for people and anecdotes. He was equally at home with the Duchess of Windsor and the market-vendor, and equally at ease with the governor of a colony, the diocesan bishop and the Pentecostal preacher. He was renowned for offering wicked and forthright rebukes to troublesome members of his congregations! He was a member of the MSF almost from its inception, serving in his retirement on the General Committee and as Overseas Secretary.[27]

Donald Soper provided an obituary for Mrs Mary Padget, a faithful member of Kingsway Hall and a convert to Anglicanism, who had been an assiduous member of the MSF and, with her husband Clifford, one of the Fellowship's former Secretaries.[28]

The Ten Propositions

The Fellowship, at its Annual General Meeting of 1976, passed a resolution noting with approval the Ten Propositions contained in the *Second Annual Report of the Churches' Unity Commission,* and earnestly hoped it would command acceptance by as wide a spectrum of Christian traditions as possible – clearly with the hope of bridging the Anglican and Free Church divide.[29]

The Methodist Church Bill

In 1976 the Fellowship sent a letter of loyal support to the President of Conference with regard to the Methodist Church Bill on its passage through Parliament. Members of the Fellowship were later told how Raymond George and Mrs Mary Lenton (as ex-President and ex Vice-President of

Conference) faced cross examination before a Parliamentary Committee. Mrs Lenton, on being asked if she could be thought a true Methodist, replied, 'Indeed I can. We entertained Mr Wesley to tea and we still have the tea service!'

New members in 1976 included Dick Westlake, a classic and endearing prep-school master who, for years, attended the Low Sunday Weekend Conferences and acted on many occasions as an unassuming but highly efficient chapel steward.[30]

The Hengrave Community

During Donald Rogers' stationing in the Wisbech Methodist circuit he and Brenda Rogers were drawn, through their commitment to the religious life, to the ecumenical developments at Hengrave Hall, Bury St Edmunds. Orginally a Tudor and Stuart mansion, the property became the nineteenth century home of the Sisters of the Assumption, who ran it as a convent school until 1974.

In September 1974 the Assumptionists founded the ecumenical Hengrave Community of Reconciliation, originally a group of families of different Christian denominations. Donald and Brenda became full members of the Community in the Methodist Connexional year of 1976. Although strongly inspired by other ecumenical communities like Taizé, the Hengrave Community had a distinctive character owing to the Sisters' continued presence, until it was dissolved in September 2005.

'Methodists and the Retreat Movement'

In the Spring of 1976 the Methodist Home Mission Division published a pamphlet, *Methodists and the Retreat Movement,* written by Donald Rogers with the encouragement of Gordon Wakefield and Mary Holliday. As he introduced his subject to Methodists Donald Rogers explained:

> Many Methodists are embarrassed by silence. Some think of it as a waste of time. Others regard it simply as free time. Still

others feel guilty if they do not fill every moment of it with prayer and meditation. As someone who used to belong to this third group, I have come only recently to see the value of silence without constant mental activity. No one who is new to retreats and quiet days should be expected to spend long periods in uninterrupted silence.

A retreat or quiet day for beginners should contain some periods of silence and others in which conversation is allowed ... A silent period can be a very creative period. It can afford a sense of timelessness, deep concentration and an extraordinary sense of fellowship. It can make us more aware of the presence of God, and help us towards a new understanding of our faith in terms of will rather than feeling.

In these days when the word 'Retreat' is often used to describe a training weekend or a social gathering the word [needs to be reclaimed] as a traditional spiritual exercise.[31]

A Letter from America

The *Bulletin* printed the first of Revd Dr John Bishop's *A Letter from America.* John Bishop had been a member of the MSF from its formative and pioneering days before he left the British stations for a lectureship in the United States. His most enduring book, first published in 1950, was *Methodist Worship* which, for a long time, held the field as the only survey of its kind. It was re-issued in the United States in 1976.

Northern Districts' Meetings

For a number of years the one day conferences of the Northern Districts were held at the Manchester University Chaplaincy. On the Eve of Pentecost 1976 the day concluded with a Sung Eucharist assisted by the Aldersgate Singers under their Churchillian director, W E Leathwood. A Deputy County Lieutenant for Cheshire and 'a Weslo-Catholic,' he had been a member of the MSF from the 1940s. The choir sang an S S Wesley *Introit,* Maunder's *Gloria, Sanctus* and *Agnus Dei* and Mozart's *Ave Verum.*[32]

New members in 1976 included Revd Dr Geoffrey Wainwright and Mrs Margaret Wainwright.[33]

Confession in the Methodist Tradition

In the second of his articles on *Confession in the Methodist Tradition* Kenneth Wilson asked two questions. Is a Methodist minister ordained to hear confessions? Would the Methodist Church tolerate the provision of an appropriate Order for Penance? Twenty years later, when the *Methodist Worship Book* was published in 1999, it contained just such a service adapted from a service of the Uniting Church in Australia.[34]

Front Page Vestments

The London MSF Meeting at Kingsway Hall in November 1977 hit the front page of the *Methodist Recorder*. A photo-shot was taken in the Little Chapel at Kingsway with the candles burning on the altar table and before it Mary Holliday, the preacher, in cassock, gown, bands and stole, Norman Beasley, the London MSF Secretary, in his habit and cross as a member of the Order of the Holy Family and the celebrant, Donald Rogers, Chair of the Fellowship, in full eucharistic vestments including chasuble! (A bit of innocent press photography – but, as Dr Rattenbury had said in his *Vital Elements of Public Worship*, such things indicate which way the wind is blowing!)

The Re-Opening of Wesley's Chapel

Members of the Fellowship (who included both the Minister and Associate Minister at City Road) were thrilled to share in the grand re-opening of Wesley's Chapel and to hear the MSF Prayer being read by the President of the Conference in the presence of The Queen and Prince Philip![35]

In the Christmas *Bulletin* of 1978 an Australian member of the Fellowship, Wesley Hartley, reported on the inauguration of the Uniting Church of Australia, bringing together 1.75

million Christians, with 1650 Methodist, 583 Presbyterian and 167 Congregationalist ministers and about a thousand parishes. Wesley Hartley felt that the Catholic presence in the Uniting Church would fare no worse than it had within Australian Methodism alone. Half the Presbyterians and a quarter of Congregationalists had stayed out of the union![36]

The Presidency of the Fellowship

In the same *Bulletin* John Newton welcomed the appointment of Gordon Wakefield to the Presidency of the Fellowship, writing of 'a Catholic Methodist steeped in the classic tradition of the Wesleys' discipline, devotion, hymnody, evangelical passion and high sacramentalism,' who would fit the MSF Presidency 'like a hand in a glove.'[37]

Stewart Denyer wrote in the *Bulletin* to mark the recognition of Donald Soper as the Fellowship's President Emeritus. Methodists were always surprised to discover that a man they cast as a liberal evangelical was in fact a convinced sacramentalist and as far removed from the Protestant underworld as it was possible to be! Soper always seemed like a man who saw the Creed as a battle cry rather than a set of theological propositions! In his year as President of Conference he had demonstrated to the entire Connexion the importance and centrality of the Eucharist by his celebration of Holy Communion in every circuit visit! He never ceased to use his commanding voice to advocate the Fellowship and he was a totally worthy successor to the MSF's previous President Emeritus, J Ernest Rattenbury.[38]

Ronald Ducker and Marcus Ward

Also in the Christmas *Bulletin* of 1978 Leslie Orchard marked the death of Ronald Ducker, a former Vice-President of the Fellowship, and recalled the Christmas Eve of 1944 when he and Ducker were both stationed in Florence. Orchard was delighted when he was told by Ducker that he had arranged for a Midnight Communion at Wesley House (the Forces'

Methodist Chaplaincy), and recalled Ducker presiding at a triumphal celebration of the Eucharist for twenty or so Servicemen.

> As I walked through the snow back to the army camp, I joined many others of my fellow Christians returning from Midnight Mass at the Cathedral and I was glad that I was, in a sense, one of them. That tells much of what Ronald Ducker stood for.[39]

Leslie Orchard also marked the death of Marcus Ward, an old Kingswood boy who had gained a first in theology at Cambridge and went on to teach New Testament at the United College at Bangalore and to be one of the architects of the Church of South India. On his return to Britain Marcus taught at Richmond Theological College in London and, in retirement, at Heythrop College, where he was regarded as having 'the natural spirit of a Jesuit.' Some of the first moves towards the MSF had been hammered out in Marcus' rooms when he was Assistant Tutor at Richmond in the 1930s, and throughout his ministry Marcus Ward had remained a faithful stalwart of the Fellowship. He had been a key player in the early years of The Ecumenical Society of the Blessed Virgin Mary and a member of its Council. As one of the Methodist representatives on the Anglican-Methodist Conversations he took the view that the South India model of mutual recognition of ministries without a service of reconciliation that included the mutual laying on of hands was not appropriate in the British situation. He was bitterly disappointed when the Anglican votes defeated the British scheme.[40]

Cardinal Basil Hume

The MSF London Meeting of February 1979 was held at Wesley's Chapel with Cardinal Basil Hume as the guest speaker. He had been invited by Donald Soper. There was a Eucharist at 6 pm and a buffet supper before the public meeting at which the Cardinal spoke and at which Kenneth

Greet, Secretary of the Conference, led the prayers. The Cardinal indicated that he wished to remain for MSF sung Compline in the Chapel. On his way out he remarked how terribly similar it was to the service they sang each night at Ampleforth! Some thought they heard a slight rustling from the graveyard. Was it the ghost of Wesley turning the pages of his *Letter to a Roman Catholic*?

Methodist Religious Communities

Following on from The Order of the Holy Family founded by Donald and Brenda Rogers, other MSF members were instrumental in the formation of The Wesley Community based at Wesley's Chapel, London. Previous ministers at City Road had raised the possibility of some kind of a community and the Methodist Conference had voted £25,000 to that end. The Wesley Community began with seven members, Ron and Olive Gibbins, two American Methodist deacons, a university music student, a stockbroker's clerk and Revd Gerald Tedcastle who, like the Gibbins, was a member of the MSF. The Conference grant enabled the provision in the Benson Building of eight study bedrooms. The Community said its own Daily Office each morning and evening in the Foundery Chapel, with a weekly Wednesday Eucharist. The members of the Community contributed to the ministry of hospitality in money, time and talent. Other Methodists in Yorkshire and North London were also forming houses of the Wesley Community, serving the estates on which they lived. In its introductory literature the Community acknowledged its debt to the ethos and practice of the MSF.[41]

1979 was also the year of the founding of the Sisters of Jesus Way at Red Acre House, West Kirby on The Wirral. Originally under the auspices of two former Wesley Deaconesses and the Guardianship of the Methodist District Chair, John Newton, the Order eventually moved into evangelical Anglicanism and now flourishes with at least a dozen sisters.[42]

The Historic Episcopate

At its 1979 Low Sunday Weekend Conference the Fellowship noted a resolution at the Methodist Conference to explore British Methodism taking the historic episcopate into its system unilaterally. In its welcome the MSF hoped that, if British Methodism moved in this direction, its bishops would be committed to increasing the missionary and pastoral potential of the Connexion. Such bishops would (it hoped) be introduced somewhere between the existing Superintendents and District Chairs. The consecrating bishops, it was also hoped, would be drawn from as wide a spectrum of churches as possible, including the United Churches in India and the Anglican Church, with an optimistic request to Rome itself![43]

Revd John Fisher was appointed Northern Districts Secretary and Revd Harvey Richardson, in relinquishing his position as Music Director, became Ecumenical Secretary in succession to Stanley Morrow. Revd Brian Pickett stood down after arranging a good number of Annual Conferences.[44]

The Community of the King of Love

A third religious community founded with the input and sponsorship of MSF members including Gordon Wakefield was The Community of the King of Love. Life within the Community was to be expressed through 'renunciation, prayer and service.' The internal life of the Community is turned outwards in work of reconciliation. The original Guardians of the Community were an Anglican priest, Neil Smith, and a Methodist minister, David Hall. Neil died in the 1990s but David is now in the 34th year of his profession within the Whaley Hall Community. A deeply ecumenical Community sponsored by the main Christian traditions, it has blossomed as a centre for corporate and private retreats and as a conference centre. Large portions of the *Methodist Worship Book* first saw the light of day in the Community and a number of the Eucharists for the new book of 1999 were first celebrated in its chapel.[45]

10
Methodist Fellowship

'The Methodist Prayer Handbook'

A footnote on the final page of the *Bulletin* for Advent 1980 drew attention to *Methodists at Prayer*, a precursor of the *Methodist Prayer Handbook*. This publication was a partnership with the World Church Office of the Methodist Missionary Society, combining the overseas *Prayer Manual* with intercessory material for the British Districts and the provision of a Daily Lectionary. The project emerged from a Conference memorial, bringing together Michael Taylor, the Editor of the *Methodist Recorder*, Keith Lewis of the Methodist Revival Fellowship and the present author from the MSF. The Fellowship's contribution has remained the consistent mainstay of the *Prayer Handbook* which, after more than thirty years, still sells in excess of 30,000 copies annually.[1] After editing the MSF *Bulletin* for twelve years the present author handed his responsibilities to Brian Pickett.

Ash Wednesday 1981

At the London Meeting of the MSF on Ash Wednesday 1981 the Fellowship celebrated the 1936 Communion Order from the *Methodist Service Book* and included the Ashing Ceremony, which was clearly a historic moment – if not for Methodism – then certainly for Wesley's Chapel, and described in the *Bulletin* as 'a unique and moving experience'![2]

East Anglia

The Methodist Conference Public Meeting during the Norwich Conference of 1981 was held out in the country, with the united Anglican-Methodist congregation of Holy Trinity, Loddon. The chair was taken by the Methodist historian and bookseller, Laurie Gage. On the way to address the meeting Lord Soper spent the entire car journey entertaining his fellow passengers with what he thought about a number of his fellow peers. The other speakers were Gordon Wakefield and the scholarly ecumenist, Alan Clark, the Roman Catholic Bishop of East Anglia.

Harborne House

Dick Westlake reflected on the Fellowships' Annual Low Sunday Weekend Conference of 1982 in the *Bulletin*:

> Throughout the Conference, at both eucharists and in the offices, the chapel resounded with the singing of the psalms and canticles. The atmosphere at Harborne House and its beautiful surroundings created an ideal setting for our thinking and discussions. The hospitality was friendly and unobtrusive. There was a good balance of familiar and fresh faces. I have now attended four annual Conferences of the Fellowship – eight days in four years – yet the people I have come to know are old and well established friends. That says something, I think, for the fellowship of our group.[3]

The Ten Propositions

Keith Burrow, the Fellowship's ecumenical secretary, gave his personal reaction following much disappointment at the failure of the Church of England General Synod to vote in favour of the Covenanting proposals in *Report of the Churches' Council for Covenanting Towards Visible Unity*. The proposals originally contained in the 1976 *Ten Propositions* asked the covenanting churches to affirm that, from an accepted date, there would be mutual recognition of communicant members and of their admission to Holy Communion, mutually acceptable initiation rites, and mutual acceptance of the ordained ministries of the other churches as true ministries of the Holy Catholic Church with an agreement that all subsequent ordinations would be according to a common ordinal which properly incorporated the episcopal, presbyteral and lay roles in ordination.

Bishop Graham Leonard and others had sounded alarm bells about interim and permissive arrangements over non-episcopally ordained moderators in the United Reformed Church, the rights of conscience for Anglican bishops in relation to Free Church women ministers and lay celebration of Holy Communion. Methodists, Moravians and the URCs voted significantly in favour but the proposals had fallen in the House of Clergy of the General Synod. John Habgood, then Bishop of Durham, viewed the decision of the General Synod as bringing to a halt the process that had started with the Lambeth Conference Appeal of 1920. Keith Burrow quoted one of his vestry stewards as saying, 'They's let us doon again.' Keith went on to warn that the current Report before Methodism on how the connexion might embrace episcopacy would not lose its relevance because sooner or later Methodism would have to return to the issue of taking the historic episcopate into its system.[4]

The Testimony of Nancy Temple

A stalwart of the Fellowship, Nancy Temple contributed an article to the *Bulletin* on *The Eucharist: Mystery and Certainty*, in which she reported both joy and frustration:

> We are one with the first Christians of Malta whose original cave and altar table I have seen. We are one with Julian of Norwich strengthened by this mysterious rite. As a lay person and a local preacher I raise the difficulties for those who seem always planned to take preaching services elsewhere when it is Communion in our local chapel. There is a case for Communion at the Preachers' Meeting. Why do some ministers still tag the service on to the end of a full Sunday service? How can there still be ministers who give out the bread and wine with no Prayer of Thanksgiving and no obvious Consecration? At times I climb the holy wall! But at the heart of it all I receive the very life of Christ.[5]

Irvonwy Morgan

In the Epiphany *Bulletin* of 1983 Ron Gibbins paid tribute to the life and work of Irvonwy Morgan. Irvonwy had been in the small group that worked with TS and AS Gregory and others in the key years and months leading to the formation of the Fellowship. After his years at Kingswood, the Guildhall School of Music and Wesley House, Cambridge, he served practically all his ministry in the London Mission. For the Connexional year 1935 to 1936 he withdrew from Methodism to consider his vocation to be a Catholic priest. He was President of the Conference in 1967. In later life he published a book of poems, *A Rent for Love and other Poems*, which revealed the tender and romantic nature of his life and spirituality.

As Secretary of the London Mission Irvonwy once warned the trustees of Westminster Central Hall to be careful about the bookings they took. He had been leaving the Hall one day when he spotted a young woman whom he knew to be a prostitute. On asking what she was doing in the Central Hall she replied that she had come to her profession's union meeting! Ron Gibbins recalled a Eucharist he and Irvonwy had shared at the East End Mission in which a well-known figure, 'Taffy,' had leapt out during the recessional and accosted Irvonwy with a whisper and then retreated. In the vestibule Irvonwy took a bank-note from his wallet and gave it to Taffy. Ron Gibbins pointed out this was not necessary because the mission had a perfectly adequate poor fund. Back came the ex-President's reply, 'Any man who can speak Welsh can have my money.'[6]

'Baptism, Eucharist and Ministry'

In the Pentecost 1983 *Bulletin*, Keith Burrow introduced the Fellowship to the far-reaching World Council of Churches Faith and Order Paper, *Baptism, Eucharist and Ministry*. One of the principal co-authors of the Lima text was a member of the Fellowship, Geoffrey Wainwright, who was quickly becoming the outstanding international Methodist theologian of his generation. After circuit ministry in Liverpool and teaching in Cameroon, West Africa, he taught scripture and theology at the Queen's College, Birmingham. After Union Theological Seminary, New York, he taught at Duke Divinity School, North Carolina. From 1976 to 1991 Wainwright was a member of the Faith and Order Commission of the World Council of Churches. His outstanding career of teaching and writing included his seminal *Doxology: The Praise of God in Worship, Doctrine and Life.*

The convergence statements in *Baptism, Eucharist and Ministry* were to prove a milestone in inter-church and international dialogue. The entire Report was to be music to the ears of the MSF, as its members encouraged Methodists and those of other Christian traditions to see themselves in what the Report had to say about the *Institution, Meaning and Practice of Baptism, Eucharist and Ministry.*

Baptism was set forth as participation in Christ, conversion, gift of the Spirit, incorporation into the Church and sign. Baptism of both Believers and Infants was defended and Baptism, Chrismation and Confirmation were seen as process. Celebration of each of the three mysteries, baptism, eucharist and ministry, was to be celebrated with the fullness of the sign.

The eucharist was set forth as Thanksgiving to the Father, Anamnesis or Memorial of the Son and as Invocation of the Spirit, communion of the faithful and meal of the kingdom. All powerfully reminiscent of the Wesleys' *Hymns on the Lord's Supper*!

The threefold ministry was expounded in terms of its calling to assemble and build up God's people, to teach them and to preside in their sacraments, worship and mission. All ordained ministry was related to the priestly service and nature of Christ and of the whole Christian community, and an episcopate that was personal, collegial and communal was at the heart of the church in its fullness. Episcopal succession was seen as a sign and not a guarantee of continuity and unity.[7]

Fifty Years of Catholic Witness

The Epiphany *Bulletin* of 1985 had its own title, *Fifty Years of Catholic Witness 1935–1985.* The present author wrote on the precursor to the MSF, *The [Wesleyan] Guild of Divine Service*, and Kingsley Lloyd and Arthur Gregory wrote about the Fellowship's beginning and continuing witness. Stanley Morrow (who had enlivened many a late night gathering at the Annual Conference with reminiscences and anecdotes about the more eccentric members) wrote about the gradual transition of the MSF from a 'High Wesleyan pressure group' to a Catholic Fellowship.[8]

The Golden Jubilee of the Fellowship – Robert Runcie

During the spring of 1984 Robert Runcie, the Archbishop of Canterbury, sent two letters to the MSF. In the first he regretted that his diary prevented him from coming to a London Golden Jubilee Event of the Fellowship in November 1985. His second letter was a greeting to be read out at the MSF Public Meeting in the Queen's College, Birmingham during the 1985 Wolverhampton Conference. (This was also the occasion on which the Fellowship launched the first of its annual published lectures, beginning with Gordon Wakefield's *Catholic Spirituality Considered.*)

> It gives me great pleasure to send the Methodist Sacramental Fellowship my greetings at your Jubilee Celebrations. John Wesley was a sacramental man, as any study of his life and Ministry inevitably shows. All progress in the ecumenical field depends upon our re-discovering the authentic roots of our own traditions and bringing them afresh as a gift to the *oikumene*. Within the Methodist tradition it is your task to emphasise that which Wesley emphasised, so that his best gifts are brought to the eventual unity he never wished to break.[9]

Though it has not survived, in October 1984 a very gracious hand-written letter was received from Michael Ramsey, regretting that he also was not able to travel from

Durham to speak at any of the 1985 Golden Jubilee celebrations of the Fellowship.

The Golden Jubilee of the Fellowship – Westminster Abbey

The MSF London Districts were given permission by the Dean and Chapter to celebrate the Fellowship's Golden Jubilee in Westminster Abbey on 2 February. The day began with a Candlemas Ceremony and a Methodist Eucharist in Saint Faith's Chapel, at which Donald Rogers presided and Brian Pickett preached. The sermon began with the memorable line, 'Recently, when I was speaking with my Bank Manager and he suggested I banked with him rather than he with me ...'

A London MSF choir sang two motets during communion and Stanford's 150th Psalm as a recessional. The congregation then processed to the John and Charles Wesley Memorial Plaque in the Abbey, where the versicles and responses concluded with the Prayer of the Fellowship.

Lunch was served in the Jerusalem chamber, followed by a lecture from the President, Gordon Wakefield, on the challenge before the Fellowship to lead Methodism into a recovery of the theology of Saint John, in which Christ becomes the exegete of the Father, and the church on earth, as successor to the saints, participates in an eternal intercession for the whole world.

The Fellowship then moved to Choral Evensong, where the Dean invited Gordon Wakefield to read the Second Lesson (which he did wearing the Dean's MA gown) and where the MSF's Golden Jubilee was commemorated in the prayers after the third collect.

The Golden Jubilee of the Fellowship – Methodist Conference

There was further involvement of Robert Runcie in the Golden Jubilee of the Fellowship. Christopher Hill, the Archbishop's Assistant for Ecumenical Affairs, had written to the Fellowship for some background on current issues in the Connexion and the hopes and dreams of the MSF. Much to the amazement of the Fellowship not only did the Archbishop's official speech as Guest Speaker at the Wolverhampton Methodist Conference contain almost verbatim what the Fellowship had told him, but he highlighted before the whole Conference the significance of the Jubilee of the Fellowship!

In October 1985 the Northern Districts celebrated the Fellowship's Golden Jubilee with a Sung Eucharist at the Heath Church in Runcorn, led by the Aldersgate Singers and culminating in Stanford's *Te Deum.*[10]

The Golden Jubilee of the Fellowship – Wesley's Chapel, London

On 2 November 1985 the Fellowship held the national celebration of its Golden Jubilee. At the Jubilee Eucharist in Wesley's Chapel the sermon was preached by Gordon Rupp. He reminded the congregation that he had been sent from college to minister to the Sidcup Methodist congregation when T S Gregory had been prohibited from his appointment by Scott Lidgett because he was on the eve of his conversion to Rome. Scott Lidgett had earlier told the Methodist Conference:

> We are here to affirm our share in the catholic inheritance of the past. Who save ourselves can separate us from it?

Rupp wanted to warn the Fellowship and all Methodists that they could not go 'back to Wesley' or to some reconstructed original Methodism. That would be to remove the clothes from the invisible man! Wesley could not be the ventriloquist's dummy speaking our words. Neither could the cut of our vestments be a driving concern (but in a memorable aside he thought that, after appearing as blackbirds for two centuries, perhaps it was an advantage that our ministers had begun to look like budgerigars!).

Looking across into Bunhill Fields he recalled an 18th century 'explosion of grace the fallout of which touched the ends of the earth.' From such Catholicity one had to move to Wesley's 'Catholic Spirit' and, more particularly, to the hymns of Charles, 'in which by grace we confess the glory of the eternal Trinity and, in the power of the Divine Majesty, we worship the Unity.' It was the doctrine of the Trinity 'that touched the mind and satisfied the heart' of the preacher. 'God for us is God in us.'

> The heights and depths of grace,
> The wounds which all my sorrows heal,
> That dear disfigured face.

Grace, said the preacher, was always evangelical, always converting. Susanna Wesley, now sleeping across the road from the chapel in Bunhill Fields, had come to the Holy Table:

> The Father then revealed the Son,
> Him in the broken bread made known,
> She knew and felt her sins forgiven
> And found the earnest of her heaven.

When Bishop Lavington spoke to Wesley of Saint Francis, Saint Dominic and Saint Ignatius as 'those nasty, ridiculous, crackbrained, wicked saints' Wesley's catholic spirit was busy putting them into the fifty volumes of his *Christian Library*!

With Bunyan we must guard the lay apostolate. More than all else Methodism offers the church good Christian people. We cannot cease from the mental fight of Scott Lidgett and Donald Soper. If the MSF is a mixture of pirates and policemen, its Magna Carta of Catholicity is *Totus Christus* – the whole Christ – head and members –

> We are here to affirm our share in the catholic inheritance of the past. Who save ourselves can separate us from it?[11]

After the Golden Jubilee celebrations a cheque was sent to Gordon Rupp for his preaching expenses. During the liturgy he had processed into Wesley's Chapel with the exceedingly ancient and frail Kingsley Lloyd in his ex-Presidential robes. As the senior founding father and surviving stalwart of the MSF, Kingsley Lloyd was propped up in the apse of the Chapel and emerged to give the Blessing. Gordon Rupp had joined the MSF in its first year but had been persuaded (probably by

Newton Flew) that it was not in his interests to remain a member. On receiving his preaching fee Rupp returned it to the Fellowship with a note, 'When I saw old Lloyd standing there – he who had borne the heat and burden of the day – as I had not – I felt such a heel. If you will now receive me back into the Fellowship I return my fee as my subscription.'[12]

The Golden Jubilee of the Fellowship – Christian Diversity and Catholic Unity

Kenneth Cracknell gave the Fellowship's Golden Jubilee Lecture on *Christian Diversity and Catholic Unity.* Though he was not a joiner of groups he testified that it was the MSF that, for him, stood closest to where he wished to see the 'great tradition' of his own church. As a catholic Christian in the Methodist tradition he gave thanks for all that he had learnt from the vision and witness of the Fellowship. He then paid his debt of thankfulness and not least to Donald Lee, 'a great exponent of all that MSF stood for' and the one who had trained him in Methodist discipleship.

Some of the church from the beginning had seen itself as 'Fortress Zion.' Mission simply involved standing faithfully in one place. 'Just keep going and one day they will come.' Other Christians were 'Frontier Riders,' like Paul in Athens, abandoning the language of Messianic expectation and translating the gospel into another way of thinking. The sixty million Methodists in America owed their existence to the entrepreneurial gifts of the circuit frontier rider!

An expanding church would often be led into Charismatic Enthusiasm. Was there a place for the gifted outsider to join the apostolic community and its leadership, either Paul or Wesley? On the frontier Christians were to expect the gifts of the Spirit. Other Christians settled down into Calm Catholicism, where faith gave way to 'The Faith,' and sound doctrine and pure faith became the order of the day. In other contexts the church had to choose between its vocation as the upholder of Law and Order and its duty to adopt Subversive Sectarianism. Every period of Christian history illustrated this choice. We might choose Fortress Zion, but the Catholic Christianity that deserved to be celebrated belonged to the frontier, was about charismatic enthusiasm and was actually politically subversive.

That there was but one form of Christianity in the New Testament is a myth, yet then and now there is but one body that breaks one bread – the whole Body of Christ, dying and rising – in Christian diversity and Catholic unity.[13]

MSF News and Business

After fifty years, with the editorship passing to Keith Burrow, MSF news, announcements and reports of Fellowship events were circulated in accompanying papers and no longer appeared in the *Bulletin*, which was given over entirely to commissioned or submitted articles and to papers or addresses given at MSF events.

The Death of Stewart Denyer

The Lent *Bulletin* of 1986 marked the death of Stewart Denyer in his seventieth year. From his native Wesleyan and Anglican roots he was remembered at school and theological college for his natural goodness and his quiet scholarship. Boatmen in the Bahamas remembered him settling down on deck with his Greek New Testament. The West Indies gave him the lively Wesleyan liturgical worship he treasured all his life. After the Forest of Dean and Cheltenham he entered into the rich Wesleyan Prayer Book tradition of Trinity, Whiteladies Road in Bristol. After Folkestone he relished the Superintendency of the Leeds Headingley Circuit.

Stewart was the first to be elected as the Chairman of the Fellowship, serving in that office from 1965 to 1974. He was deeply distressed by the failure of the Anglican-Methodist unity proposals. He was an active participant in The Ecumenical Society of the Blessed Virgin Mary from its inception and, in 1969, gave the first of the major papers of the Society on *The Magnificat.*

In Exeter, at Sidwell Street, he finally encountered a Methodist culture that he could not woo into a rich sacramental life and liturgy and, in 1974, he resigned the Methodist ministry and received Anglican orders. From 1978 to 1982 he was priest in charge of Stoke-in-Teignhead and Combe-in-Teignhead in the Exeter diocese. He served with considerable distinction, not least as Diocesan Director of Readers, thus carrying on the work he had so valuably undertaken with the Methodist Local Preachers' Department years before. He bore his final, long and painful illness with a humility and Christian fortitude which pervaded the victorious Requiem Eucharist at Saint Gregory's, Dawlish.[14]

Philip Blackburn succeeds Donald Rogers

The 1986 Low Sunday Weekend Conference of the Fellowship was held at the Ely Diocesan Retreat House. At Friday Evening Prayer, the Chair of the Fellowship, Donald Rogers, inducted Philip Blackburn as his successor. Philip was to fulfil his role with outstanding success and memorable distinction. John Newton lectured at the weekend on *The Spirituality of Edward King*, sharing out of his rich store of knowledge as the foremost scholar and biographer of the saintly and controversial Bishop of Lincoln.

Children at Holy Communion

The 1987 Methodist Conference received a Report from the Faith and Order Committee and the Division of Education and Youth on *Children and Holy Communion*. Keith Burrow set out in the *Bulletin* the reasons for a Methodist change of policy and practice. Children were able to be present at a whole service of Communion, which used not to be the case. An increased celebration of the Great Festivals had brought worship, children and communion together. Children hearing that all who love the Lord may come to the Table then felt deprived at not being able to receive the sacrament. The notion, 'Not until they understand,' had less and less credence. Other Christian traditions of a more 'catholic' sympathy allowed (baptised) young children to receive communion. Methodism was being called to look once more at the issues of baptism, confirmation, church membership and the eucharist itself. Members of the MSF were in no doubt that baptism brings adults and children into the life of Christ and into the life of the church. Catechesis with those who are un-baptised would be a crucial issue in the whole revision of current policy and practice.[15]

Altars and Altar Calls

At the 1987 Conference Public Meeting, held during the Plymouth Methodist Conference, Philip Blackburn gave his famous lecture, *Altars and Altar Calls*, in which he demonstrated with much amusement and great aplomb how he was the incarnation of the type of evangelical who still preached for conversions and decisions, but also one who put at the heart of his ministry the rites and rituals of sacramental Methodism and one to one Christian formation.

One Baptism Once – A Tangled Skein

In 1988 Methodism was beginning to move on from its 1975 initiation services to those that would eventually be provided in the 1999 worship book. In the midst of the debate a number of ministers, members and congregations were pressing for a liturgical rite (preferably with water) that would affirm those who had been led back to Christ in adulthood and to whom their baptism as infants meant little or nothing. Some were pressing for a 'real baptism' in contrast to what they regarded as a mere 'christening.' At the height of the debate Gordon Wakefield, the Fellowship's President, and Neil Dixon, a member of the Fellowship and the Convener of the Faith and Order Committee, wrote at length in the *MSF Bulletin,* defending both tradition and the pastoral requests for a service of renewal involving water.[16]

Gordon Wakefield began his article by raising what, for many, had become a basic assumption – that infant baptism is not a proper rite of Christian initiation. He argued that to deny its validity would be to repudiate the whole of Methodist sacramental history, and to regard every statement of the Conference on the subject since the union of 1932 as in error. Nevertheless there were those who believed that Methodism should go back to the practice of the first Christians and at the same time condemn the scandal of indiscriminate baptism.

It was, on the one hand, possible to justify indiscriminate baptism on the grounds that all people are entitled to claim the inheritance of what God did in Christ. Calvary was the world's baptism and we dare not deny anyone a share of its benefits. The contrary belief emphasised the necessity and awesomeness of the individual decision and the need for baptism to be the seal of a personal encounter with Jesus Christ and the sign of a new birth, which, unlike natural birth, is not without deliberate and subjective choice. Its exponents were able to point to the apparent failure of prevenient grace to be efficacious in making Christians, or in changing the world. The logic of the latter demanded a 'pure' Church, consisting only of those who were consciously born again and 'in Christ.' The former saw the Church as a mixed community, more like the harvest field of the parable, with 'wheat and tares together sown.'

A second issue was that of the unrepeatability of baptism. Wakefield realized that the Methodist Church, while re-affirming the unrepeatability of baptism, had become convinced that, in the present climate, some rite of renewal was necessary. The Faith and Order Committee was willing to countenance the use of water in such a rite, though Conference demurred. The Catholic rite of asperges, in which there was a sprinkling of the congregation with water as a reminder of baptism, had been adapted in the Uniting Church of Australia, and was surely worthy of consideration.

But where in all this was confirmation? In the East anointing with chrism is the concluding ceremony of the Sacrament of Initiation, which is a unity and takes place whatever the age of the candidate. In the West the full rite of Initiation is not delegated to presbyters, and what came to be known as Confirmation, in the sense of completion, is reserved for the bishop. Methodism was asking whether or not we should admit baptised children to Communion, which for some gave grounds for disquiet.[17]

The Aldersgate 250th Anniversary

1988 was the year Methodism celebrated the 250th Anniversary of John Wesley's Aldersgate experience. For the Sunday evening of Aldersgate Weekend the London MSF members planned and prepared the open air procession and Eucharist on the concourse of the London Museum, for the dedication of the Memorial Flame commemorating Wesley's conversion. There were approaching a thousand communicants! Wafers were the order of the day and chalices were borrowed from Methodist chapels and neighbouring Anglican sacristies all over the four London Districts!

The Death of A S Gregory

In July 1989 members of the MSF, accompanied by their president, Gordon Wakefield, made the journey to Kendal for a service of thanksgiving for A S Gegory. The Chair of the District, Norman Pickering, led the service assisted by the present author. Ivor Jones of the Methodist Church Music Society was the organist. Arthur Gregory had died in May at the age of 94. His life as one of the founding fathers of the Methodist Sacramental Fellowship and one of its venerable Vice-Presidents was recalled. He had been the most distinguished Methodist hymnologist of his generation. His *Praises with Understanding* (Epworth 1933, 1949 and 1972) had become a classic. He had lived to celebrate the Golden

Jubilee of the Methodist Church Music Society and the MSF, both of which he helped to found.

After Kingswood School and Trinity College, Oxford, Arthur Gregory served as a Lieutenant with the Royal Field Artillery. He had three great Christian passions – prayer and spirituality, the music of Christendom, and the catholicity of the Church. The first of these he expressed in his contributions to the *Manuals of Fellowship*, which were produced throughout the thirties for the Methodist School of Fellowship at Swanwick. Here, along with his ministerial cousin, T S Gregory, and the Findlays and Maltbys, he helped to develop the prayer and spirituality of Methodism. Throughout his ministry he shared his knowledge of church music and skill in its performance with many Methodist church musicians, again often at Swanwick.

When, at the time of Methodist re-union in 1932, the Wesleyan high-churchmanship of his forebears seemed to be in jeopardy, A S and others felt called to found the MSF. In the succeeding years they produced the earliest MSF conferences and the first *Bulletins*, and fended off the Methodist Conference itself, in order to breed and keep perhaps four generations of Catholic Methodists, who could live out the fullness of the Christian faith in their own tradition. Once, during the long years of his retirement, A S wrote to an enquiring Methodist student, 'You speak of the future of Methodism. I believe there is no future for Methodism outside the Catholic tradition.'[18] His memorial service began with a characteristic Bidding Prayer.

Brothers and sisters in Christ,
we praise God for the life and ministry of Arthur Gregory,
for his devotion to the church of his forebears,
his exultation in her liturgy
and his exposition of her hymnody;
but chiefly for his understanding of the people called
  Methodists
in the fulness of the Catholic faith.
From him we learnt to sing our praises with understanding;

to say our prayers in communion with the saints
and to reverence Christ in the sacraments of the gospel.
We recall his summons to the discipline and culture of the spiritual life;
his own skill in composing and making music
and his invitation to us all to glorify God and to enjoy him for ever.

The Bicentenary of Wesley's Death

On 2nd March 1991, to mark the Bicentenary of Wesley's death, members of the Fellowship prepared and led the Office of Morning Prayer in the Foundery Chapel at City Road, prepared and led Prayers in Wesley's bedroom, and prepared and led a Choral Eucharist in Wesley's Chapel.

Soper at Ninety

In the New Year of 1993 the MSF *Bulletin* celebrated Donald Soper's ninetieth birthday, giving thanks for the clarity and single-mindedness of his ministry. There was no great Methodist tradition that did not have the President Emeritus of the Fellowship at its the heart. Kingsway Hall and the West London Mission had stood for the inseparable bond between social righteousness and sacramental worship, and this was seen in the bright succession of Hugh Price Hughes, J Ernest Rattenbury and Donald Soper, and continued with John Newton, Leslie Griffiths and David Cruise.

In the tradition which married pulpit and table, the Presidency of the MSF was well blessed, in the succession of A E Whitham, J Ernest Rattenbury, Donald Soper and Gordon Wakefield.

Hyde Park, the House of Lords, Tower Hill, the Methodist Conference and the television screen had all been graced by the Protestant preacher in the Catholic cassock, whose sharpened mind and polished wit had few equals in popular and intelligent Christian apologetic.

From the '1936' Communion Service that began his week at 10 am on Sundays to the sleeveless leather jacket that warmed his sturdy frame through London protest marches, the former MSF President was all of a piece.

Members of the Fellowship could recall it being said of Donald Soper's 1957 Methodist Lent Book, *All His Grace,* that the first chapter could only have been written by a Methodist and the last chapter could only have been written by a Catholic. He who had written that Christianity was a sacrifice of the spirit and of the body went on to say of Charles Wesley's realized and sacramental sign, 'the sign has become real to me.' In one life and ministry the orthodoxy and orthopraxis of the Methodist tradition were outstandingly manifest and truly incarnate.[19]

Neville Ward

In the autumn of 1992, along with many others far beyond the bounds of Methodism, the Fellowship mourned the sudden death of Neville Ward. A son of the manse he was also a cousin of Marcus Ward, a founding father of the MSF. After Kingswood School and Exeter College, Oxford, Neville studied for the ministry in Manchester. Those who were members of his churches experienced an unforgettable preaching and pastoral ministry that left an indelible mark. His sermons, finely prepared, were short and searching and never failed to challenge, inform and teach. His conscious spiritual journey began when at Kingswood School.

> Seven years at John Wesley's school gave me the beginnings of sensitiveness to five realms – the value of reason, the goodness of the body, the pleasure and pain in personal relationships, the call to serve, the appreciation of beauty ... I had, however, experienced in my last year at school a small spiritual disturbance. It came quite unexpectedly though very vividly. So vividly that it is always associated in my mind with the actual place where it happened. I suddenly found myself, for no apparent reason, thinking about Jesus for the first time as an intriguing individual; and at that moment the pietistic,

> sentimental, Sunday School image of him that I had been hating for years dropped away for ever. And in its place was a man, unknown certainly, but real.[20]

Ward's catholicity and sacramentalism did not come until some years on in his ministry. In his early years the Eucharist had been a dead routine, until there came a time when he started to preach a sacramental Christianity with intense conviction. He came to see the Eucharist 'as a solemn, beautiful and triumphant concentration of all the Christian meanings that matter.' This view of worship remained and became so absorbing that the 'other forms of worship that we go in for seemed rather thin and uninteresting things.'

His books established him as a significant English writer on spirituality. They commanded a wide catholic readership and prompted numerous religious communities and many others to invite him to lead retreats. Prayer was at the heart of his writings and his first book, in 1967, *The Use of Praying*, came to be regarded as a modern classic. His 1971 *Five for Sorrow, Ten for Joy: A Consideration of the Rosary* was to remain in print for forty years and its contents, so remarkable for a Methodist, put the title of the book and the name of its author on the lips of countless Catholic-minded Christians. He made a huge contribution to the first years of The Ecumenical Society of the Blessed Virgin Mary. His great regret was the silence about Mary in Methodism which he thought 'positively deafening.'

His love for his family overflowed with devotion as he wrote of his sons, 'I profoundly want the aesthetic and spiritual to seize them. Those are the only dimensions I care about.'[21]

He loved his roses and his music. He transformed his Canterbury garden into one of character and great beauty and delight and, in retirement, he taught himself to play the classical guitar.

A New Look Bulletin

With the publication of the *MSF Bulletin* No 123 in 1994 there was a marked change in its appearance. After a run of sixty years, as the editorship passed to Neil Stubbens, the original pamphlet-style of the *Bulletin* was transformed into an annual journal format with card covers, its commissioned articles and reviews extending to some forty or more pages.

Patricia Billsborrow

At the Saturday Eucharist during the Low Sunday Weekend Conference of 1998 its acting Chairman, Donald Rogers, inducted Pat Billsborrow to be the new Chair of the MSF. The Fellowship had come a long way from the days when some of its leading members in the 40s, 50s and 60s wrote and spoke against the ordination of women to the presbyterate! The record of the Methodist Conference in this matter had not been a noble or notable story, with the proposal to ordain women being defeated thirty-five times in forty years! The high number of women presbyters in the active work is still not reflected within the list of District Chairs, nor in the most senior Connexional posts, nor in the number of women who have so far served as President of the Conference.

Pat Billsborrow is the only minister so far to be elected to two terms as Chair of the Fellowship. She came to the Chair having served the Fellowship with unswerving loyalty and advocacy since her ministerial student days at Queen's College, Birmingham. Her ministry in a prominent Local Ecumenical Partnership and her work as a District Ecumenical Officer fitted her well for the leadership of the Fellowship. Pat has the distinction of being the only woman presbyter (of any tradition) to celebrate the Eucharist within the Anglican Shrine of Walsingham, which she did in the Guild of All Souls Chapel. Anglican women priests were not and are not allowed to preside at a Eucharist at the Shrine or at the Parish Church. For its Sunday Eucharist the Fellowship went to the Methodist Chapel. On the Fellowship's return to Walsingham the situation was different because the Shrine's Barn Chapel had been built and made available for use by other Christian traditions.

The Death of Philip Blackburn

Easter Week 1998 was also the occasion for commemorating a significant group of recently departed members of the Fellowship who had served it with distinction, among whom were Philip Blackburn, Guthrie Burgess, Dorothy Aston and Mary Holliday. Philip Blackburn, the former Chair of the MSF, had died in office during the previous year after giving eleven years of unforgettable leadership to the Fellowship.

Under the influence of Gordon Rupp, Philip Blackburn had joined the MSF in 1953, while he was serving with the Methodist Missionary Society in Jamaica. Altogether Philip ministered for twenty years in the West Indies, before serving the second half of his ministry in West Yorkshire. From the first days of his return to MSF Weekends members were exposed, first to the Caribbean tea-shirts, then to stories of 'high chapel' colonial Wesleyanism. Late night sessions would include Philip's famous renditions of alternative ways of singing dubious mission choruses, many thumped out on the piano as he searched for the 'right note.' Members learnt how important it was in the West Indies for the choir to sing 'de an-tem.' If John Habgood was right in declaring the besetting sin of the clergy to be their dullness, then Philip Blackburn was the counter-argument personified.

Here was the jovial Wesleyan prelate who could always be relied on to play what he named in two words as 'State Church' at its own game of effortless superiority. He would address all comers as his equals and spoke to them in his own perfected version of received pronunciation. A sense of delight permeated the Methodist Conference when he stood on the podium. There was something of a reverent but impertinent challenge even in the way he pronounced the words 'Mr President' at the beginning of a speech. His famous addressing of the Conference on how to make new members and keep up a good membership by standard visitation and sound catechesis won him prolonged applause from the Conference and fifty-two votes for the Presidency!

Philip's greatest gift was to make circuit Methodism work. He presided over a swift, efficient and high chapel Eucharist. He preached short and well illustrated sermons on the Christian Year and all the offices of Christ. He was a phenomenal visitor, a meticulous administrator, and a wise and commanding superintendent. He seemed to have inherited his benevolent dictatorship from John Wesley and Jabez Bunting. In many ways he was more of a high Wesleyan than a Western Catholic.

His style of eucharistic presidency at MSF Conferences was always flamboyant. He probably had the most dramatic method of performing the Fraction in the entire history of the Eucharist.

Philip's love of the MSF and his loyalty to it were second to none. He began attending the Annual Conference of the Fellowship on his return to English circuits and he became MSF Conference Secretary from 1970 to 1972, Overseas Secretary from 1972 to 1974, and Chairman of the MSF from 1986 until his death in the early summer of 1997.

In 1987 Philip gave the MSF Conference Lecture on *Altars and Altar Calls: A Catholic Evangelical in the Circuit Ministry.* He was probably the greatest recruitment officer the Fellowship has ever known. In his visits to Cliff College, at the MSF Methodist Conference bookstall, and in his numerous contacts with the bright, the beautiful and the enquiring, Philip would distribute the Fellowship's literature, testify to an ordered life of prayer and sacrament, and overwhelm the innocent enquirer with his enthusiasm. At the Leeds Methodist Conference MSF Bookstall of 1994 he presided over the sales of Sale or Return books from the SPCK and of Fellowship literature. At the moment the takings touched £1000 he summoned those around him to render with him the entire *Te Deum* unaccompanied – which they did!

Later years at the MSF were graced by the shades, by clerical black with homburg, with the scarlet scarf, the cane and a manifold collection of pectoral crosses and patriarchal medallions. The finest of the Wesley silver medallions, with jeweller's chain, was bequeathed to Philip's successors in the Chair of the Fellowship. Not given to modern versions of inclusivity in certain areas Philip suspected he was on to a loser, but this did not prevent his pronouncing the generic 'sinful men' in such a way as to inform those listening to the Easter Four collect that they ran the danger of exchanging a new cultural literacy for the inherited purity of the Queen's English!

Guthrie Burgess

Like Philip Blackburn, Guthrie Burgess had joined the Fellowship in 1953. In the late fifties and early sixties he was Treasurer of the Fellowship with his wife Kathleen as Secretary, in the days when both the London meetings and the annual residential conferences were also their responsibilities. Guthrie Burgess had been a Chartered Accountant before entering Richmond College for his pre-ordination training, where he was a mentor to his fellow students of a 'catholic' persuasion. Because a Probationer was not, at that time, allowed to decline on conscientious grounds a dispensation to administer the Sacraments before ordination, Guthrie made sure that he didn't go into Circuit until he was ordained, and he refused to celebrate the Lord's Supper during his Circuit practice. He was a very Methodist churchman and disliked the use of vestments at MSF conferences. He believed Methodism should have the Free Churches in its ecumenical sights as well as the Church of England. He worked until he was eighty as a part time hospital chaplain.

Dorothy Aston

Dorothy Aston joined the Fellowship in 1968, after meeting Donald and Brenda Rogers at an MSF Methodist Conference Public Meeting. She very quickly became active in the residential conference and the London Meeting. As the Fellowship's Treasurer and Membership Secretary she served with distinction for about twenty years.

Mary Holliday

At the Bristol Conference of 1974 Mary Holliday was in the first group of women to be ordained as British Methodist ministers. Previously she had been a Wesley Deaconess. Much of her ministry, both as a deaconess and as a presbyter, was spent at the Farncombe Community, and for a while she was head of the Community. One of her retreat exercises was The Eucharist in Slow Motion. She would make the Eucharist last for a whole day, or even for the period of a two day retreat. Opening prayers and the Ministry of the Word would be interspersed with silences. The intercessions would usually take the form of an awareness walk. The sacrament of the altar would be the climax of the whole event.

Shortly after her presbyteral ordination she visited a Convent where she had often been before. The nun at the door recognised her face but couldn't think of her name. Mary jogged her memory by saying, 'I'm Sister Mary from Farncombe.' The nun replied, '*Sister* Mary? Aren't you *Father* now?'[22]

The Death of Donald Soper

Donald Soper, the President Emeritus of the Fellowship, died in December 1998. As Colin Morris said in his Guardian obituary, the last of the Non-conformist giants had lived to see great cracks appearing in the three pillars of his thought and life – Methodism in decline, socialism a dirty word among the Labour leadership and pacifism still rejected by the major Churches.

At the Fellowship's Annual Conference in April 1999, at Saturday Evening Prayer Gordon Wakefield gave a memorial tribute to Donald Soper during which he said:

> He became more clerical from the 1950s exchanging his frequent natty lounge suit and tie for the cassock, which became his perpetual clothing. There were inconsistencies. He lived for most of his time at Kingsway in the Hampstead Garden Suburb and sent his daughters to an independent school. He was criticised for accepting a seat in the House of Lords, which he did with schoolboy delight and in the early days signed his name 'Soper' with glee.
>
> He administered the manifold work of the West London Mission with efficiency and art including the brevity of Circuit meetings! One Christmas morning he gave breakfast to a thousand children.
>
> His remarks could cause grave offence, as when he said in the Conference that Methodism was dying; or that Britain was an American occupied country; or that evangelicals were nicer if not better people before their conversions.
>
> He only just made President of Conference in 1953. There was much jealousy of him. I remember the howls of rage in the Manchester Conference Arrangements Committee in 1955, when he asked not to serve on the preaching plan because of his commitments to Kingsway Hall and Hyde Park. And he ex-President but one!
>
> The Sermon on the Mount was the centre of his Christianity and devotion to the historic Jesus. Obedience was the secret of his ministry. 'Christianity is ninety nine per cent obedience' was a frequent saying. We celebrate the Eucharist because Christ told us to. We love our enemies because he commanded it.
>
> He was above all a Methodist preacher with a high view of ministry. He sought Anglican ordination because he did not think that this was incompatible with Methodism. He could be both minister and priest at once, but Anglicans were not in favour. His ordination charges were memorable, most of all one in which he told of Lax of Poplar's ministration to a dying old woman who longed to feel the hand of Christ 'as she

crossed over.' Stretching forth his hand Lax said, 'This is the hand of Christ' and so she died.

He may be said to have failed. The expectations of many in his earlier years that he might lead a Christian revival were not fulfilled. I remember exactly sixty years ago retired members of the Methodist hierarchy like Wardle Stafford thinking of this as a possibility, but then came the war. Christianity had a decreasing cultural influence and congregations diminished. He did not lure those who admired him from outside, the hecklers on Tower Hill and Hyde Park, in any numbers. He made a glamorous marriage and there were some happy family holidays, though there were some hints of guilt that he might have neglected his home in response to his fame. Yet he would not have had his witness otherwise and would to the last have testified in the words of one of his many favourite hymns, 'How blest is life if lived for thee.'[23]

Cell Groups

It was also in 1998 that the Fellowship issued *Guidelines for setting up Cell Groups*. The hope was that two or three people – perhaps including some housebound MSF members – would meet monthly or quarterly to say Morning or Evening Prayer or Compline, to share simple refreshments and to respond to a recent paper or book. From time to time the group might invite a speaker or go on an inexpensive outing or pilgrimage. The most successful cells have been the Delamere Forest Group, organised by Pat Billsborrow and Sue Levitt, and the Gloucestershire Group, organised by Keith Flemington.

The Rules of the Fellowship

The Rules of the Fellowship had first been agreed at Penrhos College in 1935. They had not been revised since 1950. Under the eagle eye of John Kellaway a small group re-wrote the constitution, which was ratified by the annual conference of 1998.

Methodist–Roman Catholic Dialogue

A lay member of the Fellowship with wide experience and a towering intellect, David Carter, had over the years made a unique and thorough contribution to international dialogues between Methodism and the Roman Catholic Church and between Methodism and the Orthodox Church. In the *Bulletin* of 1999 he reviewed Methodist–RC dialogue over a thirty-year period.

He drew some conclusions about unfinished agenda items on Eucharist and ordination.

> Catholics can legitimately ask Methodists why they are not prepared to go further in acknowledging the truths ... that undergird Catholic teaching on the real presence of Christ in the Eucharist. Early in the dialogue, Methodists had accepted that Christ's presence in the Lord's Supper was 'unique,' that the bread and wine of the Eucharist have a special significance that they do not have outside of that context.
>
> Why, then, may Methodists not accept the contextual appropriateness of the language of 'transubstantiation' in terms of the philosophical presuppositions that underlay it? The Methodists made an assertion about their inability to accept such definitions, but utterly failed to say *why* they did so ...
>
> From their side, Methodists could ask some awkward questions about ecclesial and ministerial recognition. Just as Catholics can validly challenge Methodists to sort out their as yet underdeveloped eucharistic theology, so Methodists can challenge Catholics concerning their failure to explicate fully some of the loose ends left over from Vatican II, and their failure to move more fully away from the rather legalistic theology of orders that has for so long prevailed.[24]

The Death of Gordon Wakefield

The death of Gordon Wakefield in September 2000 at the age of seventy-nine marked the first death of an MSF President while in office since that of A E Whitham in 1938. Gordon Wakefield had been President of the Fellowship for twenty-one years and previously a distinguished editor of its *Bulletin.* At the time of his election John Newton had written of Gordon Wakefield that, as 'a Catholic Methodist steeped in the classic tradition of the Wesleys' discipline, devotion, hymnody, evangelical passion and high sacramentalism, he would fit the MSF Presidency like a hand in a glove.'[25]

Gordon's mother had read Milton to herself while she was carrying the embryonic wordsmith in her womb. He first stepped into Methodist pulpits at sixteen and at nineteen he was an accredited local preacher. Through lack of family funds he was unable to take up his history scholarship at Manchester University, but in 1946, aged twenty-three and already a member of MSF, Gordon became a theological student at Wesley House, Cambridge under Robert Newton Flew whom he adored, and whose biography he was later asked to write, and which he published at the end of his time as Methodist Connexional Editor in 1971.[26]

In that year Gordon became Chair of the Manchester and Stockport Methodist District, a post in which he did more good work than he knew, although he was not at ease in a role he had once coveted. After eight years Gordon left his District Chair to teach liturgy at Queen's College, Birmingham and in the university, but before he arrived he had been elected Principal. It was under Gordon that Queen's had its second spring as a place of learning and piety. Uncompromising Anglo-Catholic bishops like Graham Leonard were now perfectly happy to trust their Anglican ordinands to Queen's under Gordon, the tried and trusted Catholic. He stamped his own character, style and dignity on Queen's and his charm, wit, scholarship and gift as an innocent but entertaining ecclesiastical and common room gossip came into its own. Like Ernest Rattenbury and Geoffrey Eddy, Gordon was destined to belong to that small band of gifted and distinguished ministers who never gained enough Methodist popularity to be elected to the Presidency of the Conference.

Nevertheless Gordon's immense contribution to Queen's College was recognised in 1986 when his friend, Robert Runcie, conferred on him a Lambeth DD. Gordon was proud of his place in what he called 'the guard's van of the Church of England.' He knew more bishops than most bishops and was a friend to many. He was a great raconteur with unrivalled memories of Methodism and the ecumenical scene. His students knew him simply as 'Gordon' and affectionately imitated his melodious voice in the college entertainments.

Throughout his ministry he held together the Puritan and Methodist traditions. He was Select Preacher at both Oxford and Cambridge, and was the first Methodist to preach in Westminster Cathedral. He wrote on Bunyan, the Wesleys, Newman – a wide spectrum of spirituality – and probably knew more about the 'kindly light' than any other Methodist.

Lichfield was the perfect setting for his last busy years, when past students and colleagues beat a path to his door. Here in Doctor Johnson's city Gordon watched his beloved cricket and at the cathedral, in reality if not in name, he had all the life of a canon-chaplain. He loved its liturgy as much as the cathedral community treasured the venerable scholar, preacher and spiritual director in its midst. He mounted the pulpit at Lichfield, as he had more than half the cathedral pulpits of England, clad in his doctor's robes, to deliver the Catholic faith as a Methodist preacher. It was fitting that his funeral and requiem should be in the place he so enjoyed and where he was so loved. He had been a key figure in the Methodist Retreat Movement and The Ecumenical Society of the Blessed Virgin Mary. He hardly missed an MSF gathering in his twenty-one years as President. His Low Sunday Quiet Mornings were unforgettable, not least his meditations on the wounds of the risen Christ. In his MSF Commemorative Address Gareth Powell recalled:

> From cradle to grave Gordon seemed to exude such a sense of prayer and spirituality that any attempt to offer a reflection on his life is both to dabble in holy things and to examine the very private nature of a fellow human being – a human being

who took the sacred and the secular so seriously that I often thought he was the ultimate example of the unity of those two spheres of experience. His offering on the occasion of this Fellowship's Golden Jubilee, *Catholicity Reconsidered*, was just one example of the breadth of his daily thought. Twenty-one significant publications betrayed a measured yet thoroughly scholarly output. Every one of his publications was a commissioned work. His monthly sermons for the *Methodist Recorder*, which ran for twelve years, were often testimony to his ability to be relevant yet remain timeless.[27]

When his later sermons were published in 1998 as *Medicines for the Heart* Gordon wrote, 'I issue these sermons as President of the Methodist Sacramental Fellowship. The centrality of the Eucharist is always present.'[28]

In an anthology of his sermons published posthumously by Beryl, his wife, there was included an earlier autobiographical sketch which concluded with the words:

> I never knew my father's mother. She died at fifty-two, worn out with childbearing and an alcoholic husband who would pawn the children's clothes for drink. As she died, she prayed in the words of 'Rock of Ages:'
>
> Foul I to the Fountain fly
> Wash me Saviour or I die.
>
> I have known privileges she could not have imagined, but I have no other prayer.[29]

11

Glorious Company

John Newton elected President of the Fellowship

At the Annual General Meeting of 2001 at Wydale Hall, Scarborough it was agreed to invite John Newton to be the President of the Fellowship.

After ministerial training at Wesley House, Cambridge John Newton went as Assistant Tutor to Richmond College where he became the life-long friend of one of the founders of the Fellowship, Marcus Ward, whose biography he would eventually write. After circuit work in Lincolnshire John became Church History tutor at Wesley College, Bristol and then, after five years teaching in Kenya, he returned to Wesley College as Principal. In the 1960s he wrote on the Puritan Tradition and on Susannah Wesley. He then followed Donald Soper as Superintendent of the West London Mission, where he worked pastorally and skilfully to transfer a declining congregation from Kingsway Hall to Hinde Street. He thus became the third MSF president to be associated with Kingsway Hall and Hinde Street. In 1981 he became President of the Conference and during his term of office made an official visit to Pope John Paul II. His Presidential theme, *A Christ for All, A Church for All, A Theology for All*, was fulfilled when John was appointed to the Chair of the Liverpool District, where he served until his retirement in 1995. His Liverpool ministry was one of towering ecumenism in partnership with Archbishop Derek Worlock and Bishop David Sheppard and the city's communities and churches. John served as Joint President of the Merseyside and Region Churches' Ecumenical Assembly (MARCEA), twice as Moderator of the Free Church Federal Council and as Co-President of Churches Together in England. In retirement he served on the Roman Catholic-Methodist International Commission and as Warden of John Wesley's New Room in

Bristol. The last of his significant books, leaving aside the long-awaited biography of Bishop Edward King, was *Heart Speaks to Heart: Studies in Ecumenical Spirituality* (1994). Here there were chapters on *The Merseyside Miracle, Edward King, Methodism and Orthodoxy, Methodism and Catholicism* and *Grasping the Nettle of Mary and Ecumenism.* As John Newton had written of Gordon Wakefield fitting the Presidency of the MSF like a hand in a glove so the same metaphor was once more totally apt in his own case.

A Thankful Heart and a Discerning Mind, the festschrift for John published in 2010, reprinted Henry Rack's profile which had previously appeared in the *Epworth Review*:

> John expressed much of the original Wesley spirit and concerns: what Albert Outler termed 'plain truth for plain people,' backed by serious study and wide-ranging curiosity, a spirituality which embraced elements in both Catholic and Protestant traditions with what Wesley called 'the catholic spirit' and applied in social as well as spiritual service. To these John has added a natural, unforced wit and – what Wesley perhaps lacked! – an engaging sense of humour and warmth in personal relationships along with a natural modesty. For he is still the unspoilt and unpretentious friend and recognisably the same kind person that the writer of this profile encountered over fifty years ago, but with a wealth of experience added. Long may he continue to refresh, instruct and entertain us.[1]

It was also at the MSF Annual Conference of 2001 that David Redrobe reported that he had heard the MSF referred to as 'The Methodist *Scrap Metal* Fellowship'![2]

Christopher Humble

In 2001 Christopher Humble had already given sterling service as the convener, promoter and speaker finder for a number of very successful Northern MSF meetings. At short notice he began a ten year office as General Secretary. He steered the Fellowship meticulously through its Annual

General Meetings, kept a faithful record of its decisions and appointments, and watched over the Chairs of the Fellowship and officers with due care and attention! His wry humour and gentle but blunt off-the-cuff observations added greatly to the enjoyment of some business items. He was equally gifted in both presiding and preaching at the eucharist, and had an ear for church music, both that which was good and that which was poor!

Richard Bielby

Although Richard Bielby had been in the Fellowship for twenty-five years he and his wife Susan had only recently (and innocently) begun attending the Low Sunday Weekend Conferences on a regular basis. It was a delight and relief to the Committee and the Annual Meeting, however, that Richard, with Susan's support and encouragement, was willing to succeed Christopher Humble as General Secretary. Richard's years of service as a District Synod Secretary stood him in good stead. A combination of gentleness and courtesy soon endeared him to the Committee and the Annual Meeting.

Kingsley Lloyd

In February 2004 *The Times* carried an obituary for Kingsley Lloyd who had lived to celebrate his 100th birthday. He was a founder member of the MSF and served on its General Committee for most of his active ministry. *The Times* rightly highlighted his transformation of the Methodist Church portfolio from a fund of £2 million to one that stood at £850 million at the time of his death. It was to Kingsley more than any other figure that the Connexion owed the strength of the Ministers' Housing Society and a solid basis to the Ministers' Pension Fund. *The Times* also concentrated on his work for Anglican-Methodist unity while he was President of the Conference. A few days later the obituary columns of *The Times* carried a further piece by the present author highlighting Kingsley Lloyd's part in the formation of the MSF and in the Fellowship's Golden Jubilee celebrations at Wesley's Chapel in 1985.

A revision of the Purpose, Pledge and Aims of the Fellowship

In 2004 a small working group revised the Purpose, Pledge and Aims of the Fellowship, which were then printed in a new publicity leaflet in 2005.

Purpose:
The Methodist Sacramental Fellowship exists to affirm the Catholic tradition of Christianity within Methodism. It does so in line with Methodism's emphasis on scripture, tradition, reason and experience, and with the theology and practice of John and Charles Wesley. We seek to encourage a pattern of Christian discipleship rooted in the Holy Communion enabling men and women to live creatively and well as God's grateful people and so to share in mission on behalf of God's suffering people. This eucharistic way of living inspires us to work and pray for a diverse, hospitable and inclusive Church - both within Methodism and through our hopes for greater unity with other churches – and to engage with the world through a commitment to peace and justice.

Pledge:
Members of the Fellowship commit themselves:
- to disciplined lives of prayer, study and worship;
- to receive Holy Communion faithfully and regularly;
- to uphold and cherish the faith of the Church as contained in Holy Scripture and expressed in the historic creeds;
- and to support the local church to which they belong, and promote by prayer and action the cause of Christian unity.

Aims:
- to affirm within Methodism a Catholic Christianity rooted in the doctrine of the Trinity;
- to embody the insights of Catholic Christianity in worship, education, service and evangelization; and to work and pray for the visible unity of the Church.

This was also the occasion when the new logo of 'The Chalice and the World' was adopted in place of the Penrhos Cross.

'The Grace Given You in Christ'

In the Epiphany *Bulletin* of 2008 David Carter introduced *The Grace given you in Christ*, the Roman Catholic-Methodist International Commission's Eighth Report.

At the conclusion of the Report both churches were encouraged to consider carefully what was essential within their respective traditions and what might, with integrity, be changed or 'let go of.' Catholics were encouraged to give concentrated attention to lay leadership within the Church, to the contribution of women to the Church's ministry and to 'the Church's corporate assurance as the context for the infallibility of the Pope.'

Methodists were encouraged to consider the historic succession of bishops and the individual exercise of *episcope* within a collegial ministry of oversight, and to consider the exercise of universal primacy for the sake of unity and as an expression of the universality of the Church.

Both churches were encouraged to invite members of the other to experience their forms of worship and spiritual devotion and to examine the bounds of legitimate diversity within the Church. Catholics were invited to be inspired by the example of the Wesleys and to promote the place of evangelical preaching, Bible study and hymn singing in the Church. Methodists were encouraged to consider making a weekly eucharist the norm in their pattern of Sunday worship, as well as exploring Catholic forms of devotion such as the Stations of the Cross and the veneration of Mary. Both churches were encouraged to co-operate in mission and in peace and justice projects.

These practical suggestions could, in the last resort, prove to be the most significant aspect of the report. If faithfully acted upon, they would lead to a much greater degree of growing together than had, thus far, resulted from other bilateral dialogue reports. From fuller mutual reception of each others' authentic insights into Christian faith and authentic gifts might result a vision of the catholicity of the Church fuller and richer than its previous embodiment in either communion. A key statement of faith in the ultimate guidance of the Holy Spirit occurred in the paragraph which said:

> Full communion between Catholics and Methodists will also depend upon a fresh creative act of reconciliation which acknowledges the manifold yet unified activity of the Holy Spirit throughout the ages. It will involve a joint act of obedience to the sovereign Word of God.[3]

This report, in the way in which it combined serious theological reflection with a concern for practical and practicable initiatives in Christian life and witness, represented an important methodological advance in ecumenical dialogue, and deserved to be deeply pondered, not just within the Roman Catholic and Methodist churches, but by all committed to the Ecumenical Movement. The catholicity of the Church is dynamic not static and thus develops under the inspiration of the Holy Spirit.

John Kellaway

John Kellaway, who died in December 2009, joined the MSF only in 1989, but he had a life-long dedication to the high Wesleyan tradition and was deeply devoted to a discipline of daily prayer and regular Holy Communion. Befriender and confidant of younger MSF ministers in the north-west, as soon as John joined the Fellowship he became an assiduous participant in the Northern MSF Meetings and the Annual Low Sunday Weekend Conference. Especially in widower-hood these gatherings became the highlights of his year and the MSF members a new family to him. John was keen to see the MSF constitution on a sound footing, and on the death of Stanley Morrow in 2003 John was elected a Vice-President of the Fellowship.

For fifty years or more John served the Methodist Connexion with distinction and was elected Vice-President of the Methodist Conference in 1971, with Kenneth Waights as his Presidential running partner – probably the earliest gin-drinking combination in the history of the Presidency! A son of the manse, the infant John was baptized by Scott Lidgett, which he believed placed him in an apostolic succession, since Lidgett held that he had been blessed or baptized by Jabez Bunting, who in turn, it was claimed, had received a blessing in infancy from John Wesley himself.

A Regional Director of the Midland Bank, John served the courts and structures of British Methodism with distinction, as chairman of the Central Finance Board, the Ministerial Allowances Committee, the Ministers' Pension Trust and the Methodist Insurance Company. With another MSF stalwart, Kingsley Lloyd, John helped to put the Ministers' Pension Scheme on the soundest of footings.

In 1985 the newly created ecumenical instrument for Merseyside, MARCEA, began to make its contribution to the 'Merseyside miracle' and from the beginning proceeded on parliamentary lines, electing John as its second and perhaps its most outstanding Speaker. John's speakership included the heady days of David Sheppard, Derek Worlock and John Newton.

Cedric Hallam

At the beginning of 2010 members of the MSF were devastated by the untimely death of Cedric Hallam. A more loyal, gracious person and devoted member of the MSF it was hard to find. Cedric belonged to the Fellowship for most of forty years. During that time he rarely missed an Annual Conference or a regional Day event. In his professional career he was a Senior Manager with BNP (Banque Nationale de Paris) Paribas, one of the largest global banking groups in the world, with its global headquarters in Paris and London. This, like so much else, Cedric kept in the cocoon of his modest silence.

At MSF weekends it was sometimes possible to coax him out of his modesty and persuade him to be Music Director, and this he took on with a quiet but professional air, seeing us through our paces for the Daily Offices and particularly for the Sunday morning Sung Eucharist. Succeeding John Swarbrick and Donald Rogers as the MSF Treasurer, Cedric handled the Fellowship's modest sums, year by year, with meticulous care, and his relaxed reporting of the annual accounts was always encouraging. In addition to his utter loyalty to the MSF, Cedric was assiduous in his participation in the life of The Ecumenical Society of the Blessed Virgin Mary and its sister organization, the Ecumenical Marian Pilgrimage Trust, and its regular gatherings at Walsingham.

The Fellowship's Website

Since the beginning of the new millennium the Fellowship has had its own website under the domain name www.sacramental.org, but in 2010 it was completely redesigned by the MSF's new webmistress, Sally Hall, and has become a very attractive and informative website. As well as giving information about the Fellowship and its forthcoming events there are links to other websites of similar interest. All the out-of-print lectures can now be downloaded as pdf files.

Masterminded by Alex Conn the Fellowship also has its own E-group, through which members can quickly and easily keep in contact with one another.

Howard Smith

Cedric Hallam's appointment as treasurer was temporarily and bravely filled by Cedric's close friend, Sandra Marshall, who gladly handed over the Fellowship's financial concerns to Howard Smith. Howard's financial skills and his twenty or more years in the Fellowship had prepared him to be as pastorally concerned about the membership as he was about matters of income and expenditure. His organizing of the distribution of the Fellowship's mailings have given him an almost unique knowledge of the comings and goings and the strengths and weaknesses of the membership. His unflagging support for national and regional meetings of the Fellowship have become an inspiration.

The 75th Anniversary Celebrations

In 2010 and 2011 the Fellowship celebrated its 75th Anniversary with three major events. In June 2010 the Annual Lecture at the Portsmouth Conference was given by the youngest ever lecturer, Daniel Pratt Morris-Chapman, on *Whither Methodist Theology Now? – The Collapse of the 'Wesleyan Quadrilateral.'* In a major and masterly paper an emerging scholar demonstrated that Richard Hooker had never really put together or built on the famous three Anglican equalities of 'scripture, tradition and reason' any more than Wesley had sought to build on these and add 'experience' to them.

In October 2010 the Fellowship met in London for a Friday evening 75th anniversary celebration dinner in Covent Garden, excellently arranged by Sandra Marshall. On the Saturday morning there was a celebration Eucharist at Hinde Street with the Leytonstone Methodist Youth Choir, at which Professor Frances Young preached on *The Materialism of the Christian Tradition.* In the afternoon the 75th Anniversary Commemorative Lecture was given by Christopher Cocksworth, Bishop of Coventry, on *Evangelical and Catholic in the Twenty-First Century.*

The Annual Low Sunday Conference of 2011 was a return to the Anglican Shrine and Pilgrimage Centre at Walsingham. As well as celebrating Morning and Evening Praise and the Saturday Eucharist before a splendid new icon of The Trinity, the Fellowship enjoyed three lectures from Dr Mervyn Davies on John Henry Newman – *Newman in his Time and Ours, Newman's Sermons: Prayer and Holiness in Every Day Life* and *Faith, Reason and Secularism: Newman's Response to a Contemporary Problem.*

At the Saturday morning Eucharist Pat Billsborrow was inducted for her second term as the Chair of Fellowship, only yards from where, on the previous visit of the MSF to Walsingham, she was the only woman to celebrate the Eucharist within the shrine's enclosure! On the Saturday evening the Fellowship shared in the Shrine Liturgy and Procession. The Sunday morning reflection was given by Michael Townsend on *The Dream of Gerontius*, accompanied by appropriate extracts. The Sunday morning Sung Eucharist was in Walsingham Methodist Chapel, with Pat Billsborrow presiding and Michael Townsend as the preacher, and in the chapel sanctuary it was white cassock-albs and white stoles all round!

Colin Penna

In 2011 the Fellowship had to absorb the shock of the sudden death of Colin Penna, who joined the MSF when he was an undergraduate. He would recall the Soper days with great accuracy and entertaining reminiscences! Colin was nurtured in the village Methodist chapel at Willington, County Durham. For almost fifty years he served as a Local Preacher on the Crook Circuit plan. In later years he found a second and additional spiritual home at Saint Margaret of Antioch's Parish Church in Durham, where he served as churchwarden. Had his age and his health not militated against it he had intended offering for Anglican ordination. Year by year, from the pulpits of Anglican and Methodist churches, his unmistakable voice rang out with an unforgettable clarity, as he proclaimed the Scriptures and affirmed the fullness of the church's Catholic faith.

With his London law degree and a mind and spirit enriched by the sights and sounds of the capital, Colin returned to his home county, eventually becoming a senior partner in Marquis-Penna of Bishop Auckland and Crook.

For almost twenty-five years he served as HM Coroner for Darlington and South Durham. Colin's unfailing commitment and wise counsel within MSF was recognised by his being made a Vice-President of the Fellowship in 1988. At the Low Sunday Weekend Conference of 2003 in Cheltenham he celebrated his fifty years of membership of the Fellowship by producing bottles of champagne!

Joe Farrelly

Joe Farrelly, who died in August 2011, became the second great enabler and inspiration of The Ecumenical Society of the Blessed Virgin Mary, following in the footsteps of Martin Gillett, who had founded the Society in 1967. Both were Catholic laymen, and both had an incredible network of significant contacts on which they could call, both inside and outside their own Christian tradition. Martin Gillett was an English Catholic convert where Joe Farrelly was a cradle Irish Catholic.

Beyond his wise and pastoral gifts as a devoted schoolmaster were Joe's commitments to the cause of the Catholic Marian societies and Catholic agencies dedicated to those in need. Like Martin Gillett Joe believed that Catholic, Orthodox, Anglican, Reformed and Methodist theologians and thinkers – clergy and laity alike – could be serious, spiritual and critical together about the place of the Blessed Virgin Mary in the worship, reflection and dialogue of all the mainstream churches. Often graciously and amusingly critical of those inside the leadership of his own tradition, it was out of his deep and loyal Catholicism that Joe formed lasting relationships with churches across the Christian spectrum. He sought out the key ecumenists within Orthodoxy, Anglicanism and in the Reformed traditions. He had close friends within British Methodism, and for almost twenty years attended the annual Low Sunday Weekend Conference of the MSF.

He was above all an encourager, who built on the potential he saw in the young, ordained and lay. Joe's outstanding service to British Roman Catholicism and to the crucial place of Mary in ecumenical devotion and dialogue rightly earned him the recognition of a Papal knighthood. He was never happier than being part of an ecumenical pilgrimage to Rome and Assisi. His anecdotal memory of the unofficial history of more than eight decades of English Catholicism, as he relayed it to Christians of all traditions, was a joy to experience. Joe was totally supported in his life and work by his wife Ann, and much loved in a family that had not been without its sorrows.

Gerald Tedcastle

For many years Gerald Tedcastle attended London and national gatherings of the Fellowship and meetings of The Ecumenical Society of the Blessed Virgin Mary. He was stationed for a key part of his ministry at the Leysian Mission and Wesley's Chapel, where he was associate and assistant to Colin Morris, Allen Birtwhistle and then to Ron Gibbins, under whom the return to the renewed Wesley's Chapel was completed and plans were laid for the grand re-opening in the presence of Her Majesty the Queen. For many years Gerald served as Chaplain to the City University, to Barts and to Moorfields Eye Hospital, and his commitment was recognised when he was made both a Freeman of the City of London and a Member of the Guild of Freemen.

During his Woolton ministry Gerald acted as Deputy District Chairman to his great friend, John Newton, particularly during John's sabbatical. Gerald was grieved by any odious or disciplinary matters he had to handle, but relished the ecumenical social engagements, many of which he attended with Rachel Newton. Once, at Archbishop's House, Gerald was invited to a reception for which he purchased a fine black ribbed silk clerical stock from Wippells. On his purchase's first outing Gerald bit into a *vol-au-vent* and the contents deposited themselves down his new stock! Gerald reported, 'I said to myself – Is there a God at all!'

As a Tedcastle coming from the merchant grandees of Dublin, Gerald enjoyed the romance of the high Edwardian days of his father and his Scottish forbears. When asked at college what his father did Gerald replied, 'My father doesn't *do* anything!' Gerald had an undying devotion to the Wesleyan tradition and to the Catholic Faith. He loved the days he spent as a regular guest of the White Fathers in London, and 'a Mass and a glass' with the Ampleforth Benedictines in Oxford. For a significant number of MSF Low Sunday weekends Gerald acted as chaplain and lovingly greeted and befriended newcomers to the Conference. He was particularly fond of the collect from the Gelasian Sacramentary:

> Remember, O Lord, what you have wrought in us and not what we deserve; and as you have called us to your service, make us worthy of our calling; through Jesus Christ our Lord. Amen.

Residential Renewal

The MSF was born in residence! From the inaugural weekend at Penrhos College, Colwyn Bay in 1935 the annual conference has been at the heart of the Fellowship. Numbers attending have varied from the upper fifties to the mid-twenties, but the average has been about thirty-five. There has always been a combination of ministers and laity, men and women, the old and the young, of those who were married or in a committed relationship and of those who were not. Across the years many of those attending have been weekend refugees seeking a rich diet of Easter liturgy which they were often denied in their local congregations on Easter Day.

The essential ingredients of the weekend have usually included a retreat house and chapel, a daily eucharist with all the trimmings and a rich round of daily offices with good singing, fellowship and re-union, a wide range of speakers, key business and, every other year, a half-morning of quiet reflection. From time to time the Saturday afternoon has included a visit to a holy place or a pilgrimage centre. As the weekend has proceeded the result has been greater than the sum of the constituent parts.

Low Sunday Weekend Venues

Venues have varied enormously! Occasionally the weekend at Swanwick or High Leigh was shared – once with the Regnal League! Sometimes the Fellowship has met in a college or a school. The Fellowship owes an enormous debt to the untiring efforts and often thankless task of those who have been its Conference Secretaries, finding venues, receiving bookings, procuring speakers, allocating liturgical tasks, adjusting the programme and absorbing complaints! Among the long-suffering saints who have undertaken this task have been all the early Secretaries of the Fellowship and then such stalwarts as Philip Blackburn, Arthur Saunders, Brian Pickett, John Fisher, Peter Smith, Pat Billsborrow, Sandra Marshall and Jane Cook.

By far the best venues have been Anglican or Roman Catholic religious houses or retreat centres. The chapels of these houses are already pregnant with the Paschal mystery before the Fellowship arrives. Candles, vestments and sacred vessels are always tasteful and in good supply. Over the years the indifferent quality of some of the musical instruments has presented a challenge, even under such directors of music as Francis Westbrook, Harvey Richardson, Cedric Hallam and John Swarbrick! In recent years John Swarbrick has remedied this by playing music before or after services from his stunning collection of CDs!

The business of the weekend is usually a committee meeting at teatime on Friday and the Annual General Meeting early on Saturday evening. The Annual General Meeting receives reports of regional events and of the Fellowship's finances. Plans are shared for the forthcoming public lecture at the Methodist Conference. Possible themes and speakers for future Annual Conferences are suggested. Officers are elected and a list prepared of letters of greeting or condolence to be sent. Membership figures are returned and a list is made of those who have died during the year.

Speakers from the earliest days have been drawn from Methodism and, probably more often, from other Christian traditions – Anglican, Reformed, Roman Catholic or Orthodox – sometimes ordained, sometimes lay. For many years the custom was to ring the changes on the three aims of the Fellowship – Faith, Unity and Worship. In more recent times audio-visual presentations have meant that liturgical art in particular has taken on fresh meaning. Sometimes members of the Fellowship have slept or snored during talks or lectures and sometimes all too predictable questioners have had to be reeled in by the Chair!

Late Night Sittings

On Friday and Saturday evenings, after Compline, the Fellowship retires to the main lounge. There has usually been a bookstall (once generously provided each year by SPCK, sale or return) at which to browse. Invariably there has been a bar, either *in situ* or provided by the MSF cellarer and stocked with drinks to meet all tastes! Small groups form. A few retire early. A group of survivors sits until at least midnight! This has been the time for stories round the camp-fire. Personal liturgical joys and nightmares are re-lived. Hopes and dreams are exchanged and friendships are kindled, renewed and deepened. On the Saturday afternoon there have often been car expeditions to nearby places of cultural or pilgrim interest such as Prinknash or Hexham Abbeys, Little Gidding or Birmingham Oratory. For others there is the chance (weather permitting!) of a spring walk after the hectic days of Holy Week and Easter.

Chapel Worship

The round of weekend worship is a rich liturgical fare. Friday and Saturday include both Evening Prayer and Compline. The real start of the weekend is the kindling of the Paschal light and a vigorous rendering of 'Hail, gladdening Light.' The heart of Saturday Compline includes Wesley's 'How do thy mercies close me round,' formerly sung to *Saxby*, but latterly to *Lassus*, but in either incarnation absent, alas, from *Singing the Faith*! Each night Compline reaches its climax with the Gospel Canticle, *Nunc Dimittis,* sung to *Tonus Peregrinus*, with the intoning of the Fellowship's own setting of the antiphon – 'Guide us waking, O Lord, and guard us sleeping; that awake we may watch with Christ, and asleep we may rest in peace. Alleluia, Alleluia!'

Morning and Evening Prayer have often included the chanting of the psalms and canticles and, although the singing of the *Benedictus*, the *Easter Anthems* and the *Te Deum* has largely disappeared from Methodism, the singing of these has been maintained, until fairly recently, during the MSF Weekend. In earlier days the Fellowship promoted the best of liturgy, language and idiom, revelling in Cranmer's cadences and rhythms, but now looks for the best texts and language in contemporary liturgies. The Saturday Eucharist has often been according to the rite of some non-Methodist tradition and, both at St Lazar's in Birmingham and at St Seraphim's in Walsingham, the Fellowship has crammed itself into a tiny space for the full splendour of the Orthodox Easter Liturgy! Here there were candles and processions and antidoron for all!

Quiet Mornings

The Sunday Quiet Mornings between breakfast and the final Eucharist have usually been led by MSF members. Memorable meditations have included those by Dom Robert Petitpierre, Donald Rogers, Christopher Humble, Michael Townsend, Margaret Wallwork and Gordon Wakefield, who almost certainly holds the record for the number of Quiet Mornings he has led.

A Catholic Mass

Present at the Annual Conference for many years have been not only members who are now Anglicans, but some who have been cradle or convert Roman Catholics. None were more faithful than Joe and Ann Farrelly and Amanda Hill of The

Ecumenical Society of the Blessed Virgin Mary. They came to MSF weekends until Joe was well into his eighties. Either within the retreat house or at a nearby church they would attend a Saturday or Sunday Mass. In recent years they have been joined at the mass by Jane Cook, a key officer of the Fellowship, once a Methodist minister but latterly heavily involved in Diocesan catechesis as a Roman Catholic. One year a Catholic priest contributing to the MSF weekend made it abundantly clear that he would be very surprised if the Methodists present didn't receive at the Catholic Mass!

The Sunday Morning Eucharist

The highlight of every Low Sunday Weekend is the Sunday Easter Eucharist before final drinks, lunch and departure. This liturgy is always a Sung Eucharist with *Gloria*, *Sanctus* and *Agnus Dei* sung to settings rehearsed earlier in the weekend. If it hasn't been sung earlier in the weekend the service often includes what, by some, came to be regarded as the Fellowship's 'national anthem,' 'Christ the Lord is risen again:'

> He who slumbered in the grave
> Is exalted now to save;
> Now through Christendom it rings,
> That the Lamb is King of kings: Alleluia!

There have been some memorable sermons, including those by Colin Penna, Marcus Ward, Kenneth Cracknell, Peter Howard, Brian Beck and Gordon Wakefield and, in earlier days we are told, by A E Whitham, J E Rattenbury and Kingsley Lloyd.

Perhaps the most moving moment each year is the reading of the names of those members of the Fellowship who have died during the year. The silence speaks, the memories crowd in and the tears come unbidden.

The first time the fellowship met in Walsingham the Sunday morning Eucharist was in the Georgian Methodist Chapel in Friday Market Square. At the beginning of the sermon by John Fisher, Philip Blackburn, the celebrant, noticed he did not have about his person the slip of paper containing the list of those to be remembered! He whispered to the present author on the front row, 'The dead! The dead! I haven't got the dead!' The author left the service, discovered a bicycle against the chapel wall and pedalled through the main street back to the pilgrim centre to retrieve 'the dead' and returned before the preacher had finished his sermon!

The sharing of the Peace at the final Eucharist exemplifies the word 'Fellowship' in Methodist Sacramental Fellowship, as does the sharing of the Body and Blood of Christ before the members go their several ways. Some have attended only one or two MSF weekends, others have been a living part of such weekends for five, six or perhaps even ten years. Yet others have made their way with the *stabilitas* of a life-time, ending their tryst only through frailty or death, thus handing on a bright succession of commitment which began at Sidcup with the very first retreats and has spanned eighty years!

12
Liturgical Tradition

The Role of a Service Book

The *Bulletin* for 1997 published two papers by Neil Dixon, the first on *The Making of a New Service Book* and the second on *The Role of a Service Book in Methodism.* In his paper on *The Role of a Service Book in Methodism* Neil Dixon suggested seven functions for a printed book of services. The first of these was to provide texts that can be used to glorify God, because we must aim, to the best of our God-given ability, to provide material that is excellent. The contents of a service book must stand the test of time.

A second role was to provide a norm and a standard. In the Methodist tradition, many services do not involve the use of a book, other than the hymn book. It was hoped, for instance, that many would learn from the *Methodist Worship Book* what basic elements should be in the eucharistic prayer.

A third role was to teach individuals the faith. This had once been the role of the hymn book. The role of the service book in this regard was therefore especially important. *Lex orandi, lex credendi* speaks of the profound relationship between prayer and belief.

A fourth role of a service book was to express the faith of the Methodist Church. If one asked what Methodists believed about, say, baptism or ordination, one needed to quote from authorised services. The official liturgy of a Church was a major doctrinal statement.

A fifth role was to provide a link between our tradition and the future. Any new worship book must recognize where we have come from and try to read the indications as to where we are going. This meant keeping an eye on tradition.

A sixth role was to reflect ecumenical consensus. The new worship book was to use the English Language Liturgical Consultation texts of the Lord's Prayer, the Nicene and

Apostles' Creeds, the *Gloria in excelsis*, the *Sursum Corda* and the *Sanctus*.

A final role of the worship book was to extend horizons. A function of a new book ought to be that of introducing ministers and congregations to treasures, well-known in other traditions, but not so familiar to us.[1]

The Prayer Book Tradition

Towards the end of his life Wesley realized that, in Britain and America, most of his followers had found faith independently of the established church and of existing Dissent. In their new mid-week meetings and in the Sunday worship at their preaching houses the Methodists needed the opportunity to be fed on the sacraments and liturgy of the Church that had fed their founders.

Accordingly, in 1784 and 1786, Wesley revised the 1662 *Book of Common Prayer* in *The Sunday Service of the Methodists*. The long continuous Anglican fore-noon experience of Matins, Litany and Ante-Communion as one service was shortened by Wesley to provide a briefer version of Morning Prayer and a very slightly amended version of Cranmer's Holy Communion Office. The Psalter was reduced by a third, and a number of services, including Confirmation, were omitted from the revision. Wesley retained an Ordinal for Superintendents, Elders and Deacons.

Between 1860 and 1912 the non-Wesleyan Methodists provided short service books using some of Wesley's amendments. These included forms for the Methodist Covenant Service, for Baptism and the Lord's Supper, and an outline for a Preaching Service, with hymns, readings, prayers and sermon.

In 1882 the liturgically conservative Wesleyan Conference revised its double inheritance of texts – the 1662 *Book of Common Prayer* and Wesley's *Sunday Service*. Liturgical revision after the 1932 re-union of the Methodist Church resulted in the 1936 *Book of Offices*. The most enduring services in this order were the 1930 Covenant Service and the

Wesleyan revision of Cranmer's Communion Office. A second communion order was provided for those unfamiliar with the Cranmer-Wesley text. It consisted mostly of extracts from the Prayer Book communion tradition. In addition it included the *Agnus Dei* and two verses from Charles Wesley's Easter hymn beginning at verse 2, 'Love's Redeeming Work is done.' Though Maldwyn Edwards called it 'The Liturgy of the Mule, having neither pride of ancestry nor hope of posterity,' it served well, introducing 'non-Wesleyan' congregations to 'the book' and, in some ways, it was more suited in structure to follow the preaching service than the second part of the Cranmer-Wesley Communion Office.

The Order for Morning Prayer

Residual Wesleyanism in the earlier part of MSF history brought with it a devotion to the Order for Morning Prayer. Until 1882 Wesleyan preachers and ministers had read the service from the *Book of Common Prayer* (not from Wesley's abridgment, as they did for Communion) and changed the more priestly texts as they went along. In 1882 the Wesleyan Conference published a Methodist revision of the 1662 Order for Morning Prayer in the *Book of Public Prayers and Services*. Evening Prayer, though appearing in Wesley's revision, was dropped as it had perhaps never been used in Methodist Sunday public worship! The Wesleyan Order for Morning Prayer of 1882 was printed as the first service in the 1936 *Book of Offices* 'for the convenience of the Methodist churches where it is in use.' The Order for Morning Prayer had probably only ever been used in about seventy or eighty chapels in the whole of England, with probably about thirty of them in central or outer London and probably about forty of them mostly in the Wesleyan merchant suburbs in the provinces. By the late 1970s many of the Morning Prayer Chapels had closed, dropped 'the liturgical service' or reduced its use to monthly or quarterly. The two national occasions on which it survived in the Connexion were the Sunday morning service at the Methodist Conference (often broadcast, with inevitable complaints about the 'Anglican service') and on the Sunday morning of the MSF Conference, before breakfast! Since the Uniting Conference of 1932 (and until 1975) the *Te Deum* had been sung unaccompanied, by the whole Conference, at the opening of the Representative Session after the Presidential Address!

The Full Communion Order

Of much more concern to the MSF – apart from a well ordered Preaching Service – was that of the full Order for Holy Communion, using the first order in the 1936 *Book of Offices*. The common custom in most chapels – of all pre-union branches – was to have a preaching service (with the sermon before the final hymn). After the blessing the minister would go to the porch to say goodbye to the majority of the congregation who were then departing. The faithful remnant would gather in the central pews and, with or without the service book in their hands, the minister would give out a communion hymn and then begin the Lord's Supper somewhere in the second part of the communion order. The longing of the MSF was that its ministers and members would do their utmost to see that, on Sunday mornings, the full order with hymns and sermon was the norm at the time of communion. Linked with this innovation was the hope of making the quarterly morning 'town' communion into a monthly one. In the 1960s a number of ministers began introducing elements of the pre-communion, such as the Collect for Purity, the Collect of the Day and the Prayer for the Church Militant, into the Preaching Service.

'The Methodist Service Book' 1975

Inter-church conferences, the work of the Methodist Renewal Group, publications of the Liturgical Movement and trial services at MSF gatherings all influenced the move towards *The Methodist Service Book* of 1975. Primarily the work of Raymond George, but with considerable input from David

Tripp, Geoffrey Wainwright and such MSF members as Marcus Ward, Arthur Nelson and Keith Beck, the *Methodist Service Book* was among the first of the 'modern' liturgical movement service books to be published.

The most significant feature of *The Methodist Service Book* was the marrying of the traditional Methodist preaching service to part one of the Eucharist – the liturgy or ministry of the Word. The content of the eucharistic prayer now moved away from Cranmer and adhered to the outline of the second century text of Hippolytus. All this resulted in the general loss of the tagged-on communion service and the virtual ending of the practice of folk leaving before communion. There were practically no congregations that did not have the whole of *The Methodist Service Book* or 'the little red books' for Communion, *The Sunday Service.*

The 1968–75 period leading up to the publication of the *Methodist Service Book* also marked the other great revolution accompanying 'everyone staying for communion,' namely the bringing of the Bible readings and the sermon into close relationship with one another by taking the sermon from its climactic position at the end of the preaching service and placing it next to the gospel or second reading, with a second group of prayers after the sermon.

'The Methodist Worship Book' 1999

The publishing of *The Methodist Worship Book* in 1999 brought into Methodism a collection of liturgies the like of which the founders of the Fellowship could have only dreamt. The very success of *The Methodist Service Book* meant that, by the late 1980s, Methodists were asking for more material and greater variety of imagery in Sunday services and in eucharistic worship. The Methodist Conference of 1990 directed its Faith and Order Committee to start work on a successor to the 1975 book. The principal directives were to take into account the issue of inclusive language and to provide a richer variety of eucharistic material. The new Liturgical Sub-Committee of fifteen (with more than half of them MSF members!) met for the first time in Oxford in November 1990. At its request the present author drew up a possible list of contents which, apart from a catechism, was adhered to for the nine years of preparation and appeared practically intact in the new worship book.

The 1991 Methodist Conference gave permission for its Faith and Order Committee to publish draft services drawn up by its Liturgical Sub-Committee. These camera-ready originals could be copied without further permission, to allow experiment and wide circulation. The Liturgical Sub-Committee met thirty times in eight years for a total of seventy-one days. Over twenty thousand originals of the draft services were ordered from the Faith and Order office. In response to a request for comments, the Faith and Order Convener received over a thousand letters.[2]

The book had a number of new and key features. By design every member of the church who owned the book now had complete access to all the services at every level of the church's life, not just liturgical texts for use in the local congregation (rather on the model of the original *Common Prayer*). So, for instance, alongside the sacraments there was material for private daily prayer, for every liturgical moment surrounding death, and for national ordination services. Following the practice of the Anglican Province of South Africa, every group of rites had a short introductory section, setting out the history and meaning of the rite. So there were brief introductions to the church's understanding of the meaning and purpose of Daily Prayer, The Liturgy of the Word, Initiation, Holy Communion, Holy Week Services, the Covenant Service, Ordination, Commissioning Services, Marriage, Pastoral, Healing and Funeral Services, Blessing and Dedication Services and the Calendar and the Christian Year. New aspects of the services included the greater use of the rubric beginning, 'This, or some other,' to provide a normative form at every point but with the possibility of the presiding person finding alternatives. Very few of the liturgies required the presiding person or worshippers to turn to another part of the book, between the beginning and the end of the service. Even the collect of the week or the season could be replaced by a standard form printed in the text of the service.

Daily Prayer

The provisions for Daily Prayer were intended for daily personal or corporate devotion, but not as a basis for public worship on Sundays. 'O Lord, open our lips ...' and scripture sentences for times and seasons began the offices, and these were followed by an invitatory psalm, an office hymn, a prayer for morning and evening, a psalm, a short reading, a canticle and concluding prayers. An act of penitence was included in Prayer in the Evening.

The Preaching Service

The one Methodist service for which no provision had been made in most previous service books was the so-called Preaching Service. In early Methodism this began life as a supplementary service of two hymns, a short intercession or bidding prayer, a scripture text and a sermon. In time it expanded to become the main Methodist Sunday diet of non-eucharistic worship. The Sunday Preaching Service appeared in the new *Worship Book* under the guise of Morning, Afternoon, or Evening Services. Two complete forms were provided, with alternative examples at each prayer point in the service. The outlines fell under the headings of The Preparation (Gathering, News, Approach, Penitence, Praise and Theme Prayer), The Ministry of the Word (Scripture, Praise, Exposition and Peace), The Response (Thanksgiving, Intercession, Lord's Prayer, Collection) and The Dismissal (Praise, Blessing and Dismissal).

Initiation

The initiation services, entitled Entry into the Church, occupied over forty pages of the book. The forms provided catered for the various combinations of young children and those able to answer for themselves, who may be candidates for baptism or candidates for baptism and confirmation. Baptism was stated to be a gift from God which declared God's love and grace, and a celebration of the life of Christ laid down for us, the Holy Spirit poured out on us and the living water offered to us. In the sacrament candidates were claimed and cleansed by God, rescued from sin, raised to new life and planted in the church, where they were to be sustained and strengthened by the Holy Spirit. These gifts of grace God offered to all. All candidates for baptism were assured, in the words first used by the Reformed Church in France, that all the benefits of Christ's incarnation, example, passion and victory were present for each baptizand before they could know anything of it. In both baptism and confirmation the promises made by the candidates or their parents, and by god-parents and by the church are made *after* the baptism and *after* the confirmation.

Communion Orders

The orders of service for Holy Communion were preceded by an Introduction and by Notes. In the introduction Holy Communion was said to be *the central act* of Christian worship. (And this seventy-five years after the Methodist Conference hoped the newly-formed MSF would remove the word 'central' from its aim concerning Holy Communion in Methodism!) The classic themes of the Wesleys' eucharistic hymns of 1745 were then set out, corresponding as they did to the famous Lima headings. There was a reminder that baptized children should be admitted to communion. The peace was seen as the hinge point between 'The Ministry of the Word' and 'The Lord's Supper.' In the Notes there was a reminder that the presiding minister was a presbyter or 'a person with an authorization from the Conference to preside at the Lord's Supper.' The presiding minister was not to delegate to others the beginning and ending of the service, the greeting the people at the peace or the presiding over the fourfold eucharistic action. The juice of the grape was to be used, thus declaring all eccentric and unspeakable substitutes unacceptable. What remained of the elements was to be reverently consumed or otherwise disposed of at the end of the service.

There were sixteen complete communion orders – one for each of the following days or seasons – Advent, Christmas and Epiphany, Lent and Passiontide, Maundy Thursday, Easter including Ascensiontide, and for Pentecost and other times of Renewal in the life of the Church, and there were a further three communion orders for use in 'ordinary time.' There were another seven complete communion orders, one for each of the following: The Housebound and those in Hospital, Extended Communion, Renewal of the Covenant, Ordination of Presbyters, Ordination of Deacons, Marriage, and Healing and Wholeness.

The Advent Communion Order included the Commandments of the Lord Jesus and the *Benedictus* or *Magnificat* instead of the *Gloria*. The intercessions were partly dependent on the Advent antiphons. Like all the new Methodist eucharistic prayers, the specific season or occasion was reflected in the first part of the prayer. The institution narrative was rehearsed between the *Sanctus* and the acclamations of faith. The anamnesis and oblation followed, together with a single or double epiclesis moving into an act of doxological praise and the Amen of the people.

The Christmas and Epiphany communion order provided *A Song of the Incarnation* as an option to the *Gloria*. The communion order for Ash Wednesday used the Ten Commandments, and the Lent and Passiontide order had Henry Allon's *Salvator Mundi* in place of the *Gloria* and included, in the invitation to communion, John Hunter's famous bidding, 'Come to this sacred table, not because you must but because you may ...'

Each of the communion orders had its own post-communion collect. These were some of the best new compositions in the book and reflected the strong eschatology in Methodist eucharistic theology. In the Ascensiontide part of the great fifty days of Easter, the *Song of Christ's Glory* (Philippians 2.5–11) was offered as an alternative to the *Gloria*. The final blessing in the Pentecost order used the Pratt Green phrase, 'Spirit, Son and Father.'

Of the three orders for use in 'Ordinary Seasons' the first was the normative model, with everything in its conservative form and place. The second communion order for use in Ordinary Seasons was an 'all-age' form with simple music provided, and with all the words in the eucharistic prayer being easily signed for those having a hearing impediment. The third of the communion orders for Ordinary Seasons was the most radical of the three in avoiding 'Father' and 'Lord' imagery for the first person of the Trinity.

Marriage

The Marriage Service spoke of 'a life-long unity of heart, body and mind' and of 'comfort and companionship, enrichment and encouragement, tenderness and trust.' Both the bride and the groom could, if desired, be 'presented' by a relative or a friend to avoid the archaic 'giving away' of most earlier marriage services.

Healing and Reconciliation

The various forms of service for anointing and the laying on of hands were followed by A Service of Repentance and Reconciliation. Based on the form in the Australian *Uniting in Worship*, the service included a formal and an informal confession of sins and a declaration and assurance of forgiveness.

During the consultation process there was pressure on the Liturgical Sub-Committee to provide two forms of every absolution and blessing in the book, one form for 'low church,' the other for 'high church.' This they did. Every act of penitence in the book is followed by a 'you' and 'your' declaratory form of absolution and by a 'may' and 'us' petitionary form. Similarly the blessings preceding the dismissals appeared either in two forms side by side, or with the *you/us* in italics.

Funerals and Related Services

In the Funeral and Related Services there were Prayers in the Home or Hospital after a Death, An Office of Commendation, A Vigil, A Funeral Service leading to a Committal, A Funeral and Committal followed by a Thanksgiving, A Funeral of a Child, A Funeral for a Stillborn Child and A Service for the Burial of Ashes.

Blessings and Dedications

The Blessing and Dedication Services consisted of orders for the Blessing of a Home, the Laying of a Foundation Stone and an order for the Dedication of a Church Building and its Furnishings. In the last of these there was the hint and hope that there would be only one place for both the reading and the preaching of the word, and not the provision of both a lectern and a pulpit.

Calendar and Lectionary

The Calendar and Lectionary was loyally dependent on the international *Revised Common Lectionary* and included a set of collects drawn partly from traditional Anglican and Roman forms, and partly from the composition of the Methodist Liturgical Sub-Committee itself. The very strong emphasis on the Christian Year reached its climax in the provisions for Holy Week. Encouraged by the ecumenical work of the British

Joint Liturgical Group the Methodist Church provided forms for the whole of the Easter Triduum. Palm Sunday was designated The Second Sunday of the Passion, and provision was made for the traditional Liturgy of the Palms, with a form for the traditional blessing, distribution and procession. The Ministry of the Word consisted of the solemn reading of The Passion. The lectionary gave readings for the Monday, Tuesday and Wednesday of Holy Week, and there followed a complete communion order for Maundy Thursday with penitence, *Gloria*, readings, foot-washing, intercessions, Peace, eucharistic prayer, Fraction, *Agnus Dei*, *Pange Lingua*, traditional collect, *Tenebrae* or the Gospel of the Watch, the Stripping of the Table or a Prayer Vigil. The Good Friday liturgy consisted of the traditional psalm and readings, the Passion according to John, a sermon, The Proclamation of the Cross, the great intercession and the final collects. The Easter Vigil included the preparation of the Easter candle and began with the traditional set of readings, psalms, refrains and collects. The Service of Light began with the kindling of the Easter fire and continued with the procession, the *Exultet*, the Easter Thanksgiving, *Gloria*, collect, psalm, epistle, gospel, Re-affirmation of Baptism and the rest of the Easter eucharist.

Renewal of the Covenant

The renewal of baptismal vows at Easter was new to most Methodists and, of course, could pose some problems to those reflecting on the liturgical theology of the Methodist Covenant Service. Wesley's 1780 version of this searching service was a monologue read at great length by the minister. Not until the form in the 1936 *Book of Offices* did most Methodists receive the Renewal of the Covenant in the sectional and responsive form which became so popular in ecumenical circles via its inclusion in *The Book of Common Worship* of the Church of South India. The 1975 British *Methodist Service Book* strengthened the link between the Covenant and Holy Communion. Some of the familiar and much loved passages which were lost in 1975 were re-worked and re-included in the 1999 *Worship Book*.

In the Introduction the Renewal of the Covenant was seen as a transaction, not only between individuals and God, but as an act of the whole faith community. The service being so solemn it was still recommended for use only once a year in each congregation. The opening section of glory and blessing was a re-working of the 1936 act of thanksgiving. The collect was drawn via 1975 from the Church of South India. The idea of reading from both the Law and the Prophets was new as was also the inclusion of special responses after all the readings. The introduction to the Covenant and the act of confession had been re-worked. The classic bidding to the actual covenant prayer beginning 'Christ has many services to be done' was slightly amended. The Covenant Prayer appeared in two forms. The first form was new and of a quality to stand its ground alongside the more traditional form. For the first time ever, the Covenant Service had its own eucharistic prayer and post communion collect. These came from the same gifted hand as the new covenant prayer.

Ordinal and Commissioning Services

One of the crucial acts of Methodist separation from the Church of England was the decision by John Wesley to ordain some of his itinerant preachers as deacons and elders. In his revision of the 1662 *Prayer Book* Wesley provided a three-fold ordinal for the ordaining of Superintendants (sic), Elders and Deacons. Later Methodist service books contained only the Ordination of Ministers. However, after the 1975 service book was issued British Methodism developed its diaconal order into a permanent diaconate of the Church of God. The new ordinal in the *Worship Book* therefore contained forms for the ordination of both presbyters and deacons. The Introduction to the Ordinal declared that deacons were ordained to the ministry of service and pastoral care and were to seek to equip God's people for service in the world. For both presbyters and deacons ordination was to a permanent lifelong office of ministry. The Methodist Church ordains to the presbyterate and the diaconate in the One Holy Catholic and Apostolic Church. The ordinal said that it 'looks for the day when in communion with the whole Church such ministries are recognized and exercised in common.' The Ordinals had their own communion orders and eucharistic prayers with newly composed prefaces. Just as important as the national services of ordination, which most British Methodists never see, are the circuit services for The Admission of Local Preachers. The circuit superintendent minister presided at the Admission Service. Existing local preachers were encouraged to take part in the service by reading the scriptures, leading the intercessions, preaching the sermon and assisting in the distribution of Holy Communion. In the Preface to the Admission the superintendent reminded the congregation that the duties of Local Preachers included being worthy in character, leading God's people in prayer and praise, sharing in the Church's mission in the whole world and bringing the message of salvation to all, in season and out of season.

Liturgical Actions

Within the worship book there was a new emphasis on actions and 'eye-gate' during the services. These included water being poured into the font during the baptismal liturgy, the manual acts in baptism, the use of the Advent Wreath, the wrapping of the stole in marriage, the laying on of hands in reconciliation and anointing, and the laying on of hands in healing. New actions and developments also included the burning of Palm Crosses and the 'ashing' on Ash Wednesday, a Palm Sunday procession, the Exaltation of The Cross on Good Friday, the use of a paschal candle at Easter, music printed in one of the communion orders and a full listing of the liturgical colours for Sundays and holy days.

Open Air Liturgy

Though contemporary Methodism has largely abandoned open-air preaching it has taken to open-air liturgy! The great Christmas and Easter events proclaiming that 'the best of all is God is with us' and that 'Christ has died, Christ is risen' are capable of significant open air procession and pageant. Often and best undertaken ecumenically, an open-air Nativity or a public enactment of the Passion brings the central events of the faith before bystanders and gathered crowds.

'Prayers for the Sunday Preaching Service'

The MSF published two of the present author's collections of prayers, *Prayers for the Sunday Preaching Service* in 1987 and *More Prayers for the Sunday Preaching Service* in 1994. Unlike the other Free Churches, Methodism had provided few 'models' of succinct prayer to be used at each of the key points in the preaching service. The aim of the two popular books was to demonstrate best practice, for invocation or adoration, penitence and absolution with the collect of the day in the first part of the preaching service, and thanksgiving, intercession, offering and blessing in the second part. Most significant of all was the emphasis on a prayer of thanksgiving as well as one of intercession in the second part of the service, and the difference between the later thanksgiving and the earlier prayer of adoration in the first part of the service. There was little understanding by many ministers, local preachers or worship leaders of adoration celebrating *who God is* and of thanksgiving celebrating *what God does*. This was often jumbled together in the earlier prayer time and lost sight of in the second.

'Prayers for the Waiting Times: Prayers for use during Communion'

Francis and Margaret Henman joined the Fellowship in 1968 and, in addition to an almost unbroken contribution to MSF gatherings for 45 years, they were founding figures in the Methodist Retreat Movement. Part of their gift to the

Fellowship was their production of a devotional anthology to accompany those precious moments before going down to or coming back from communion, when so many Methodist communicants are slightly at a loss what to think, pray or do. Master copies were available so that the prayers could be produced as bookmarks and distributed to the congregation in their hymn books.

Charles Wesley's Hymns

Almost twenty years ago the author of this book contributed an article to the *MSF Bulletin* of 1994 asking *Is there a future for any of Charles Wesley's hymns?* Building upon the author's researches Norman Pickering wrote a further article in the *Bulletin* of 1995 entitled *Charles Wesley's Hymns beyond 'Hymns and Psalms.'* Between them the writers established two lists. First a 'top list' of 40 Wesley hymns (in 'popularity' order), emerging from an ecumenical comparison of 67 hymn books.

Love divine, all loves excelling
Hark! the herald angels sing
Rejoice the Lord is King
O for a thousand tongues to sing
Jesus, lover of my soul
Forth in thy name, O Lord, I go
Christ the Lord is risen today
Lo! he comes with clouds descending
Soldiers of Christ, arise
Ye servants of God, your Master proclaim

And can it be that I should gain
O for a heart to praise my God
Come, thou long-expected Jesus
O thou who camest from above
Christ whose glory fills the skies
Hail the day that sees him rise
Come, let us join our friends above
Come, Holy Ghost, our hearts inspire

Jesus, the name high over all
Author of life divine

Christ, from whom all blessings flow
Come, let us with our Lord arise
Come, O Thou traveller unknown
Jesus, Lord, we look to thee
O love divine, how sweet thou art
Give me the faith which can remove
Help us to help each other, Lord
A charge to keep I have
Away with our fears, Our troubles and tears
Jesus, we thus obey

Thou hidden source of calm repose
God is gone up on high
To us a child of royal birth
Come, thou everlasting Spirit
My God, I know, I feel thee mine
Let earth and heaven combine
Happy the souls to Jesus joined
All praise to our redeeming Lord
Jesus, united by thy grace
Glory, love and praise and honour
Victim divine, thy grace we claim[3]

A second list was published of another 30 Wesley hymns that might remotely survive within the Methodist community.

All glory to God in the sky
All things are possible to him
Behold, the servant of the Lord
Come, divine Interpreter
Come, Holy Ghost, thine influence shed
Come, let us use the grace divine
Come, sinners, to the gospel feast
Earth, rejoice, our Lord is King
God of all redeeming grace
God of almighty love

Granted is the Saviour's prayer
Great is our redeeming Lord
Hail! Holy, holy, holy Lord
Head of thy church triumphant
How do thy mercies close me round
Jesus, the word bestow
Jesus, thy far extended fame
Jesus, thy wandering sheep behold
Jesus, we look to thee
Lord we believe to us and ours

O heavenly King, look down from above
O Love divine, what hast thou done
Open, Lord, mine inward ear
See how great a flame aspires
Spirit of faith come down
Thou God of truth and love
Thou Shepherd of Israel and mine
What shall I render to my God
What shall I do my God to love, My loving God to praise
Where shall my wondering soul begin?

It is interesting to compare these 70 Wesley hymns of 1995 with the 80 Wesley hymns remaining in *Singing the Faith* in 2011, not a few of which had to swim upstream to survive.

The classic collection of 1780 contained approximately 500 Wesley hymns. The 1933 *Methodist Hymn Book* contained about 250. *Hymns and Psalms* had approximately 150. This figure was almost halved again for *Singing the Faith*. This was a hymn-book designed out of necessity, not only for the traditional Methodist with some devotion to Wesley, but for the average busy Methodist church where most of the worshippers might not be traditionally Methodist at all. Many fine hymns and songs have arrived, but many hymns in the great tradition have been removed, and a fair amount of shallow verse has been placed in the new collection. The result may be that side by side with the most Catholic worship book Methodism has ever had it now has the most Protestant hymn book it has ever known!

A third question was suggested in the original MSF article. What makes a good hymn – by Charles Wesley or anybody else? A working definition was quoted from Donald Allchin.

> A true hymn is neither simply a statement of doctrine nor simply an expression of devotion. It is a text in which thought and feeling, imagination and reason, have been fused together by the poet's craft and vision, through the gift of the Holy Spirit.[4]

'Singing with the Saints'

In 2005 the Fellowship published a 170-page companion to the collects and readings for the Festivals and Lesser Festivals of the Church of England appearing in *Exciting Holiness.*[5] Although *Exciting Holiness* was intended for use at eucharistic celebrations, it was argued it could be used with a daily office, but in either case the propers lacked an appropriate hymn. In *Singing with the Saints* Margaret Wallwork provided a hymn for each of these commemorations. The hymn was either written by the person commemorated or was based on his or her writings, or the hymn celebrated some characteristic of the person commemorated or an incident in his or her life, or the hymn was based on one of the readings for the day. The choice represented many rich storehouses of hymnody. Some were very old. Some were very new. Some were well known. Some were known only to a few. Suggested tunes were given for each hymn. Beyond its use by individuals *Singing with the Saints* found its way into a number of larger parish churches where small groups met for daily worship, and soon a second printing was required.

The Creed

In the Wesleyan-Catholic tradition there had always been a great devotion to the Nicene Creed, the Creed of the Mass. Gordon Wakefield recalled the Ecumenical Methodist

Conference at Oxford in 1951, during which a service was held in the University Church to commemorate John and Charles Wesley. The preacher was John Scott Lidgett, then aged 97.

> [Lidgett] entered by the north door, supported by two sticks and several dignitaries, his aged and emaciated face rising shrunken from his red doctor's robes. Throughout the service he remained seated, but in the hymn before the Nicene Creed he insisted on being raised to his feet. Like some old soldier, pulling himself to attention before the flag, he would, to the last, salute the great symbol of Christian faith.[6]

At the Annual Low Sunday Weekend Conference in 2010 John Swarbrick, the Fellowship's Director of Music, presented a fascinating and absorbing paper on *Music – a Way to God.* The most memorable and stunning section was devoted to the *Credo* in Bach's *B minor Mass.* Some of those listening cast their minds back to Francis Westbrook telling MSF members that the *B minor Mass* was the nearest thing to heaven they were likely to encounter this side of eternity. So John Swarbrick invited the MSF Conference to listen to the setting of the Creed from the *B minor Mass* or, as Bach entitled it, reverting to patristic usage, the *Symbolum Nicenum.*

> We begin the first section with a fugue, '*Credo in unum Deum.*' Bach treats it with appropriate austerity, notating it in a deliberately old-fashioned *alla breve* style: the five vocal parts are in big fat breves (ironically, once regarded as a *short* note!), semibreves and minims, a deliberately archaic throwback to the notational style of the polyphonic composers of a hundred and fifty or two hundred years earlier; and he uses as the theme the original plainsong melody in an ambiguous key somewhere between the medieval mixolydian mode and A major. And then some fascinating pieces of number symbolism: in the figure alphabet, CREDO equals 43; so Bach makes 43 entries across the five voices of the plainsong melody, which represents God's law. At the risk of sounding like a complete anorak, there are 45 bars in this opening fugue, then 84 bars in the '*Patrem omnipotentem,*' which sets

the rest of the text of the first clause of the Creed. How is your arithmetic? 45 + 84 = 129 which is 3 x 43 – an explicitly trinitarian piece of number symbolism. (We know that Bach intended such things, because he would scribble numbers in his score, presumably to check up on his sums, and we have the manuscripts. Clever stuff!)

If all that seems quite stern, we then move on to the second clause '*Et in unum Dominum [Jesum Christum]*,' and the musical interpretation of the second person of the Trinity in the luminous key of G major, the key of blessedness; it's a duet for soprano and alto, written in canon at the distance of a beat to symbolize the mystic union of the Father and the Son – and done so subtly and intimately entwined with itself that the ear can hardly separate the two voices.

Next the '*Et incarnatus*' for full 5-part choir, and a swift change of mood to B minor. Like a number of other movements in the Creed, this one makes a backward reference to the '*Gloria*' which has preceded it. Here the '*Et incarnatus*' is linked with the '*Qui tollis peccata mundi*:' the same key – B minor, the same triple time, a bass pulsing in crotchets, with obbligato strings in quavers; and again a theme based on falling minor triads which, for Bach, are a musical symbol of death, which is in this case also a birth. (T S Eliot's *Journey of the Magi* – *was* it a birth or a death?) The Word dies into the flesh, that the flesh may become Word, and the incarnation is heard as bittersweet mystery.

That intensifies with the '*Crucifixus*,' which is a passacaglia in E minor, the key of crucifixion, a passacaglia being a musical form with a constantly repeated bass line – in this case just four bars – over which, within the limits imposed by the baseline harmony and melody, weave varied patterns. Bach uses a chromatic line, descending in semitones, which musically accentuates the idea of extreme pain through extremely unstable chromatic harmony and angular, anguished vocal parts and piercing dissonances (in yet another example of numerology, he repeats that ostinato 13 times, a number which has traditionally stood for Christ and the twelve apostles), yet right at the end, and without warning, in the final two bars it twists and comes to a close – a final blessed release – in G major.

Then out of nowhere, comes the '*Et resurrexit*' in a blaze in D major and a spine-tingling burst of trumpets and timpani – D major the key of glory (and for 'natural' brass instruments an easy and brilliant key in which to play). After all the descending, drooping grief of the '*Crucifixus*' we have breathtaking joy.[7]

The Original MSF Daily Offices 1935

To assist each member of the Fellowship in their daily discipline of prayer and devotion, from the very beginning the MSF provided its own form of the Divine Office. The original Order for the Morning Office closely adhered to An Order for Prime in *The Prayer Book as Proposed in 1928*. The MSF version from 1935 consisted of:

In the Name of the Father ...
The Collect for Purity
O God, make speed to save us ...
Glory be to the Father ...
Here may follow a hymn, or a psalm or other act of praise
A Scripture Lesson
A Responsory
Nicene Creed
Kyries and Lord's Prayer up to '... deliver us from evil.'
Versicles and Responses
Confession and Prayer for Pardon (priestly absolution omitted)
The Prayer of the Fellowship
A Morning Collect
Final greeting
A blessing

The original Order for the Evening Office closely adhered to An Order for Compline, also from the Prayer Book of 1928. The Prayer Book version contained all the familiar elements of Sarum Compline as it had been handed down in an Anglicised form since the 1850s. The MSF version from 1935 consisted of:

The Lord Almighty . . .
O God, make speed to save us ...
Glory be to the Father ...
Here may follow a hymn, or a psalm or other act of praise
A Scripture Lesson (or short verse of the season)
A Responsory
Nunc Dimittis
Apostles' Creed
Kyries and Lord's Prayer up to '... deliver us from evil.'
Versicles and Responses
The Prayer of the Fellowship
Private Prayers and Meditations with Thanksgiving and Intercessions
One or more of five collects ...
  Visit, we beseech thee, O Lord, this place ...
  Lighten our darkness ...
  O Lord Jesus Christ ... who at this evening hour ...
  Look down, O Lord, from thy heavenly throne ...
  Be present, O merciful God, and protect us ...
Versicles and responses – We will lay us down and sleep ...
Final greeting
A blessing

At the beginning these simple offices were printed in a tiny booklet containing the *Rules and Pledge* of the Fellowship, and were designed to slip into the *Book of Offices*, the Hymn Book or the pocket.

In about 1964 *The Order for the Morning and Evening Offices* booklet contained two versions of each office, one 'For Private Use' and one 'For public use when said in company' and containing the rubric *All kneel.* Although originally for private daily prayer, by the 1960s the gatherings of the Fellowship began to use the Office each time they met, and each day at the Annual Conference.

'Forms for the Divine Office' 1975

In 1975 the Fellowship published a greatly expanded version of daily prayer, *Forms for the Divine Office: Private and Communal orders for Morning and Evening Prayer.* Once each day the Primary Office was based on the Liturgy of the Word or the first part of the Eucharist. The Second Office had the form of a more familiar office. There was a table of psalms for every day of the liturgical year. The shorter lessons, the collects and the thanksgivings and intercessions were all printed in full. The offices were now moving away from Prime and Compline and were moving towards Morning and Evening Prayer – or Lauds and Vespers – and were built around the *Benedictus* and the *Magnificat.*

Morning and Evening Prayer and Compline 1978 and 1981

By 1978 there was a move towards three new MSF services. The offices of Morning and Evening Prayer were based on those appearing in Anglican Series Three, and Compline was a contemporary language version based on the 1928 Prayer Book Compline. In 1981 the Fellowship produced a full version of Compline with a hymn, psalm and lesson for each day of the week. This was reprinted in 1984, revised for Easter 1992 and reset in June 1997.

'Morning and Evening Praise' 1995

The advent of the new pattern and rich content of the Anglican Franciscan *Celebrating Common Prayer* in 1992 influenced the Fellowship to produce its fullest version of daily prayer in its 1995 *Morning and Evening Praise.* A complete office was provided for each day of the week consisting of:

Opening Praise
Hymn
Psalm
(optional Old Testament Reading)
Old Testament Song

New Testament Reading
New Testament Song
Silence
Collect of the Morning or Evening
Prayer of the Day or Season
Prayer of Thanksgiving
Prayer of Intercession
The Lord's Prayer
Silence
(optional hymn, song or chorus)
A Blessing

Evening Praise was provided with an optional preface, The Blessing of the Light.

The kindling of light
'The Christ Light' versicle and response
The Light Prayer
Lighting of other candles
Hymn: 'Hail, gladdening Light'
The burning of incense
The Incense Psalm: Psalm 141
Evening Psalm Prayer

The full version of Compline, as reset in June 1997, was designed to follow Evening Praise at a later time in the day.

The daily offices of the Fellowship have been the backbone of its life and at the heart of its discipline. It was the testimony of Peter Hills, when serving as an army chaplain in the field, that he had been significantly sustained and upheld by the Fellowship's *Morning and Evening Praise.*

13
Marian Pilgrimage

Wesley and Catholic Devotion to Mary

In the 1750s John Wesley issued three anti-Roman Catholic tracts, in each of which he challenged what he believed to be erroneous teaching concerning the place of the Blessed Virgin Mary in Catholic doctrine and devotion. The first, published in 1752, was entitled *A Short Method of Converting all the Roman Catholics in the Kingdom of Ireland.*[1]

The second, published in 1753, was entitled *The Advantage of the Members of the Church of England over those of the Church of Rome,*[2] and, the most significant from the Marian point of view, was Wesley's work of 1756, *A Roman Catechism, faithfully drawn out of the allowed writings of the Church of Rome, with a reply thereto,*[3] unique among Roman Catechisms in that it was compiled by Wesley himself!

Wesley's main problem with Catholic devotion to the Blessed Virgin Mary was that, as he saw it, Mary was not merely held in reverence by Roman Catholics but actually worshipped. In his reply to his own Q.46, *On the veneration of Crosses and Crucifixes,* he did in fact distinguish between *latria* (worship) and *doulia* (reverence), but in Q.38, on *Devotion to the Blessed Virgin,* he failed to understand the distinction between veneration and adoration and asked his readers to consider, 'What is the worship (Roman Catholics) give to the Virgin Mary?'[4]

Wesley critically observed: 'they fly unto (Mary) as the advocatrix of the faithful, the mother of God; that by prayer to her they may obtain help through her most excellent merits with God.'[5] In answering his own question Wesley was happy to claim for Methodists and Protestants, 'We honour this blessed Virgin as the mother of holy Jesus, and as she was a person of eminent piety; but we do not think it lawful to give honour to her which belongs not to a creature, and doth equal her with her Redeemer.'[6]

Wesley went on in his reply to Q.39 (about forms of devotion to Mary) to remind his readers that, concerning Mary's acts on earth and her power in heaven, Scripture was either very sparing or altogether silent.[7] There was nothing in Scripture about her bodily assumption into heaven, nor of her exaltation to a throne above angels and archangels, nothing about her being the mother of grace and mercy, or the queen and gate of heaven, nothing about her being advocatrix of sinners, of her power in destroying all heresies, nor of her being all things to all. Two years later, in 1757, in his pamphlet, *The Doctrine of Original Sin*, Wesley lamented that most Catholics in Ireland knew the names of God, Christ, and the Virgin Mary, they knew the *Ave Maria* and the *Pater Noster*, they knew how to do penance and how to hear Mass, 'but they know little more than the beasts about the nature of true religion.'[8]

In 1779, following the Catholic Relief Act of 1778, Wesley issued his *Popery Calmly Considered*. He was still insisting that Romanists offered to the Virgin Mary worship which was beyond what they gave either to angels or saints. 'They pray to her to bring light and to cause their hearts to burn with Christ.' He insisted that such worship cannot be given to any of God's creatures 'without gross, palpable idolatry.' Methodists on the other hand, he said, 'honour the Virgin as the mother of holy Jesus, and as a person of eminent piety: but we dare not give worship to her; for it belongs to God alone.'[9]

John Wesley and Walsingham

John Wesley's only visit to Little Walsingham was on Tuesday 30th October 1781. He wrote in his journal:

> At two in the afternoon I preached at Walsingham, a place famous for many generations. Afterwards I walked over what is left of the famous Abbey, the east end of which is still

standing. We then went to the Friary: the cloisters and chapel whereof are most entire. Had there been a grain of virtue or public spirit in Henry the Eighth, these noble buildings need not have run to ruin.[10]

The Myth of Wesley's Rosary

On 3rd September 1756, in a letter he wrote from Kingswood, Bristol to Nicholas Norton, Wesley sought to correct a number of spurious opinions held by one of his erstwhile preachers, Charles Perronet. One of Perronet's assertions was, 'A man may be circumcised, *count his beads,* or adore a cross, and still be a member of your society.' Wesley's response was, 'I know no such instance in England or Ireland.'[11] Wesley clearly took the view that Jews and Roman Catholics who joined his Societies renounced their former faith and practices, and that Irish Papists who converted to Methodism ceased saying the rosary or 'counting their beads.'

But this was not to be the last of John Wesley and the Rosary. In his classic Fernley Hartley Lecture of 1967 J Neville Ward re-opened the subject with his never-to-be-forgotten and often quoted sentence, 'Not many (Methodists) know that John Wesley himself used the Rosary; and the one he used is at present to be found among the archives of The Leys School, Cambridge.'[12] Neville Ward's assertion went unchallenged for over forty years. There is indeed a rosary at the Leys School and it is accompanied by some correspondence implying that it had belonged to Wesley. Sometime in 1950, along with other Wesleyana, the rosary was presented to the Leys by L H R Rigg of Grove Avenue, Muswell Hill, London. The school prepared a news item at the time which contained the words:

> Mr L H R Rigg has presented to the School some mementoes of John Wesley which were given to Mr Rigg's mother by her sister, Maud, who married into the Wesley family ... the third memento is a rosary; of this Mr Rigg writes: – 'I am assured that the small type of rosary is quite genuine and was worn [sic] by Wesley ...'[13]

Other notes kept with the rosary and headed *The Wesley Relics* contain the paragraph:

> Rigg wrote that he wished his old school 'to have these articles as I feel they are not fully appreciated by my family now but may be by the Greatest Methodist School.' Rigg's mother had been given them by her sister who was married to 'Sebastian Wesley – a descendent of the Wesley family.'[14]

Who was the Sebastian Wesley who was married to the sister of Rigg's mother? There were, of course, two known generations of Sebastians in the Wesley family tree. Charles Wesley the hymn-writer had a bachelor son, Charles Wesley (1757–1834), and another profoundly gifted musician son, Samuel [the Bach Wesley] (1766–1837). Among Samuel's second and illegitimate cluster of children was the great Samuel Sebastian Wesley himself (1810–76). Samuel Sebastian Wesley had five children, all sons, and the first born, who arrived in 1836, was named John Sebastian Wesley after J S Bach and, like one of his other brothers, trained to be a doctor and practised in Yorkshire. Was there another Sebastian Wesley, perhaps the son of John Sebastian Wesley the Yorkshire doctor, who fell heir to a family rosary? Samuel Wesley, son of the hymn-writer, became a Roman Catholic for a few short years from about 1784 to about 1790, this much to the grief of his uncle, John! But did some Catholic friend give a rosary to Samuel Wesley's descendants?

In a recent and definitive book on Walsingham, Fr Michael Rear cites John Wesley's Journal entry recording his visit to Walsingham on 30th October 1781 and concludes with the almost casual remark:

> A rosary sometimes said to have belonged to Wesley, passed down from his family, actually contains a Miraculous Medal, indicating a nineteenth century origin.[15]

The first Miraculous Medals of Mary were made in 1832 and the devotion quickly spread across the Anglo-Irish and European Catholic community; in subsequent years copies of the medallion were incorporated into rosaries. It is clear from

Fr Michael Rear's observations that the Leys School rosary could never have belonged to the founder of Methodism, for in Wesley's life-time this particular type of rosary did not exist!

The Virgin Birth

The Methodist scholar, Vincent Taylor, in his first significant publication, *The Historical Evidence for the Virgin Birth*, wrote:

> The ultimate considerations which determine a true estimate of the Virgin Birth tradition are doctrinal ... But the historical and the theological aspects of the problem overlap; we cannot determine the question by weighing evidence alone. If we are to confine ourselves to a purely historical inquiry the verdict must be, 'Not proven.' All that we can reach is a primitive belief, generally accepted within New Testament times, which presumably implies an earlier private tradition. On the theological side, the question is probably more far-reaching than is commonly supposed. Individual Christian doctrines can never be treated *in vacuo*; they are inter-related one with another. It is often said those who reject the Virgin Birth reject also the physical Resurrection of Jesus, the Ascension, and many other miracles reported in the Gospels. The statement is largely true; it is possible we ought also to include in it the doctrine of the Pre-existence of Christ. The reason is that these denials belong to the same general habit of mind; they are part of the content of what has been called a 'reduced Christianity.'[16]

'Five for Sorrow, Ten for Joy'

In 1971 neither Neville Ward nor a brave Epworth Press imagined that *Five for Sorrow, Ten for Joy: A Consideration of the Rosary* would remain in print for forty years! Its contents put the title of the book and the name of its author on to the lips of countless Catholic minded Christians of every tradition, and no one now disputes the fact that the best book on the rosary in the English language is by a Methodist! Neville Ward believed that every Christian needed to be open to praying in a new way, and that must include Methodists who needed to break their deafening silence about Mary and be open, in an ecumenical climate, to a nervous interest in Mary's mysterious being. He wrote:

> People unused to the rosary may hesitate over its most frequently repeated prayer:
>
> > Hail Mary, full of grace,
> > the Lord is with thee.
> > Blessed art thou among women,
> > and blessed is the fruit of thy womb, Jesus.
> > Holy Mary, Mother of God,
> > pray for us, sinners, now and at the hour of our death. Amen.
>
> The first part of this prayer, from Luke 1.28 and 42, is a way of bringing to mind our belief that the Incarnation of the Son of God is the most wonderful thing that has ever happened in history. Our joy comes through God's favouring another human being.
>
> The second part of the prayer is a reminder that Christ has abolished our loneliness, that we pray within the fabulous community of faith, live within it, owe more than we know to it, and particularly rely on the prayers of others, the whole communion of saints, of which the Blessed Virgin Mary is the representative figure.[17]

Mother of God

In 1978 Neville Ward wrote his fourth book, *The Following Plough.* In the last chapter, entitled *Mother of God,* he says:

> If there is a world of growth beyond this one, a satisfactory meaning for good and evil could well be there. It is to that world of meaning which alone gives mortality an acceptable face that the Blessed Virgin Mary belongs. She does not represent its fulness and triumph as Christ does, but she is part of it. Her special significance in the Christian mind lies in the fact that she is one of us, as fully and only human as the rest of the cloud of witnesses, so that in principle every prayer

> invoking her name gives us once again the feel of death's feebleness and makes the beyond familiar since it is inhabited by men and women who are prayed for and loved.
>
> That is too important a belief to leave just a belief, something you say in a creed on Sundays. To anyone who thinks it is true it is like the invigorating air of break of day. Devotion to the Mother of Jesus is one of the means of breathing this deeply thought happiness about our human future. She is one of the ways Christians talk about life and live it.[18]

In 1982 Neville Ward gave an address to The Ecumenical Society of the Blessed Virgin Mary entitled *Mary: Intercessor,* in which he brought together what for him was the true nature of prayer with what for him was the true nature of the Mother of Jesus:

> Altogether I personally much prefer to keep to the practice of normally asking the Blessed Virgin Mary, and the saints generally, simply for their prayers. However, I interpret such prayers in terms of an undefined openness and presence of loving, since prayer is not just a matter of saying some words but a giving of oneself to God, and being summoned by God, more deeply into the realm of concern which stimulates the prayer.
>
> Prayer is also an abandoning of self-preoccupation and an entry into the wider world of faith. In devotion to the Blessed Virgin Mary we may find in her a point of hold for our Christian love of her as the Mother of our Lord. On another occasion the praying mind may be glad to sense in her the presence of many meanings or choose some other particular aspect of all that Christian believers want to think about, as indeed is the case in the use of the Rosary. But sooner or later we are brought to Christ ... All of the saints point to Christ both positively and negatively, but of course none with the loveableness and radiance of the Mother of our Lord whom the fourth gospel sees as the Saviour's last gift to the disciple.
>
> And when we ask the saints to pray for us we are commending ourselves to the supernatural love of the blest communion. So I have to say that I see the invocation of the

saints, and particularly of her known as the Queen of saints, as one of the Christian ways of humanising religion and bringing the warmth of personal feeling into it, as an expression of our faith in the oneness of life in time and the beyond, and of our belief that in God's providence the saints have some share in his aid to us and we in his aid to them.[19]

Martin Gillett

The Ecumenical Society of the Blessed Virgin Mary owes its origins to the vision and dogged determination of Martin Gillett. Though from an Anglican and Free Church background he was received into the Roman Catholic Church in 1932 and became an authority on Marian shrines, both in England and throughout the world. He despised the word denomination and always spoke of the various Christian traditions. With his great capacity for friendship he enabled Protestant, Catholic, Anglican and Orthodox Christians to speak to one another on quite delicate theological issues. Following the Second Vatican Council he asked Cardinal John Heenan if he would bless Martin's vision – a new venture called The Ecumenical Society of the Blessed Virgin Mary. The Cardinal responded, 'By all means start an ecumenical society, but with a title like that it will never get off the ground.' Martin Gillett joined the MSF in 1972 and was a member until his death in 1980.

The Ecumenical Society of the Blessed Virgin Mary

Plans were drawn up for the Society in 1967 and formally adopted at a first General Meeting at Westminster Central Hall in March 1969. The purpose of the Society was:

> ... to promote ecumenical devotion, and the study, at various levels, of the place of the Blessed Virgin Mary in the Church, under Christ ...

The first three papers of 1967 were given by a Benedictine monk from Downside Abbey, Dom Ralph Russell, by an

Evangelical canon from Sheffield Cathedral, John de Satge, and by one of the first co-Chairs of the Society, Gordon Wakefield. In his paper, *The Methodist Point of View*, Gordon singled out the work of two notable Methodist scholars, John Lawson and Kingsley Barrett, who had had occasion to deal with Mary and the Virgin Birth in the course of their researches.

In 1948 John Lawson had received his Cambridge BD for *The Biblical Theology of Saint Irenaeus*, and Wakefield wrote:

> John Lawson endorsed the verdict of Vernet that 'St Irenaeus was the first theologian of the Virgin Mary' but he shows with meticulous care that Irenaeus is dominated by the idea of *anakephalaiosis,* and just as Christ is the second Adam, so, for him, Mary is the second Eve whose virginal obedience loosens the knot of virginal disobedience and performs 'a subsidiary recapitulating action.' Hers is 'that pure womb which regenerates men unto God.' There is a distinct value in the place given by Irenaeus to the Virgin in the scheme of salvation, nor need the honour be limited to her. There is, however, no evidence in *Adversus Haereses* to support Vernet's claim that it is reasonable to see in Mary as the advocate of Eve the power of the Virgin to intercede in heaven.[20]

Gordon Wakefield wrote of Kingsley Barrett:

> In his great Commentary on St John's Gospel, C K Barrett sees in John 1.13, 'born not of blood, nor of the will of the flesh, nor of the will of man, but of God,' a Johannine allusion to the Virgin Birth and clear evidence that the Evangelist knew of the tradition.[21]

In an earlier work on the Holy Spirit Kingsley Barrett had written:

> ... the entrance of Jesus into the world was the inauguration of God's new creation and therefore has its only true analogy in Genesis – the work of the Spirit in the entrance of the Redeemer upon the stage of history speaks of a miraculous

creation of the child, but not of a miraculous begetting by a divine agent.[22]

'Magnificat'

In October 1969, in the seventh of the *Mother of Jesus Pamphlets*, Stewart Denyer wrote on the *Magnificat*.

> We are here, I assume, primarily as Christian men and women, to share our treasures, just as our Lady in the Magnificat shares some of those things she treasured and pondered in her heart, as we are told. In this field I think a Methodist has little that is distinctively Methodist to share, but very much to learn and even to covet. All I shall say is what I have come to treasure and value through that interchange of spirituality which is a signal mark of the work of the Holy Spirit in our generation. *Magnificat anima mea Dominum* has been a part of the daily worship of the Church of Christ since St Benedict, at the beginning of the VIth century, appointed it as a canticle at Vespers in the western Church. It was sung with special antiphons and with a censing of the altar at Solemn Vespers. In the Greek Church it has for a similar period formed part of the morning office, the *Orthros,* on certain days, sometimes with the Benedictus. And of course it came from Vespers into Evensong in the *Book of Common Prayer*.[23]

'Intercession'

In November 1969, in the eighth of the *Mother of Jesus Pamphlets*, Gordon Wakefield wrote on *Intercession*:

> Richard Baxter's hymn, 'He wants not friends that hath thy love,' was written with the dispersed dissenting congregations in mind after the repressive laws of 1662. They who had once met together to worship God are scattered and assemble under grievous restrictions and not without danger, but:
>
> In the communion of the saints
> Is wisdom, safety and delight

And when my heart declines and faints,
It's raised by their heat and light!

As for my friends, they are not lost;
The several vessels of Thy fleet,
Though parted now, by tempests tost,
Shall safely in the haven meet.

In 1681, Baxter's wife, Margaret died. Almost thirty years younger than himself, she had been a sweet and restraining influence on his controversial temper and as close and congenial a companion as a man could wish. Now his hymn took on a deeper meaning: and the fellowship of those separated by earthly vicissitudes was affirmed beyond the gulf of death:

Still we are centred all in Thee,
Members, though distant, of one Head,
In the same family we be,
By the same faith and spirit led.

Before Thy throne we daily meet,
As joint petitioners to Thee;
In spirit we each other greet,
And shall again each other see.

God has given us our friends and fellow-Christians to pray with us and for us and it is artificial to regard death any more than life as making this impossible. Catholic and Orthodox Christians ascribe to Mary a supreme and for some Protestants embarrassing place in this community of prayer because she is seen as the first member of the Church, the link between the old Covenant and the new, bestowed on us by Christ with all the other saints to be our helpers and comrades in His Body the Church. It would seem illogical to rule out prayer *to* the saints, if we accept prayer *with* them.[24]

'Marialis Cultus'

In 1974 Geoffrey Wainwright reviewed *Marialis Cultus – To Honour Mary,* Pope Paul VI's Apostolic Exhortation of February 1974. The reviewer questioned the kind of biblical interpretation which was used:

> If all that is false and legendary is to be eschewed by the church where does that put the Immaculate Conception and the 'bodily' Assumption of Mary? Though Methodists consent to Mary's co-operation with divine grace can they really accept that she 'offers Christ' at the foot of the cross? Is there still the risk in Roman Catholic theology that Mary has been put on the wrong side of any necessary distinction between the human and the divine? Methodists will indeed recognize Mary as the perfect model of discipleship and as a woman of prayer attentive to the word of God and as the one who stands out among the poor and humble of the Lord.[25]

'Mary and Methodism'

In a paper he gave to The Ecumenical Society of the Blessed Virgin Mary in 1975 on *Mary in Methodism* Geoffrey Wainwright looked in turn at six of the doctrinal or spiritual characteristics of Methodism, and looked for the nearest corresponding feature in Roman Catholic doctrine or emphasis with regard to Mary. His six Methodist emphases were: Faith as active receptivity – 'the o'erwhelming power of saving grace;' Entire sanctification – 'a heart in every thought renewed ... perfect, and right, and pure and good;' Assurance – 'the witness in himself he hath and consciously believes;' The universal offer of the gospel – 'for all thou hast in Christ prepared, sufficient, sovereign, saving grace;' Social implications of the gospel – 'constrained by Jesu's love to live, the servants of mankind;' The communion of saints – 'one family we dwell in him, one Church, above, beneath.' Each of these six characteristics of Methodist doctrine and devotion he then sought critically to parallel with classic Roman Catholic teaching on Mary.

> I think that Methodists might well see in Mary 'the perfect model of the disciple of the Lord,' a woman of prayer and attentive to the word of God. Her example we ought to be willing to follow. But what of her intercession for us? Again, the associated notion *of merit* makes us suspicious of Roman Catholic talk of the prayers of the saints. But if, without that, Mary may be seen as part of the 'one family,' then we ought to be glad for her prayers.[26]

'The Mother of Jesus in the New Testament'

In 1975 the Roman Catholic New Testament scholar (who was later to be an MSF Weekend lecturer), John McHugh, wrote a major book of five-hundred pages on *The Mother of Jesus in the New Testament.* At the time of its publication Geoffrey Wainwright cynically remarked to the present author that he could have compressed all we know about the Mother of Jesus in the New Testament into ten pages, though later that year he went on to write a five page review of the book for *One in Christ!*

> Let me confess that by his careful exegesis Dr McHugh has almost completely won me round to the view that Mary is here [in Luke 1–2] presented in terms of the daughter of Zion, the personification of the faithful remnant waiting for deliverance. He has made a definite convert to the view that John 1:13 referred originally to *Jesus*: the internal arguments outweigh the external attestation. (I should, however, deduce no more from this than that the notion of the virginal conception of Jesus was familiar to the author of the Johannine prologue: McHugh wants to link the Fourth Gospel very closely to John the son of Zebedee, to whom Jesus entrusted Mary, and to whom Mary entrusted her secret.) Dr McHugh's exegesis of John 2:4f also deserves attention: he translates 'Of what concern is that to thee and to me?' – 'The only satisfactory interpretation of these words is that Mary (like Jesus) knew that his mission was not of this world ... The mother of the Lord is represented as believing in her son *before* the first miracle.'[27]

The Methodist Conference

At Westminster Central Hall, during the Methodist Conference of 1979, the President of the Conference, Bill Gowland, referred to God saying to Mary, 'I'm trusting my boy to your care.' John Newton took up this remark as he addressed the President and the Conference in the course of a debate on the Report of the Ecumenical Committee.

> I want to suggest to Conference a number of reasons why, I believe, the time may well be ripe for a fresh look at the place of Mary in the Church and in the Gospel. We have seen recently a reaction against the traditional male domination of theology in the Christian Church. Mary may prove the true corrective here. Again, recent years have brought us a renewal and deepened understanding of the crucial importance of good mothering for a child's whole future development. Dr Frank Lake has coined the phrase 'the womb of the spirit' to underline the fact that for the first year or two of life the child is as much part of the mother – emotionally, personally, spiritually – as he is, biologically, during the nine months preceding birth. The doctrine of the Immaculate Conception may not feature largely, or at all, in our Christian thinking. Yet if we put this understanding of mothering together with our belief in our Lord's real humanity – its complete, unspoilt integrity and goodness – then are we not saying something of supreme significance about the quality of Mary's mothering of her son?
>
> ... May I ask Conference to take note of the work of The Ecumenical Society of the Blessed Virgin Mary, which brings together Christians from many different traditions, including a number of Methodists. The Society exists 'to promote ecumenical devotion, and the study, at various levels, of the place of the Blessed Virgin Mary in the Church, under Christ.' Its members believe that, through this shared seeking, Mary may be, not a source of division, but of unity and renewal.[28]

'The Ecumenical Office of Mary, the Mother of Jesus'

In 1981 the present author prepared for The Ecumenical Society of the Blessed Virgin Mary an office of prayer to be used at its gatherings. It arose out of an attempt by the compiler to build some basic devotions around a commonly accepted version of the *Magnificat*. Prior to its publication gatherings of the Society found it impossible to recite a common version of the Song of Mary without a printed text in front of them. The first version of the Ecumenical Office was a simple pamphlet with Scripture Sentence, Penitence, Versicles and Responses, Office Hymn (George Timms' 'Sing we of the Blessed Mother'), Psalm, Canticle, Scripture and Responsory, *Magnificat*, Litany of Thanksgiving and Intercession, Lord's Prayer, Collect and Conclusion to the Hour. In 1990 there was a *Revised Edition*, properly type-set and printed with Appendices of Scripture Sentences, additional Office Hymns all set to music, additional Scripture Lessons, a variety of Collects, and a selection of Votive Texts. This became the definitive version of the office of the Society. It was printed in its entirety as the conclusion to John Macquarrie's *Mary for All Christians*, published in 1990 and 2001, and an embossed copy bound in white leather was presented to Pope John Paul! In 2002 a ninety-page book, *A New Ecumenical Office of Mary, the Mother of Jesus*, was published in which the 1990 version was further expanded and enlarged, with complete offices for four mornings and four evenings for use at ecumenical Marian congresses and pilgrimages. The type-setting of the Society's *New Ecumenical Office* was undertaken by Margaret Wallwork and printed by the Methodist Publishing House!

'Mother of Faith and Hope'

In 1982, for the first time in the history of the Fellowship, an entire *Bulletin* was devoted to The Blessed Virgin Mary. Brian Pickett, under the title *Mother of Faith and Hope*, wrote on *The Blessed Virgin Mary in the Thought of the Wesleys*, centring on Charles Wesley's amazing verse linking the three great mysteries of the incarnation, the resurrection and the indwelling Christ.

The only sinless Man and just
He cannot mix with common dust,
But born of a pure virgin's womb,
Must rise out of a virgin-tomb;
The tomb is new where Christ is laid,
New is the heart for Jesus made,
And all His purity receives,
While God in man for ever lives.[29]

Pauline Webb, who always described herself as a 'Weslo-Catholic,' contributed *A Song of High Revolt*, a reflection on the *Magnificat* for the contemporary church and its current needs. The *Bulletin* then included a sermon, *The Mother, the Neighbour and the World*, that Gordon Wakefield had preached the previous autumn at the International Congress of the Blessed Virgin Mary. This was during a Communion Service at which the celebrant was John Newton, then President of the Methodist Conference. The last of the Marian pieces in the Bulletin was a 1978 hymn by Fred Pratt Green, moving through the joyful, sorrowful and glorious mysteries of the Rosary.

Never was a day so bright,
Never maid so gentle;
Brighter than the brightest light
Shone the Lord's archangel.
Lady, you tremble at the news!
Tell us you will not refuse
To carry
Our little Lord of Love
And Glory.

Soon a sword shall pierce your heart,
Sadden your tomorrows;
All too soon you too must start
Up the Hill of Sorrows.

Lady, they will respect your grief,
When in darkness past belief
You tarry,
Bearing the cross that love
Must carry.

There's a crown upon your brow
You alone are wearing.
Mother of all mothers now:
In his triumph sharing.
Lady, you were God's home on earth:
Now your Son must come to birth
Within us,
By nothing else than love
To win us.[30]

Pieta

In 1986 Frances Young, a patristic scholar and pastoral theologian, published the first version of her apologia based on her journey as mother to her profoundly handicapped son, Arthur. In it she provided the context for a poem addressed to Our Lady:

> In 1982 the local convent invited all the residents of Selly Park to a carol service during the week after Christmas. I took Arthur along in his wheelchair. He loves singing and music. There in the chapel I was very conscious of his presence, especially since many people there did not know him and it is impossible to keep him quiet. In the chapel was a statue of Our Lady. Out of that combination of circumstances came this:

> Mary, my child's lovely. Is yours lovely too?
>   Little hands, little feet.
>   Curly hair, smiles sweet.
> Mary, my child's broken. Is yours broken too?
>   Crushed by affliction,
>   Hurt by rejection,

Disfigured, stricken,
Silent submission.

Mary, my heart's bursting.
Is yours bursting too?
Bursting with labour, travail and pain.
Bursting with agony, ecstasy, gain.
Bursting with sympathy, anger, compassion.
Bursting with praising Love's transfiguration.

Mary, my heart's joyful. Is yours joyful too?[31]

A Methodist Looks at Walsingham

In May 1983 Geoffrey Thackray Eddy delivered a paper at the East Anglia Branch of the Wesley Historical Society meeting in the Methodist Chapel in Walsingham. He described how Walsingham had been transformed in fifty years. He related the mediaeval origins of the shrine, its pilgrimages and priory, its dissolution, Wesley's preaching visit and his criticism of Henry VIII. He then told of the Anglo-Catholic revival of the Shrine under Alfred Hope Patten, of the Kensitite protests and of the Methodist butcher who brandished his carving knife at one Kensitite and shouted, 'Don't say that about our Vicar!' He spoke of Hope Patten's collapse and death during the historic visit of bishops during the Lambeth Conference of 1958. He noted the restoration of the Slipper Chapel and the establishing of the Roman Catholic Shrine, 'perhaps a little more English than its Anglican counterpart!' He welcomed the presence of the small Orthodox Chapel within the Anglican shrine.

The later part of Geoffrey Eddy's paper asked 'How does a Methodist look at Walsingham? Were there three great Christian traditions in Walsingham or four? What more could Methodism do in Walsingham beyond its small and faithful Sunday afternoon congregation?' Methodists elsewhere, he noted, had moved into pilgrimage in a big way. Methodist heritage tours invaded Epworth Rectory, Wesley's Chapel, the New Room and Gwennap Pit in significant numbers. From most of these places they left with knick-knacks, including carvings from wood in Epworth Rectory garden! For Wesley Walsingham had been 'famous for many generations.'

> There is some deep need of the human spirit to which veneration of the Virgin Mary ministers. Methodists need to discover and share what Catholics, Anglicans and Orthodox understand about a part of the Faith that all of us hold. After all *Theotokos* – the Godbearer – is essentially about the Incarnation. We do not honour the Son by dishonouring the Mother! As Wesley himself said, in his comments on the *Roman Catechism*:
>
> > We honour this blessed Virgin as the mother of the holy Jesus and as she was a person of eminent piety; but we do not think it lawful to give that honour to her which belongs not to a creature, and doth equal her with her Redeemer.[32]

Thackray Eddy reminded his listeners that Walsingham was here to stay! Its Catholic piety could only grow. Walsingham Methodism needed to make sure that its treasured and historic site was part of the itinerary of all pilgrims to Walsingham. Year by year the life of the Methodist community needed to proclaim:

> Our God contracted to a span,
> Incomprehensibly made man.[33]

Methodist Stations of the Cross

Although the writer and broadcaster Frank Topping became a Methodist Minister as well as an actor he came from a Roman Catholic family and has found the two Christian traditions interpenetrative. For many years he has belonged to the MSF. In 1986 he published a remarkably popular book of prayers and meditations on the Stations of the Cross and indeed of Stations beyond the Cross. His reflection on the station *Jesus Meets his Sorrowing Mother* includes the words:

> Mary, by love's sacrifice,
> your heart is pierced.

Mary, by love's generosity,
you are emptied.

Mary, in temptation
may we imitate your obedience.

Mary, in the hour of trial
may we know the love
you gazed on at Calvary.[34]

Theotokos

In the Epiphany Bulletin of 1987 Marian Jones published a poem, *Emmanuel – God with us*, which began:

Mary,
Theotokos,
Bearer of God,
I am a God-bearer too!
With the rest of God's creation
I, too, am called to bring Christ to birth.
Christ, within me, waiting silently,
Waiting for the quickening,
Waiting for me to realise,
To realise that he is here,
Here in me.

The poem ended:

Mary,
Theotokos,
Bearer of God,
In your fear and your pain,
In your hope and your joy
Help me to labour for Christ, our God.
Help me to help others to bring him to birth,
For we are God-bearers too.[35]

Eamon Duffy and the 'Epworth Review'

For the January 1989 issue of the *Epworth Review* the editor, John Stacey, commissioned an article by the Cambridge Roman Catholic scholar and historian, Eamon Duffy, on *The Place of the Blessed Virgin Mary in Roman Catholicism.* Typically the article and the statements were clearly crafted with careful footnotes. After outlining the scriptural bases – the passages in the gospels, in the Pauline corpus and in Revelation 12 – Professor Duffy then explained the origins and development of the Cult of the Virgin, the Immaculate Conception and Marian Intercession. He also provided a Guide to further reading. John Stacey had invited five responses. Geoffrey Ainger and Myrtle Langley were eirenical but critical in their responses, particularly in relation to issues concerning social justice and the place of women in Christian life and ministry. John Job, despite the efforts of Eamon Duffy, still believed Catholics 'worshipped' Mary! Howard Marshall wanted everyone to work and pray for the day when all the churches would get rid of their unbiblical ideas and come closer to the truth and purity of the gospel of Christ.

It was left to Gordon Wakefield, in the fifth and final response, to invite Methodists on a pilgrimage of discovery:

> ... in spite of everything, one is haunted by Aristotle's words about fiction being truer than history, while, as this paper illustrates, human hearts cry out for poetry, of which Mary has so often been the inspiration and will be as long as Christians and human beings exist.[36]

Mary, Icon of the Covenant

One of the most profound insights linking Methodist tradition with Marian devotion has been provided by the MSF member and ecumenist, David Chapman, who sees a deep parallel between the liturgical theology at the heart of the Methodist Renewal of the Covenant and Mary's total sacrificial obedience to the Divine will:

Now there are many saints and martyrs, ancient and modern, whose lives may reveal something of what is involved in the new covenant in Christ. Nevertheless, it is the figure of Mary, the Mother of the Lord, who most fully images the dynamics, divine and human, found in the new covenant. From the divine perspective, at the Annunciation Mary is invited to enter into the new covenant in Jesus Christ. Through prevenient grace she is enabled fully to accept that invitation. From the human perspective, Mary makes a free and considered decision in faith: 'Behold, I am the handmaid of the Lord; let it be to me according to your word' (Luke 1.38). Although her own role in the new covenant is uniquely hers, Mary may also be looked upon as the first to accept the invitation to participate in the new covenant. Thereafter the same invitation is issued to humankind in general through the ministry of Christ and his Church.

And like Mary, only not so fully, through prevenient grace we are enabled to respond to the covenant. Altogether, Mary's obedient acceptance of the new covenant in Christ is archetypal for the response of faith. With imagination the Methodist covenant prayer can be seen as an elaboration of Mary's glad acceptance of the new covenant:

> Put me to what you will, rank me with whom you will;
> put me to doing, put me to suffering;
> let me be employed for you or laid aside for you,
> exalted for you or brought low for you;
> let me be full, let me be empty;
> let me have all things, let me have nothing.[37]

Mother of Jesus and the Beloved Disciple – First Members of the Church

In a paper, *Mary, servant of the Word,* which David Carter gave to The Ecumenical Society of the Blessed Virgin Mary at Norwich in 1994, he clearly saw the Mother of Jesus and the Beloved Disciple as the first members of the Church and indeed as iconic for all future members of the community of faith.

To return to Mary and John at the foot of the cross: I see them as constituting, in conformity with Christ's promise that 'where two or three are gathered together in my name, there am I' (Matthew 18.20), the first 'local' church, model for every subsequent local church. They are there committed utterly to each other, to care for and to serve each other, and to journey onwards in the Saviour's love. As Charles Wesley puts it:

Didst Thou not make us one,
That we might one remain,
Together travel on,
And bear each other's pain;
Till all Thy utmost goodness prove,
And rise renewed in perfect love?

They are committed at the foot of the cross as the first of all those whom Christ will 'draw to himself' (John 12.32). They stand there as the first members of the Church, the original witnesses of the saving event which constitutes the foundation of the Church Universal. Christ bows his head towards them and breathes out the Spirit which is to join them as one and keep them and all later Christians in fellowship. He cries, 'It is finished' in acknowledgement that the first fruits of his sacrifice have appeared in the founding of his Church and its equipping with the Spirit.[38]

Mary in the work of salvation

Richard Clutterbuck gave a paper to The Ecumenical Society of the Blessed Virgin Mary's Chester Congress in September 2002 on *Helpmate of a self-sufficient God: the Servanthood of Mary in dialogue with Karl Barth* in which, at the close, the lecturer drew his own personal conclusion:

Mary's solidarity with the crucified God is surely a wonderful participation in the work of salvation. If God has, in Christ crucified, placed the very triune life of God at the mercy of human beings, Mary's faithfulness at the cross was a true sharing of that moment. The artistic and devotional depiction of Mary reinforces this – in the poem *Stabat Mater,* in the great

Isenheim altarpiece of Matthias Grünewald, in the depictions of the *pieta*, and in the Eastern icon, the virgin *eleousa*. This virgin of mercy is one who stands by the Son of God in his hour of need.[39]

'Mary – Mother of all God's Children'

In 2010 the present author contributed to the festschrift for John Newton with a chapter on *Mary – Mother of All God's Children.* In the first section of the paper on *Mary: Mother of Jesus Christ the Son of God* he argued:

> ... it is within the burgeoning and foundational Christology of the first Christian writers, when the full implications of the true nature of Christ are tested, rehearsed, celebrated, debated and consolidated that a similar and parallel process of reflection, revelation and consolidation attaches itself to the church's understanding of and devotion to Mary.
>
> It is quite impossible to maintain that while there was a dynamic movement within the New Testament concerning the evolution of Christology, there was no fairly early movement in the church's understanding of and devotion to Mary. All four gospels have a primitive, rich and developing Christology and out of these Christologies Luke and John in particular formed a rich foundation for the church's understanding of and devotion to Mary.
>
> For Luke Mary is 'favoured by God,' 'full of grace,' 'handmaid of the Lord,' 'virgin mother,' 'overshadowed by the Spirit,' and 'blessed among women.' She is the one who 'ponders all things in her heart.' She is a prophetic voice in the Magnificat, she is a representative in the Temple of the poor of Israel, she is the recipient of the piercing sword and she is with the twelve at the descent of the Spirit on the Day of Pentecost. Here is the beginning of the church's rich understanding of and devotion to Mary from the seventies of the first century.
>
> Only slightly later, in the Fourth Gospel, does Mary first carry the enigmatic title 'Mother of Jesus.' Then she has a decisive role in the first of the signs of Jesus at Cana, when he

first reveals his glory. Then, ultimately, in the Fourth Gospel, at the foot of the Cross, Mary becomes the mother of all loved disciples of the Lord.[40]

The Ecumenical Marian Pilgrimage Trust

Under the auspices of the Ecumenical Marian Pilgrimage Trust Anglicans of various shades, Roman Catholics, Scottish Presbyterians, Orthodox of several Patriarchates and Methodists now make a significant biennial visit to Walsingham. Over the past ten years the Trust has run a number of residential ecumenical pilgrimages which have included participation in each tradition's distinctive liturgies, enjoying the fact that Walsingham is blessed with Anglican, Roman Catholic, Orthodox and Methodist churches. There has been great gain and blessing in the exchange of views, the unique ecumenical ethos and in the formal and informal conversations, reminding us all that there are rich and diverse patterns of doctrine and devotion, some comfortable and some less so. Talks, homilies and papers have provided a balanced programme.

One highlight has been the regular contributions of the Methodist local preacher, Margaret Barker, a former President of the Society for Old Testament Study and a co-founder of the Temple Studies Group. She is the originator of Temple Theology, which seeks to show the extent of Temple influence in Christianity. Her books and papers have revisited a lost and significant strand relating Mary of Nazareth to the Wisdom tradition.[41] These have clearly interested and stimulated a wide variety of ecumenical pilgrims who have numbered between eighty and a hundred on each occasion. Each year the welcome given by the local churches to the clergy and people of our disparate community has always left very positive memories.

Little Walsingham Methodist Church

We began this chapter with John Wesley's visit to Walsingham in 1781. The Methodist Society in Walsingham had been founded in 1779. The present Georgian chapel stands close to the main street and in sight of regular Marian pilgrims. Many of them seek to enter the chapel as it is customary for pilgrims to visit all the 'holy' houses while in Walsingham.

The tiny Methodist congregation shares in the various events arranged by the Walsingham churches during the Week of Prayer for Christian Unity and during Holy Week. In Lent 2013 the Methodist minister, Jenny Pathmarajah, provided a contemporary meditation on the Stations of the Cross. Year by year the stewards, Tommy and Sylvia Seaman, welcome Methodist and ecumenical groups to the chapel to celebrate the Eucharist and to give thanks for the Mother of Jesus. The MSF, The Ecumenical Society of the Blessed Virgin Mary and the Ecumenical Marian Pilgrimage Trust have all celebrated liturgies in the chapel, and the visiting Methodist and Reformed preachers have taught a fullness of the Christian faith that has brought honour to Mary and offered worship to her incarnate Son. Two of the MSF's youngest ministers have made significant contributions to the Ecumenical Marian Pilgrimage Trust at Walsingham. Mark Rowland was probably the first Methodist to preach in the Shrine church itself, at a farewell Office of the Pilgrimage. Adam Stevenson not only preached at an opening pilgrimage Eucharist in the Methodist Chapel but also chose the Chapel for the celebration of his first Eucharist after ordination.

Friends of Our Lady of Tintern

Visitors walking into the remains of the Abbey Church at Tintern, Monmouthshire will see a statue of the Virgin and Child, sculpted in the Abbey and dedicated in 2007. It was carved with hand tools, in local stone, to recreate the late 13th Century figure that once graced the Abbey. The original statue was broken into pieces at the dissolution in 1536.

Philip Chatfield first heard of the existence of these fragments in October 2005 and made the suggestion of carving a replica, based as closely as possible on the old fragments. During the following months a group of local people considered this suggestion and in due course approached Cadw, the custodians of Tintern Abbey, about the feasibility of such a project. Their response was encouraging and The Friends of Our Lady of Tintern was formed to put together a formal application, which was approved in June 2006. A small group commissioned the new statue and underwrote the cost. From its earliest days the committee of The Friends of Our Lady of Tintern has drawn in Anglicans, Roman Catholics, Moravians and Methodists. In 2007 the present author was invited to join the committee and assist in drawing up a Simple Office of Prayer and the Friends' own Prayer of Our Lady of Tintern. Each September, following the dedication of the statue in 2007, the Abbey Church has been filled for open air Sung Vespers in the presence of the Anglican Bishop of Monmouth and the Roman Catholic Archbishop of Cardiff, with Catholic and Protestant pilgrims from Wales and the South West of England. Orthodox, Moravians and Methodists have all preached at September Vespers. The present author's prayer concludes the Friends' Simple Office of Prayer.

God, our Father,
by the overshadowing of the Holy Spirit
and the loving obedience
of Our Lady of Tintern,
Virgin and Mother,
you gave your Son to be our Redeemer.
By the same Spirit
fill us with your grace,
heal the nations
and renew your creation,
until with Mary and all your saints
we are crowned for ever in the glory of heaven;
through the merits of Jesus Christ our Lord.
Amen.

14

Arminian Testimony

The Conference Annual Lecture

Peter Baldwin, an Anglican priest and a one-time 'Recognized and Regarded Methodist Minister,' was of the opinion that the Methodist Conference was more like the Edinburgh Festival than the General Synod of the Church of England! This was in the 1980s when what took place on the periphery of the Conference during the day and what took place in the local churches in the evenings after the Conference had risen was almost as important as what took place during the business sessions. The 1980s and the 1990s were also the last decades in which there was any significant engagement between the members of the local Methodist churches and circuits of the host Districts and the membership of the Conference. Many of the personalities of the Conference and the representatives who were ordained or local preachers often led Sunday morning worship in the surrounding chapels. Members of the Conference were for the most part billeted with local Methodists. In the fifties and sixties an evening Conference Public Meeting of the MSF, with Donald Soper as one of the speakers, could draw several hundred from the local Methodist congregations and the membership of the Conference.

In the 1990s, for logical and demographic reasons, the link between the local Methodist population and the visiting Methodist Conference grew weaker. The evening Conference Public Meetings that survived changed their nature. They came to rely on the Conference representatives and the loyalty of keen supporters.

Until the mid-1980s the MSF Conference Public Meeting had consisted of a short service or an Evening Office, usually followed by two speakers often chosen for being well known rather than for the subject. But in the MSF's Golden Jubilee year of 1985, when the Methodist Conference was meeting in Birmingham, the Fellowship chose to inaugurate an annual lecture. These lectures would be published on the day of their delivery. They were free to members as one of the two mailings per year. The other mailing of the year was to be the MSF *Bulletin*. The Annual Lecture was to be available for purchase and was often sold on the MSF Conference bookstall, or the official Conference bookstall, when the bookstalls of the voluntary Methodist societies were marginalized and priced out of existence by central Methodist policy!

'Catholic Spirituality Reconsidered'

During the 1985 Birmingham Methodist Conference the MSF Jubilee Lecture was given at The Queen's College, Birmingham by its Principal and Chair of the Fellowship, Gordon Wakefield. The title *Catholic Spirituality Reconsidered* was negotiated between the lecturer and the editor. It was designed to mark a significant stage in the evolution of the Fellowship, the opportunities for ecumenism still open to Methodism and the spiritual journey of the lecturer. In many ways the tone and content of what was said and written offered the MSF an agenda for the next thirty years and threw out a challenge to Methodism – before it was too late – to live on a large ecclesiastical map and set its ecumenical sights high.

> The universality of the Roman Church still offers hope for the unity, not of all Christians merely, but of all mankind. More than any other communion of Christians it is *elect from every nation, yet one o'er all the earth.* And it is a Church, which, when freed from the lust for uniformity and submission, includes wide varieties of temperament, theology and prayer. And more than any other it is the Church of the poor. This was what helped to convert John Henry Newman, as his novel *Loss and Gain* makes clear. The critical Protestant will retort that it too often leaves the poor in their poverty and ignorance, and that the religion of the criminal classes, if they have any, is most often Catholic. There is cause for disquiet here; but a

Mass where all races and classes may be together, and no one is rejected because of poverty or imagined ethical inferiority, where the philosopher may worship with the illiterate or mentally handicapped, and the barmaid may have attained supernatural sanctity beyond the priests or the obviously virtuous, is an *antepast of heaven.* The most terrible fear is that the hope of this adumbrating a world Church and a renewed civilisation is vanishing on the tides of history.[1]

'Blackbirds and Budgerigars'

Given by the present author at the Stoke on Trent Methodist Conference in 1986, *Blackbirds and Budgerigars: A Critical History of Methodist Liturgical Dress 1786–1986* ran to at least one re-print! It was admitted from the outset that to many minds the whole topic was trivial. The title was drawn from an aside (not in the manuscript of Gordon Rupp's Jubilee Sermon, preached at Wesley's Chapel) in which he opined that, having looked like blackbirds for two hundred years, perhaps it was no bad thing that the liturgical attire of Methodist ministers was now making them look more like budgerigars! He had been particularly struck by the appearance of Ron Gibbins, the minister of Wesley's Chapel, whom he described afterwards as looking like the Abbot of Glastonbury!

The lecture surveyed ministerial dress from the time of Wesley's death, when a number of his preachers began wearing the surplice or cassock, gown and bands. Conference then ruled against all gowns – and the like – in Methodist pulpits. A few ministers however persisted across the nineteenth century. Mainly as a result of First World War chaplaincies in the forces more and more Methodist ministers began to dress like their counter-parts in the Church of Scotland or the other Free Churches. During the sixties and seventies cassock, gown and bands, or gowns over suits became the majority practice. From the eighties onwards black clerical stocks and black clerical shirts were giving way to other colours, including various shades of episcopal maroon and purple; some ministers were even asking the bride what colour she would be wearing! In an attempt to be more 'catholic' and 'universal' some Methodist ministers began appearing in white or oatmeal cassock-albs, with or without an appropriate seasonal stole. For some ordained ministers this became part of the journey from minister to presbyter!

In part *Blackbirds and Budgerigars* was an attempt to expose the custom of Methodist ministers and local preachers dressing in clerical garb without regard to the rules and customs governing clerical dress in other more systematized traditions, where logic and uniformity had generally prevailed. Some Methodist ministers who believed they were being 'ecumenical' or 'proper' by donning ecclesiastical dress were anything but when they appeared in the 'wrong' or 'inappropriate' colour or garb at an inter-church service! The ultimate argument of the lecture was an invitation to take the trouble to conform to the general practice of those who have been at it for a long time or just abandon clerical dress altogether! Clearly the preferred MSF option for a presbyter or deacon of the Western Catholic tradition was a white cassock alb with an appropriate stole. Blue preaching scarves and black gowns had been encouraged for local preachers. New look cosy and relaxed worship and the carpeted sitting-room-style conversion of chapels was going to dilute the debate until it disappeared altogether!

'Altars and Altar Calls'

By the time Philip Blackburn came to give the Portsmouth Conference Lecture he had had plenty of time to test out in Leeds and Harrogate the Wesleyan high churchmanship he had inherited and celebrated in Jamaica and the Bahamas. The full title of his lecture was *Altars and Altar Calls: A Catholic Evangelical in the Circuit Ministry.* His lecture was his testimony to the effectiveness of a fully integrated catholic and evangelical approach to day to day ministry:

> It never occurred to me that there could possibly be any incompatibility between simultaneous membership of the Methodist Sacramental Fellowship and the Methodist Revival Fellowship (as it then was) until some time after I returned to work in an English circuit, following nineteen years with the Methodist Missionary Society. This was through a chance remark, not unkindly spoken, by my Superintendent, the Revd W Norman Stainer-Smith, that *in spite of* my 'high chapel' practices, including strict adherence to the *Book of Offices* and the regular chanting of canticles and psalms, the congregations in my pastoral care were growing, large numbers of young people were being converted and confirmed, and there was a steady flow of candidates requesting 'notes' to preach.[2]

Philip had relished the rich Wesleyanism of the West Indies and looked back on it with both delight and conviction:

> Everywhere I served for the first nineteen years of my ministry the main Sunday morning worship was liturgical – according to the 1936 *Book of Offices* – either Morning Prayer with four hymns, four chants and sermon, or the first office of Holy Communion, with hymns, psalms and sermon. The evening services were less structured – more like the contemporary services in English Methodism, but in the Jamaican country circuits we used Cliff College choruses along with the *Methodist Hymn Book*.[3]

The other mighty string to his bow was catechesis!

> While serving in Wesley College, Belize, I was invited by the circuit Superintendent, the Revd T Stanley Cannon, to take the confirmation classes at Wesley Church, the mother church of the District. The date of the first class was duly announced in the Sunday service at Wesley Church, and also during prayers in Wesley College. I expected about a dozen to turn up, but forty-seven candidates appeared. During four years I was privileged to prepare hundreds of people for church membership. Out of my *last* class of eighty-four, seventy-seven persons were approved by the Leaders' Meeting for

> confirmation in Wesley Church by the Chairman of the District, the Revd W Hartley Totty.[4]

On his return to the English work and his taking up of his Yorkshire appointments Philip gave the same outstanding priority to confirmation and church membership classes:

> [Jamaica and Belize] have been an inspiration to me for the rest of my ministry. There are more people than we realize in our congregations who are ready to commit themselves openly to Christ. Like most evangelicals, I have emphasized commitment to Jesus, but also I equally emphasize the need for committed Christians to *belong* to the church, the Body of Christ. This is catholic and evangelical teaching.[5]

'What I owe to the Wesleys'

For the Conference Public Meeting of 1998 John Newton and Donald Soper each gave a short paper on *What I owe to the Wesleys*. In his paper John Newton wrote:

> The Wesley brothers steadfastly resisted every move in the Conference of preachers which favoured a formal breach with the Church of England. They remained loyal to the last, urging Methodists to attend their parish churches to receive the Sacrament, and warning the preachers not to make personal attacks on the Anglican clergy, however much of their ministry might be open to criticism.
>
> Yet Methodism continued to grow apart from its Mother Church, and the breach was sealed by Wesley's ordination of preachers for America and Scotland.
>
> Charles, who was always less inclined to 'filial disobedience' than John, saw with brutal clarity that 'ordination is separation' and so it proved. With the death of the Wesleys, the remaining links between Methodism and the Church of England were steadily eroded.
>
> What, then, does the reaction of the Wesleys to their Mother Church have to say to us today? They challenge us in a twofold sense ...[6]

As Methodists, we have to face the disturbing growth of new movements, both inside and outside the mainstream of our church life. How are we going to respond to them?'

> Do we not need to take serious stock of the proliferations of new groups and movements among Christians today, and ask what the Spirit is saying to us through them? Movements of Charismatic Renewal; house churches; independent Christian fellowships; and the many new forms of religious community, both Evangelical and Catholic: and all these pose sharp questions for Methodism. Their growth and dynamism highlight our own areas of decline and low morale.
>
> If we are to be true to the Wesleys, we shall be open-minded in our appraisal of such new movements; not blind to any faults they may display, but ready to receive the new life that may flow from them.[7]

Donald Soper concluded with an acknowledgement of his debt to J E Rattenbury and the MSF as much as to the Wesleys themselves. It was through his introduction to the Methodist Sacramental Fellowship and his friendship with Dr Rattenbury that he came to see that in both the Wesley brothers there was a profound sense of the sacramental nature of the Christian faith.

> Maybe Methodism has from time to time either forgotten or ignored this central element in the ministry of both John and Charles. What is beyond any doubt is that their evangelical fervour was rooted in sacramental worship and was, they believed, indispensible to its advocacy.
>
> I was brought up within the framework of Wesleyan Methodism, and I realise now how far much of it had departed from the sacramental element. As a boy I remember the Communion Service seemed to be an optional extra, appended to the 11 o'clock or 6.30 service, and often carelessly undertaken. I have learned since, and owe it to the Sacramental Fellowship, that the disciplined practice of sacramental worship is inseparable from a comprehensive presentation of the Christian faith in practice. To put it in quite personal terms, I need to stretch out my hands for the

> bread on Sunday morning if I am to offer that bread in Hyde Park later in the day. That perhaps is my deepest gratitude for the life and work of the Wesleys.[8]

'Whatever Happened to Heaven?'

Separated by only four years Michael Townsend delivered two Annual Lectures on the mystic union that binds together the church on earth and the church in heaven. His first paper, *Whatever Happened to Heaven? Worship, Prayer and the Communion of Saints,* given in 1989, was based on *lex orandi, lex credendi.* In the lecture he exposed the strengths and weaknesses of Methodist hymnody and liturgy in relation to a fully fledged faith and practice regarding the communion of saints. One of his great laments was the disappearance, after the 1933 hymn-book, of 'Jerusalem the golden,' 'the omission of which is quite incomprehensible.' He spoke of the contemporary removal of any language hinting that heaven was the believer's home. He noted that the 1936 *Book of Offices* had not the slightest hint at prayers for the dead in the Burial Service. The 1975 *Methodist Service Book* got as far as 'We commend our *brother* (......) to your perfect mercy and wisdom.' In the second half of his paper Michael explored some of the reluctance about prayer and the departed, leaning on the combined faith and spirituality of John Henry Newman and Gordon Wakefield:

> The objections to prayer for the departed arise largely from the fear that we should be somehow introducing a notion of purgatory, with an apparatus of prayer as a means of securing release. That, of course, is quite untenable. The salvation of believers depends upon the finished work of Christ and the graciousness of God, not upon whether they have sufficient friends on earth to intercede for them at the throne of grace. But the notion that there is still some work for God's grace to perform in us after death is anything but untenable. The insight of J H Newman is precious. When, after death, Gerontius receives his momentary glimpse of the Divine Glory, he cannot bear it: 'Take me away.' So Gordon Wakefield is

right when he says: 'The grace of God will make us fit for his presence, partakers of the divine nature, to be one with him in the company of heaven. And he will not do this by magic ... He will do it through a process of education, which enlists the co-operation of my own so feeble will, intelligence and love. There will be pain in it, even frustration at times, but all is of grace and on the morrow there is joy unspeakable and fullness of glory.'[9,10]

'Norah and Her Ark'

By 1990 churches, Bible translators, hymn-writers and liturgists were beginning to face the challenge of inclusivity in language and imagery both for God and humans. The dominant mode had been to think and speak of God using masculine language and pronouns. In every aspect of the church's life and liturgy there was a general paucity of feminine imagery and characteristics when celebrating the Godhead. Linguistically the challenge to the churches was the secular shift away from presuming that the generic 'he,' 'him,' 'himself,' 'man,' 'men' and 'mankind' could any longer serve for women as well as men.

In *Norah and Her Ark: The Dilemma of inclusive Language for Humans and God* the present writer sought to establish that the challenge of inclusivity must be taken seriously by the worshipping community. A number of recent contributions were of great beauty, as in Janet Morley's third collect for Easter Day:

> O God, the power of the powerless,
> you have chosen as your witnesses
> those whose voice is not heard.
> Grant that, as women first announced the resurrection
> though they were not believed,
> we too may have courage
> to persist in proclaiming your word,
> in the power of Jesus Christ. Amen.[11]

The ultimate challenge of inclusivity was to see the great Biblical images of patriarchal power and the culture they had perpetuated transformed by a gospel of the vulnerable, self-giving and unquenchable love of God. Part of the problem with the language and models of inclusivity was that, at the beginning, their advocates didn't know when to stop. Profoundly problematic were the alternatives to the classical Trinitarian formulae. 'God, Christ and the Spirit' had permeated a number of Reformed churches. 'Source of all Being, Eternal Word and Holy Spirit' preserved the objectivity of the Godhead but lost any sense of inter-personal relationship. 'Glory to the Lover, and to the Beloved, and to the Mutual Friend' was not likely to catch on! Naming God as 'Mother,' from time to time, was tolerable in Protestant worship, but totally confusing in a Catholic culture where the title of 'Mother' had already been given to 'the mother of Jesus' as early as the Fourth Gospel, when Jesus said to the beloved disciple, 'Here is your mother.' It was recognized that to deliver Christian theology, life and liturgy entirely or adequately from 'God *the Father*' and 'God *the Son*' was impossible and that some sensitive and deeply thinking feminist theologians and writers would finally part company with historic and Biblical Christianity as irredeemably patriarchal. 'Let us re-write the Salvation history Text Book to fit in with our improved perceptions.'[12]

'An Hour to Raise the Dead: The Art of Performance in Sunday Worship'

Cruelly, in the midst of his ministry Michael Austin was taken from his family and from Methodism by an early death. He had been a refreshing gift to his congregations because he had wedded his natural gifts and understanding of drama with his deep understanding of worship as performative action and dynamic event.

> What makes a good performance? A good performance in the theatre occurs when all the elements are brought together in

> harmony with each other. When this occurs the script will be enhanced by the performance of the actors; the performance of the actors will be enhanced by the space in which the performance occurs; and the set, the costumes, the sound and the lighting, if these additional elements are being used, will add to the meaning of the drama. When we see a good performance we do not think about the elements that have gone to make it up. They are brought together in harmony, and we remember only the total effect of the performance ... If the script is poor, if the costumes clash with the scenery, if the lighting dominates the production, then the performance suffers. The key to a successful performance is to enable all the elements to work together in harmony.[13]

Michael Austin demonstrated that a sense of event, a good script and a good director, space and level and how they work, scenery and props, light and sound, gesture and action, signing and symbol, shape and movement, banners and costume can be brought together in harmony to enable worship to be a dynamic and life-changing celebration of the liturgy, 'the work of the people,' offered to God.

'Protestant Evangelism or Catholic Evangelization?'

As an international Methodist scholar and a renowned student of missiology Kenneth Cracknell was well placed to invite British Methodists to appreciate that the Catholic term 'evangelization' was much more akin to Methodist understandings than the Protestant term 'evangelism.'[14]

The Wesleys, from the very beginning, were committed to permanent quality rather than transient quantity. The British Methodist figures of growth between 1768 and 1798 from 40 circuits to 149, and from 27,341 to 101,712 members were 'not the statistics of a great ingathering or mass movement.'[15]

> For the Wesleys, primary evangelism (a term they never used) was the midwifery of the Spirit, enabling the new birth. The goal was not merely conversion, a term Wesley rarely used. No more was it justification, nor a sense of pardon, nor a claim to

be *born again*. The goal was nothing less than the 'restoration of the soul to its primitive health,' 'a recovery of the divine nature,' a life lived 'in righteousness and true holiness, in justice, mercy and truth.'

For the Wesleys, initiation was into community. There was no point in scattering the seed for the birds of the air to pluck it up. Preaching at random simply meant that the preachers could not instruct the hearers in justification, but more serious even than that, the believers were not able to bear one another's burdens, and so to build each other up in faith and holiness. John Wesley, Albert Outler remarked, 'had grasped the secret of the Word made social.'

Woe to him, whose spirits droop,
To him who falls alone!
He has none to lift him up,
To help his weakness on;
Happier we each other keep,
We each other's burdens bear;
Never need our footsteps slip
Upheld by mutual prayer.

For the Wesleys, discipling was sacramental. Attendance upon the Means of Grace was obligatory, and among these was 'the Supper of the Lord.' It is rather endearing that in 1788 John Wesley should have reprinted 'a Discourse written some fifty-five years ago, for the use of my pupils at Oxford,' entitled *The Duty of Constant Communion*. But this fifty-five year old sermon was needed lest Methodists should forget in 1788 that which Wesley had intended in the *General Rules*. John and Charles Wesley, we may add, had grasped the secret of the Word made sacramental.

Come, to the Supper come,
Sinners, there still is room,
Every soul may be His guest,
Jesus gives the general word;
Share the monumental feast,
Eat the supper of your Lord.[16]

'Our Friends in Light'

Written as a sequel to *Whatever happened to Heaven?: Worship, Prayer and the Communion of Saints*, Michael Townsend's second MSF Annual Lecture, *Our Friends in Light: Praise and Prayer in the Communion of Saints*, moved on from whether we may pray for the departed to whether or not we believe the departed pray for us! The context for the debate was 'our total understanding of the communion of saints, the nature of prayer and the finished work of Christ.'[17] The writer understood there were basically four objections to invoking the saints.

> The invocation of the saints is simply unnecessary since we already have Christ to pray for us and need no other. The invocation of the saints comes dangerously close to undermining the unique High Priesthood and mediatorship of Christ himself. In naming the saints in such prayer we appear to pre-empt God's prerogative of judging who the saints actually are. The practice is open to severe abuse which opens the door to a syncretistic or even polytheistic understanding of faith.[18]

The principal argument of the paper was that for the saints to pray for us was simply an expression of their continuing Christian love. As we do not compromise the sole and unique mediatorship of Christ when we ask our earthly friends 'in Christ' to pray for us, neither do we when we ask for the departed 'in Christ' to pray for us. Just as we do not grade the sanctity of those who pray for us here, so we do not need to grade the holiness of the departed when we ask for their prayers. We pray equally to those formally canonised as to those who are not. The strategy of Christian mission from the start was, on the whole, one of reticence about condemning any pre-conversion fellowship of ancestral prayer. Worshipping ancestors was one thing. Excluding them from our memorial before God was quite another.

> I am certainly not pleading for the immediate wholesale incorporation of traditional Catholic veneration of the saints

into the public liturgies of our beloved Methodism, but I do think it is possible that some tentative steps would not be foreign to the tradition of the Wesleys. We do seem (by and large) to have accepted that recognition of Advent, Christmas, Epiphany, Lent, Easter, Pentecost and even All Saints is not a sectarian High Church Anglican invention, to be resisted at all costs in the cause of Protestant purity, but rather the possession of the Holy Catholic Church, in which Methodism, according to the Deed of Union, 'claims and cherishes its place.' Might we now take the next step, which is to remember that the Holy Catholic Church, in both its public and private praying, recalls particularly those of our friends in light whose lives have indeed been a commentary on the Gospel, and does so at specific days and times?

If we are concerned lest the Christian calendar be cluttered up with much multiplication of saints – a legitimate concern, to be sure – perhaps we might also reflect that, just as the Lord's Prayer is a pattern prayer, containing within it all that needs to be said in Christian prayer, so there is an ancient prayer of the Christian Church which perhaps says all that needs to be said about the way in which we may ask for the prayers of the saints. It also has the advantage of being addressed to God through one about whose historical existence we need have no doubt, unless we disbelieve Holy Scripture. It is about the one who, in assenting to God's call, in being willing to allow the sword of sorrow to pierce her heart, in standing at the foot of the cross, and in being found with the company of believers after the resurrection, has rightly been seen by Christians of all ages as the representative friend in light. It runs:

> Hail Mary, full of grace, the Lord is with you. Blessed are you among women, and blessed is the fruit of your womb, Jesus. Holy Mary, Mother of God, pray for us sinners now and at the hour of our death.[19]

'Presbyteral Ministry in the Catholic Tradition or Why shouldn't women be priests?'

Rowan Williams wrote of Frances Young's 1994 MSF Annual Lecture, 'a study that manages to be both judicious and imaginative, and goes straight to the heart of our problems about ordained ministry. It is a substantial and valuable contribution and should be of enormous ecumenical importance.'[20]

From her rich Biblical and patristic scholarship Frances Young demonstrated that neither the Protestant nor the Catholic reading of the historical evidence was likely to be adequate. The presbyterate did not arise where and how it is generally assumed. It had a quite different origin from 'the bishop' and 'the deacon.' In the New Testament the priesthood of believers was always corporate and never assigned to any individual other than Christ. An *episcopos* was the steward or manager of a complex household – perhaps three generations – and all serving within it. The *episcopos* represented God the Father. The *diakonoi* were servants within the household and 'deacons' and 'deaconesses' represented Christ and the Holy Spirit. The 'presbyterate' was a corporate parish council in origin and at the beginning it was their corporality and not their individual office that was of significance. Eventually the presbyters took on the bishop's role in his absence. It was Cyprian who equated presidency at the Eucharist with that of the one who 'imaged' the priesthood of Christ – hence the bishop was the *sacerdos*. Types however are like ikons – symbols that bear the presence. The paper presented the weaknesses in the two principal arguments normally advanced against the priestly presbyterate being open to women:

> In the first place, the very notion that precedent is needed sits oddly with the Catholic tradition. It was the Protestant Reformation which argued a return to origins. Catholics have accepted later developments in the tradition, even up to certain notorious doctrinal innovations of the Nineteenth Century. That Cyprian could develop clerical institutions,

along with their theological justification, in response to a pastoral crisis is surely a precedent for taking seriously the pastoral imperative of an entirely unprecedented change in social values and expectations. Of course there are always problems about discerning the movement of the Spirit, but in principle, in the Catholic tradition, a possible such movement is not to be outlawed on the grounds of lack of precedent. Even Protestants must admit that the Spirit blows where it listeth, since it says so in scripture.

In the second place, the claim that no woman can be a 'type' of Christ is an extraordinary misunderstanding of the dynamics of typology. To return to Cyprian, it is clear that anything in creation is potentially a 'type' of Christ, and especially every baptised Christian. Baptism produces 'christs' by anointing with the Holy Spirit. The one who 'puts on' Christ in baptism is a living 'type' of that new creation in Christ, humanity re-fashioned in God's image. The signing with the cross in baptism marks the Christian as one who 'images' Christ in patience, obedience and humility. Thus baptism initiates the life of a 'type' of Christ.

This is most dramatically fulfilled in the sacrifice of the martyr ... there is, then, nothing to stop a woman being a 'type' of Christ in the Catholic tradition. Gender is irrelevant; it is not the point of comparison. As already noted, to literalise the typology of Christ's priesthood in terms of role-play is to miss the dynamics of typology. To declare that a man must play the role of Christ is to compound the misunderstanding.[21]

'John and Charles Wesley's Hymns on the Lord's Supper'

At the Bristol Methodist Conference of 1995, to celebrate the 250th anniversary of the Wesleys' first edition of *Hymns on the Lord's Supper*, Donald Rogers provided an introduction to a new MSF publication, *A Selection of John and Charles Wesley's Hymns on the Lord's Supper.* The book contained sixty-six of the eucharistic hymns in whole or in part. They formed the cream of the original collection and were helpfully provided with the metre of the hymn and a suggested tune, in all but one instance to be found in *Hymns and Psalms.*

'The Far Side of the Cross: The Spirituality of R S Thomas'

There was a high demand for this lecture and more copies had to be printed. Unique among MSF Annual Lectures Leslie Griffiths' paper was dedicated to the writing and spirituality of one person – indeed one Welsh literary spirit reflecting upon another! Leslie Griffiths wrote:

> This octogenarian Anglican priest has been battering the world with his rugged and relentless verse since the mid-1940s. I used to meet him from time to time when I lectured at St David's College, Lampeter in the 1960s. He and Geoffrey Beaumont were occasional visitors to the high table and no greater contrast can be imagined. Beaumont, whose hymn tunes we used to think modern, was the life and soul of the party, always ready to jolly up an evening with his anecdotes and piano-playing. Thomas, on the other hand, then serving the Cardiganshire parish of Eglwysfach, was already the 'bad-tempered old bugger' described in a *Church Times* article several years later.[22]

Leslie Griffiths believed there was no other poet alive who had wrestled so consistently with the devotional life nor thrown himself in quite the same way on his God. The intimations of immortality and the glimpses of glory were all enfolded within the profundity of all-engulfing silence.

> Thomas somehow keeps alive the possibility presence-in-absence. This counterpoint is exquisitely conveyed in his *Via Negativa.*
>
> Why no! I never thought other than
> That God is that great absence
> In our lives, the empty silence
> Within, the place where we go
> Seeking, not in hope to
> Arrive or find. He keeps the interstices

In our knowledge, the darkness
Between stars. His are the echoes
We follow, the footprints he has just
Left. We put our hands in
His side hoping to find
It warm. We look at people
And places as though he had looked
At them, too; but miss the reflection.

Here all our themes come together – the darkness and the silence, the absence and the waiting for signs of God's love. Our exploration of the regions at the far side of the Cross, at the back of the mirror, have shown us, I trust, how deep is the mystery of God, how easy it is to trivialise him with our piety. The immensity of that darkness, the profundity of the silence, the desolation of the absence, the awesomeness of the stillness – all conspire to make us feel just how little we are, how pathetic our attempts in liturgy, prayer, or devotion to get anywhere near the Great Mystery who is God.[23]

'The Fragrance of the Spirit: Towards the Sacramental Use of Oil in Methodism'

John Wesley argued that the anointing of the sick with oil, clearly attested in scripture, had died out in the life of the churches through unbelief! In his paper given at the 1996 Annual Conference of the Fellowship David Chapman took the view that the time had come for Methodism to strike a middle way between the high-church ritualist view of anointing and the negative attitudes of classical Zwinglian disdain. As in so many other aspects Methodism had much to gain from re-visiting Cyril of Jerusalem and, in this instance, his insistence that only through the invocation of the Spirit could the material gifts of bread, wine and oil confer sanctifying grace received by faith.

All in all, the sacramental use of oil ranks among the means of grace by which the Church cares for the faithful so as to bring them safe home to God. Just so, anointing is a powerful sign of salvation and the triumph of the gospel over the forces of evil, among which death ranks as the last enemy. In the light of Jesus the Christ we discern new significance in the familiar words of the psalmist:

> Thou preparest a table before me
> in the presence of my enemies;
> thou anointest my head with oil,
> my cup overflows.
> Surely goodness and mercy shall follow me
> all the days of my life;
> and I shall dwell in the house of the Lord
> for ever.[24]

By happy coincidence the Methodist Faith and Order Committee had recently prepared *An Order of Service for Healing and Wholeness*, which allowed for the blessing of oil to be used in an act of anointing. Uniquely the MSF act of worship in Hinde Street Chapel, during the London Methodist Conference of 1997, was a Eucharist which included the act of anointing. The sermon by David Chapman was a synopsis of the paper he had given the previous year at the MSF Low Sunday Weekend Conference.

'With Clouds Descending'

In 1998 the MSF published the present author's book, *With Clouds Descending: The Recovery of the Christian Year in the Methodist Tradition with all-age and other resources celebrating the Church's Festivals and Seasons.* Its primary purpose was to introduce Methodists to the gift of liturgical time, with an invitation to move beyond praying, singing and listening to drama, movement and action, in which anamnesis brought together past, present and future through calendar and festival as much as through baptism and eucharist. Within its fifty pages a ten page introduction was followed by short liturgies for A Ceremony of Candles for Advent, The Chrismon Tree, The Jesse Tree, A Christingle Service, The Blessing of the Crib, The Blessing of the Gifts of the Magi, The

Blessing and Procession for Candlemas, The Lenten Cross, The Blessing and Distribution of Palms, The Seven Candles of Failure, A Service for Good Friday, A Blessing of the Paschal Candle and Easter Garden, A Festival of White Flowers for All Saints Tide and The Advent Antiphons.

'At Your Service Again!'

In 1976, as an introduction to the *Methodist Service Book* of 1975, the Epworth Press published a commentary by Neil Dixon entitled *At Your Service*. As an introduction to the new *Methodist Worship Book* of 1999 the MSF invited Neil Dixon to undertake a similar task to the one he had done in relation to the previous worship book some twenty or so years before.

The dominant changes between 1975 and 1999 were a much richer provision of communion orders, much more material for services surrounding death, substantial provision for Lent and Holy Week, significant imagery celebrating the inclusivity of God as 'fundamentally loving, fundamentally gracious and fundamentally self-emptying,' the use of inclusive language for people, a greater use of poetic imagery, the return of angels, archangels and all the hosts of heaven and a conscious celebration and commemoration of the departed.

> Finally, *The Methodist Worship Book* has a much stronger sense of the power of signs and symbols. This is a theological point, because an incarnational and sacramental religion depends upon the belief that God uses material things to convey grace. The 1975 book had bread and wine at the eucharist, water and an optional candle – though only for infants – at baptism, rings at a wedding (though it was the giving of rings, rather than the rings, which God was asked to bless). In 1999, we still have all these, except that candles may be given to the baptized, whatever their age, and we do not shrink from asking God to bless the rings themselves. We also have the opportunity for *ashing* at the start of Lent, for *foot-washing* on Maundy Thursday, not to mention the *stripping of the communion table* later that day, for the *lighting*

> *of an Easter Candle* at the Easter Vigil and subsequently at Baptisms, *for the laying on of hands and/or anointing with oil* at a Service for Healing and Wholeness, and for the *dedication of domestic buildings* as well as of church buildings and their furnishings. I suggest that it is an important theological truth which many Methodists have still to embrace that worship is not words alone.[25]

'A Sense of Déjà Vu?'

George Guiver, of the Community of the Resurrection, was the first non-Methodist and the first Anglican to give an MSF Annual Lecture. His subject was eighteenth century liturgical reforms on the continent and some food for thought about ourselves. He gave examples of Roman Catholic continental liturgical reform in Germany, France and Italy – all carried out in the teeth of fierce opposition from Rome – a century and a half before Vatican II!

> The main principles of the French Catholic reformers were preference for scriptural texts for antiphons and responsories, a concern for language and its style, the purging of hagiographies, the spreading the Psalter through the week, the importance of Sunday, participation with understanding, liturgical catechesis of the laity, the moderating of devotion to saints and to the Blessed Sacrament and recovery of the old local usages of dioceses.[26]

The principal attempts at Catholic liturgical reform in Germany were:

> Vernacular hymn-singing, only one parish church service each week with no vestments, no altar candles, no Latin or Gregorian chant, an abandonment of the complications of the liturgical year, an evening devotion should replace Latin vespers on Sunday, consisting of church hymns and bible reading, community worship should be communal and participatory.[27]

As in France so in Germany, from the 1830s onwards the Enlightenment reforms ended up being expunged and vilified.

The principal attempts at Catholic liturgical reform in Italy included:

> The liturgy as a common action of priest and people, the priest is to say mass audibly, the liturgy should have a more simple form, it should be in the language of the people, people should be encouraged to communicate each time they attend mass, communion should be from elements consecrated at the same mass, only one altar in the church, encouragement to receive communion at every mass, and at the proper place, Bible-reading encouraged, people encouraged to attend the offices, catechumens and children born in the period from Maundy Thursday to Holy Saturday are to be kept for the solemn baptism of the Easter ceremonies or at Pentecost.[28]

These late eighteenth and early nineteenth century attempts quickly collapsed, but have never been forgotten.

'The Eucharistic Community: The Community of Saints'

The Methodist Conference Public Meeting at Ipswich in 2001 took the form of a eucharist at which Dr Kenneth Wilson preached the sermon. He reminded his hearers that it is by God's grace alone that we are brought together into the eucharistic presence. There we are not alone. We stand with others, with our mothers and fathers in the faith. Our eucharistic thankfulness includes them all and we hold out our arms to embrace them. However little we understand of what we owe to them they stand with us, urging us on with cries and tears.

> Our unity of aspiration, faith and love is renewed in our sharing in the Body and Blood of Jesus Christ, by the God who is the One and Only Spirit, whose lively presence witnesses with our spirits that we are one in Christ, the One, Holy, Catholic and Apostolic Church. Christ makes this possible because He is the One and Only Celebrant at our feast, the One and Only Sacrifice, the One and Only Gift. And in Him we stand. The Communion of Saints is the Body of all God's People, in whose faithful remembering, praising and

thanking there is the real possibility of offering to God, in God's timeless presence, the sacrifice of praise and thanksgiving which, in our thrilling freedom, we are constrained to want to offer.[29]

'Whatever Happened to the Father? The Jesus Heresy in Modern Worship'

The 2002 MSF Lecture at the Wolverhampton Conference was by far our best-selling lecture and many extra copies had to be printed. Susan White, who gave the lecture, reminded her audience that heresy is about choice. The New Testament was not clear about putting Jesus at the centre of worship. Jesus himself was centred on the Father. Early Christian prayers addressed to Jesus were usually devotional rather than liturgical. Liturgical prayer addressed to Christ was originally petitionary or penitential. It was in this mode that Charles Wesley himself was most at home, addressing Jesus his 'strength and hope.' In the modern scene attention to the Triune God was decreasing as liturgical attention to Jesus was increasing. In many places Jesus of Nazareth had become the sole focus of worship. The Christocentric piety of the Wesleys had its centre of gravity in the grace of the Christ who was incarnate, crucified, risen and ascended – the work of the Father.

Many evangelicals had entered into 'Jesus-olatry' –

> When the music fades,
> all is stripped away ...
> I'm coming back to the heart of worship
> and it's all about You, all about You, Jesus.[30]

'This is our God, the Servant King' is simply wrong, theologically. Our God is not the 'Servant King:' our God is the Triune God, Father, Son and Holy Spirit. And liking the tune, or the sound of the words, or the way the hymn makes us feel does not make up for the fact that the powers-that-be are encouraging a congregation to express in song an unorthodox Christology ... Will people look back on the late 20th, early

21st century and see it as a time when an essential split within Christianity occurred? Are these two theological and liturgical streams, the one which has Jesus at the centre of its faith and worship, and the other which has the one God, Father, Son and Holy Spirit at the centre of its faith and worship, are these two streams irrevocably dividing from one another as we speak? Is there a day coming when we will not recognize one another as members of the same Christian family, because of the choices we are making about the object of our worship?[31]

'"Jesus the Soul of Musick Is": Music and the Methodists'

John Swarbrick, the longest serving Music Director of the MSF, delighted those attending the 2003 Conference Public Lecture in Llandudno with a musically accompanied account of some of the popular melodies and tunes at the heart of the Lutheran, Reformed and Methodist traditions.

The singing of metrical psalms moved on apace from the 1560s. Psalm tunes were employed for some of the hymns of Watts and Wesley. Outside Britain a different strand of hymn-singing had developed with Lutherans and Moravians – chorale tunes having a life of their own. Older mediaeval and folk tunes were often wedded first to Latin hymns and then to their translations. Eventually the people's music was placed on an equal footing with that of professional musicians. The driving principle was Luther's *musica praedicat evangelium* – music preaches the gospel. The music and hymnody promoted by Johann Crüger, Paul Gerhardt and Count Zinzendorf stimulated the Wesleys' drive to supplant the likes of Sternhold and Hopkins (the popular name for *The Whole Book of Psalmes*, the English equivalent of the *Genevan Psalter*, published in 1562) and publish their own tune books as well as hymn collections. Among his illustrative material John Swarbrick traced the evolution and use of the tune *Vater Unser*.

VATER UNSER, a German chorale, was one of John Wesley's favourites. It first appeared in Luther's *Geistliche Lieder* of

1539 (one of the early Lutheran tune books) set to Luther's metrical version of the Lord's Prayer, hence its short title, VATER UNSER. Later, Bach was to use it on three occasions: once in the *Saint John Passion,* with a direct reference to its origins with a petition from the Lord's Prayer; again in Cantata BWV 102; and finally and most extraordinarily in Cantata BWV 90. (For good measure, Mendelssohn uses the tune as the basis for his sixth organ sonata.)

The melody passed into the Anglo-Genevan Psalter of 1561, then into the English Psalter of the same year set to William Kethe's metrical version of Psalm 112, and so it received its English name of OLD 112TH. Wesley included it in the first tune book which he edited, *A Collection of Tunes, Set to Music, As They are commonly sung at the Foundery* of 1742, or the *Foundery Collection* for short. VATER UNSER has not survived into *Hymns and Psalms.* In the 1933 *Methodist Hymn Book* it was set to John Wesley's translation of Gerhard Teerstegen's 'Lo, God is here, let us adore' and to one of Charles Wesley's hymns on the Lord's Supper, 'O God of our forefathers, hear.'[32, 33]

'The Forgotten Trinity in Contemporary Methodism'

In many ways the present author's MSF Annual Lecture of 2004 was a sequel to Susan White's *Whatever Happened to God the Father? The Jesus Heresy in Modern Worship.* Though John Wesley wrote and preached comparatively little on the doctrine and mystery of the Trinity he everywhere assumed it and declared, 'knowledge of the Three-One God is interwoven with all true Christian faith; with all vital religion.'[34] Richard Watson, who taught the generation of Methodists that followed Wesley, devoted four chapters and nearly a hundred pages of his *Theological Institutes* to the doctrine of the Trinity, declaring that all heresies could be traced back to inadequate attempts to understand and celebrate the mystery.[35] W B Pope, who succeeded Watson as the leading Methodist theologian, declared the doctrine of the ever-blessed Trinity to be essential to Christianity and that there was no theology or Christology without it.[36] Geoffrey Wainwright, Methodism's leading contemporary systematic theologian, insisted that there were no sound doctrines of the atonement that were not profoundly dependent on an adequate understanding of the nature of the Trinity.[37]

The present author argued that it was with a certain strain of *imported liturgy* and *imported hymnody* that Methodism faced the whole-scale watering down of classic Trinitarian praise and prayer. Among others he cited the *Iona Abbey Worship Book* of 2001.

> The book contains 250 pages. Apart from the *Lord's Prayer* and the *Apostles' Creed*, for which alternatives are provided, there is not a single reference, by name, to God the Father. The references by name to God the Son are sparse. Because the book is heavily influenced by so-called Celtic spirituality the liturgies are strongly Trinitarian in atmosphere, yet almost every Trinitarian reference is either to *God, Christ and the Spirit*, or to *God, Jesus and the Spirit*, or to the *Creator [or Maker], Christ and the Spirit.* What is completely lacking from all 250 pages is any use of a Trinitarian formula that implies there is any relationship between the persons of the Godhead. Throughout the book there is not a single reference to the eternal relationship between God the Father and God the Son. This tendency, on the grounds of a genderless Trinity, brings the users of Iona liturgies well inside the bounds of incipient Unitarianism ... On July 13th 1771, Wesley referred to this very custom in a letter to Jane Catherine March, in which he observed, 'The quaint device of styling (the Trinity as) three offices rather than persons, gives up the whole doctrine.'[38] [39]

'Resisting the Tyranny of Genesis Three'

The longer title of Kenneth Cracknell's 2005 Annual Lecture was *Resisting the Tyranny of Genesis Three: Frederick Denison Maurice, John and Charles Wesley and a Eucharist of Creation.*

F D Maurice believed that the Evangelical movement rekindled in the English nation a faith that would have otherwise died. Nevertheless, he thought that the movement had made *sinful man* and not the *God of all grace* the foundation of Christian theology. Though this may have been true of much nineteenth century Methodism and evangelicalism, Kenneth Cracknell advanced the theory that the insistence of John and Charles Wesley on the goodness of a creation pervaded throughout by grace had significant and different consequences. Both Catholic and Protestant classic theologies had made much of The Fall in Genesis Three. Together and separately they had built their doctrines of redeeming grace on the need to reverse the depravity brought about by the primordial 'Fall' and its consequences. In this crucial matter the Wesleys stood against both Calvin's *Institutes* and the *Westminster Confession*, most memorably in the original seventeen-verse hymn, 'Father of everlasting grace.' For both the Wesleys, the light of the Logos shone on *every fallen soul*. The redeeming goodness of God was present and at work both in the renewal of the entire fallen race and of the whole of the fallen creation:

> Spirit Immense, Eternal Mind,
> Thou on the souls of lost Mankind
> Dost with benignest Influence move,
> Pleased to restore the ruined Race,
> And new create a world of Grace
> In all the image of Thy Love.[40]

To the witness of Maurice and of the Wesleys Kenneth Cracknell added the creation theology at the heart of the best of contemporary liturgy, particularly in what he called 'the remarkably varied versions of the Eucharistic Prayer used currently in the *Methodist Worship Book* (1999).'

> Advent
> God of all glory and light of our salvation,
> we offer you thanks and praise
> through Jesus Christ your Son our Lord.
> By your living Word you called all things into being,
> breathed into life the desire of your heart
> and shaped us in your own likeness.

Lent and Passiontide

Blessing and praise belong to you,
gracious and eternal God.
Through your living Word you created all things,
the majesty of the heavens and the glory of the earth.
In your wisdom and goodness
you have made all people in your image and likeness.
Therefore with saints and angels and with all creation
we lift up our voices to proclaim the glory of your name:

Easter Season

Blessing and honour, glory and power,
are rightly yours, all-gracious God.
By your creative word you brought the world to birth;
in your generous love you made the human family,
that we might see your glory
and live for ever in your presence.[41]

'Imitating Christ: Wesley's "Christian Pattern" and Spirituality for Today'

Robert Jeffrey, the former Dean of Worcester and Sub-Dean of Christ Church, Oxford, had been a colleague and friend of Gordon Wakefield's for forty years, from their days together in the Newcastle Theological Society in the late 1950s. It was therefore natural and appropriate that Canon Jeffrey dedicated the MSF Annual Lecture of 2006 to his late friend and colleague. Robert Jeffrey had undertaken considerable research into the *Devotio Moderna*, the fifteenth century movement of the Sisters and Brothers of the Common Life, most prominent among them being Thomas à Kempis. At the invitation of Penguin Classics, Robert Jeffrey was working on a new and contemporary translation of *The Imitation of Christ.*[42]

In the course of his background research the lecturer had spent a considerable amount of time looking into the part *The Imitation* had played in the spiritual development and practice of both Dietrich Bonhoeffer and John Wesley. Bonhoeffer,

Wesley and the Sisters and Brothers of the Common Life were open to a renewal of spirituality which existed only in community, but often outside the church.

> Thus, as predicted by Bonhoeffer, the church has become a society for its own self-preservation. (Or, as Hollenweger put it, 'There abideth faith, hope and charity, and the greatest of these is the status quo.') So evangelism becomes an attempt to keep the institution going, rather than an engagement with God in the world. Tacey points out that the religious conservatives argue that they are conserving tradition; but by refusing to make way for the new, they are destroying the tradition they profess to love. Real tradition has to be open to the inwardness and spiritual meaning found outside the Church. He sums it up by quoting Pablo Picasso who said, 'Tradition is having a baby, not wearing your grandfather's hat.'
>
> In a strange way this is not far from the call of Wesley for scriptural holiness, expressed in a secular culture. One community, expressing something of the pattern of the *Devotio Moderna*, is the Iona Community. A paper of theirs on spiritual formation, published in 1989, lists the following marks of a meaningful spirituality:
>
> 1 It has to be reconciling and integrative with the world around.
> 2 It has to be incarnational, being sensitive to culture, language, symbolism and history.
> 3 It has to be rooted in scripture and nourished by prayer.
> 4 It has to be a costly and self-giving spirituality.
> 5 It has to be life-giving and liberating.
> 6 It has to be centred in community and rooted in the Eucharist.
> 7 It has to be expressed in service and witness.
> 8 It has to be open to God's new initiatives.
> 9 It has to be seeking God's love in today's world.
> 10 It has to be open to the wider world and all sorts of diverse patterns of spirituality.

> Here is a summary of a *Devotio Moderna* for today. Of necessity, such spirituality produces communities of protest against what is dehumanising in modem society. How is this to come about? It will not come from an institutional base, but from groups of people seeking these ends; not by rejecting the institutional church, but not taking it too seriously either.[43]

'Theology in Ashes'

John Lampard spent over fifteen years representing the Methodist Church on the Churches' Funerals Group and has been a member of the government's Burials and Cremations Advisory Group. He played a key part in the formation of the *Methodist Worship Book* and in its new series of Funeral Services, of which he later came to be critical. Out of his rich experience he reached the point where he felt it was time to challenge the theology, liturgy and ritual surrounding crematoria and the churches' involvement with them. The very question, 'Will it be a burial or a cremation?' he believed was neither an appropriate nor an accurate one. The false choice had arisen from the very beginnings of modern cremation, when the church had failed to think theologically about what it was doing. The church had failed to accept that the disposal of the ashes of a dead person was as important as the disposal of the body. In both cases there were sacred remains. It was supremely odd that there were strict legal rules about the burial or cremation of a body but none about what happens to a person's ashes. Theologically and liturgically the remains of a Christian – their ashes or their body – need to be 'buried with Christ.' This was contrary to the general view of the churches that the funeral ends with the body being committed to the cremator, and that the Christian disposal of the ashes was of no liturgical or theological significance.

The Orthodox Church had taken the view that burial of the ashes in the ground was the equivalent of burial, and a number of Anglican liturgies made it clear in the funeral rite that the body was 'given' to the flames and not 'committed' at the crematorium, 'in preparation for burial' which would be 'the committal.' The service at the crematorium, whether a 'complete' service or just 'a committal,' was not really the equivalent of a funeral rite in church and should never have been regarded as such. Towards the end of a seriously argued and well-presented thesis John Lampard says:

> I would like to see the Methodist Church moving towards following the practice of the Church in Wales, which insists that cremated remains must be buried. The clergy of the Church in Wales are forbidden either to permit the scattering of ashes, or to do it themselves. The theological conviction which underlies that discipline is the traditional understanding that the body has an integrity about it which is not diminished either in death or by cremation. In this we can hear an echo of the doctrine of the resurrection of the body, which is symbolised by the return to the dust of the earth from which we came, and which should be the destiny of all human remains.[44]

'Immense, Unfathomed, Unconfined: Gospel Grace in the Methodist Mode'

The present author suspected that the deeply inclusive journey and theology of Inderjit Bhogal was sufficiently embedded in Methodism that a fruitful lecture could be built around three of Charles Wesley's inclusive polysyllables, 'undistinguishing,' 'incomprehensibly' and 'inextinguishable.' Inderjit Bhogal immediately saw the possibilities of a paper built on the characteristics of the Trinity as Charles Wesley had himself perceived them: God the Father who had *undistinguishing* regard for all, God the Son, who was *incomprehensibly* made man for all and God the Holy Spirit, burning with *inextinguishable* blaze in the hearts of all. For Inderjit Bhogal, who is both Sikh and Christian, God is without boundaries – 'immense, unfathomed, unconfined.' All, regardless of gender, skin colour, ability, disability, sexual orientation or age, are created in the one image of the one God. The incarnate, ecclesial and eucharistic Body of Christ is one fully integrated mystery signifying and incorporating both equality and diversity. That diversity includes the poor among whom some of the best theology has been born. Prevenient grace is a jewel entrusted to Methodism for the acceptance of all and the healing of all.

As he explored the question of 'uniqueness' Inderjit Bhogal gave his long-considered reflection on the controversial verse in John 14.6:

> I come to [Jesus' saying: No one comes to the Father except through me] from a particular perspective:
> I believe God is one and 'enlightens everyone.'
> I believe people all around the globe have, for centuries, been responding to the one God's light and self-revelation, and that great histories of response have developed into what we call Religions or Faiths – shaped by different languages, foods, climates, colours, dreams, visions, great messengers of God. Consequently all religions are different.
> I believe that the existence of people of many faiths is within God's purposes. I rejoice in this diversity and thank God for it.
> I believe that each tradition of faith enjoys special, distinctive and unique gifts, riches and insights. Christians have the life-giving, life-transforming story of Jesus as a special gift to share and live by, without arrogance. It is a story by which we can interpret and give meaning to all life.[45]

'The Extempore Sacrament: Finding words in and for the present'

Despite opinions to the contrary the tension between structure and form and freedom and spontaneity as an experience of God's presence has always existed, and Helen Dixon Cameron's exploration of the extempore prayer tradition in Methodism was an examination of but one example of it. The MSF Annual Lecture of 2009 invited reflection on why, in contemporary Methodism, the extempore tradition of prayer and preaching was on the wane. Why were so many student ministers lacking confidence in and experience of the extempore tradition? Could and should the extempore tradition be taught? Isaac Watts taught that extempore or 'conceived prayer' demanded preparation and learning. It was possible that the profusion of liturgies militated against new ministers and preachers having a store of words, phrases and concepts on which to draw as they pray extempore. This recalled the third-century injunction of Hippolytus, 'Let each [bishop/presbyter] pray according to his own ability.' Ruth Duck reminded her readers that the ultimate preparation for extempore prayer is a daily life of prayer and commitment![46] In his *Sunday Service* Wesley inserted a rubric encouraging the Elder 'to put up an extempore prayer' at the close of the Communion Office between the Gloria and the Blessing. Wesley wrote to Freeborn Garrettson, 'I constantly add extempore prayer both to the Morning and Evening Service.'

Helen Cameron believed there was something profoundly sacramental about the gift and practice of extempore prayer – 'the concept of digging God out of our deep places in order that God's voice can be heard is very powerful.'[47]

> The experience of the Methodist Church has been that God has worked through tradition and spontaneity, yet we have seemingly lost some confidence in some of the forms of spontaneity, such that many student deacons and presbyters have low confidence in their ability to pray extemporaneously, or to give an account of their experience of God at work in their lives through testimony, or be clear about how they might draw on the extemporary tradition in prayer and preaching.
>
> I would suggest that there needs to be a renewed confidence in the Methodist narrative which forms and shapes our identity which offers us a vision of tradition renewed and informed by spontaneity which leads, not to an abandonment of that tradition, but to its reviving and renewing.[48]

'Whither Methodist Theology Now? The Collapse of the "Wesleyan Quadrilateral"'

In the year of its 75th Anniversary the MSF chose its youngest ever lecturer, a ministerial student, Daniel Pratt Morris-Chapman, to give a substantial paper on *Whither Methodist Theology Now? The Collapse of the 'Wesleyan Quadrilateral.'* The paper quickly established that it was the nineteenth century Bishop Francis Paget who invented the notion that the Elizabethan divine, Richard Hooker, 'gave equal loyalty' to scripture, reason and tradition. Albert Outler's taking of the Anglican 'triad' and adding experience to make 'the Wesleyan Quadrilateral' was a misreading of Wesley erected on the pedestal of Paget's mistake. The complete Wesley was influenced first by the scriptural and holiness traditions of Puritan spirituality, then by the Patristic tradition through the doctrines and devotions of the Caroline Divines and the Non-jurors, and then by the spirit of theological enquiry and experiment leading up to and away from Aldersgate.

In the second part of the paper Daniel Chapman asked whether the Wesleyan Quadrilateral, in itself, could properly be regarded as a fitting theological method for contemporary Methodism. Building on the writings of William Abraham and others the paper established that the interplay of scripture, tradition, reason and experience never worked! The best that could be achieved by this method was a conversation but never a conclusion. It begged the need for a magisterium, be it the papacy, an ecumenical council or the Methodist Conference! For Daniel Chapman the true vocation of contemporary Methodist thinking and resourcing lay in William Abraham's movement of Canonical Theism.

> Canonical theism is dispersed in the Scriptures, the Nicene Creed, the iconography, the liturgy; it is enacted in the life of the saints; it is summarized and worked through in the work of the Canonical teachers of the Church prior to the great schism; it is implicitly received in baptism; and it is handed over in ordination to the diaconate, priesthood, and episcopate from generation to generation. The intellectual core of

> Canonical theism is a rich vision of God, creation and redemption.[49]

Daniel Chapman feared for a Methodism that took a functionalist view of Christian faith and practice:

> The contemporary Church needs to make full use of the Canonical heritage. Unfortunately the popularity of 'fresh expressions' of Church, and other *ad hoc* approaches to ecclesiology, has distracted Methodism from embracing the fullness of the Church Catholic. While mission is a 'crucial dimension of the essence and life of the Church, it is not the only dimension.' The consequence of a purely functional ecclesiology is that it can disconnect theology from episcopal oversight.[50]

'Look, no Mitres!'

The sub-title of Samuel McBratney's 2011 Annual Lecture was *A Conversation on Bishops and Leadership in British Methodism.* He reminded those who heard or received his paper that most Methodists in the world and the vast majority of Methodists who settle in Britain from elsewhere have never know their own Methodism without bishops! Episcopacy might be about the historic succession in the end but such a succession didn't have to dominate the character and life of every episcopally led church in the interim.

Personal episcopacy has been a gift within American Methodism from the very beginning, as has succession in the episcopacy by ordination. When Lutherans, Anglicans and Methodists in the United States conferred over church order the issue was not over episcopacy but simply over the nature of episcopacy and episcopal succession. Anglicans and Methodists in Ireland had entered into a covenant which included the participation of episcopal ministers from both traditions in each others ordinations and a mutual recognition of orders.

British Methodism probably needed to take episcopacy into its system for two primary reasons. The first was that without it perhaps there could be no serious in depth and country-wide engagement with the Church of England. The second was whether a personal model of episcopal superintendency was a necessity for serious leadership in mission in the current ecclesial and social context.

> I remain undecided as to the next step for British Methodism with regard to bishops. Indeed, I am left with the strong impression that it is an issue that may have been overtaken by events, both within the Churches and beyond. The real struggle in British Methodism is one for a clear purpose and mission. Whether that requires a recognized and personalized episcopal leadership is a moot point![51]

'Belonging and Believing: The Dilemma of Methodist Identity'

Dr Paul Kybird worked for twenty years in the Anglican Church, including time in Nigeria and the Selly Oak Colleges, Birmingham before serving for over thirteen years with the Methodist Church as a Training and Development Officer. During that time he combined his skills in understanding how adult Christians learn with his discoveries about the relationships that exist between belonging to a worshipping community and the nature of personal belief and credal faith.

In his 2012 Annual Lecture to the Fellowship he demonstrated that every part of the church had the ability to abuse and misuse the Bible at every level of its life. Most of those who belonged to the Methodist community – anywhere – had few Methodist roots and were unfamiliar with the Methodist story. How did we belong if we had lost the story? How many in all our churches had few Christian roots or knew the Christian story – or the Bible's story? There was a huge gap between the teacher and the taught. Preachers and teachers in the Methodist tradition had to be recalled to this huge primary responsibility. Those on whose shoulders the responsibility rested for training and formation needed to rediscover the art of inspired communication.

If we believe that there are distinctive narratives, or even the resources for building them within Methodism, that have value in the movement of God in the world today, an urgent and demanding task is ahead of us. It is not just an historical task, because that only makes us more coherently irrelevant. Nor is it even just a doctrinal one, given the marginality of religious knowledge. It has to be an apologetic task that searches the deeper narratives of our post-modern condition (including the narrative of the TV programme *Rev*) and finds congruence. It has to be a work of learning, though it need not be entirely intellectual. For a community that has faith – some faith – in a God at work in the world, calling the church to discern in order to participate in that activity, this should not be impossible. It should be at the heart of our identity.[52]

Notes

Introduction

1 William J Abraham, *Crossing the Threshold of Divine Revelation*, Eerdmans, Grand Rapids, MI, 2006, pp. 6–9 and Daniel Pratt Morris-Chapman, *Whither Methodist Theology Now? The Collapse of the 'Wesleyan Quadrilateral,'* MSF Annual Lecture, Portsmouth, 2010, p. 20

Chapter 1: Wesleyan Legacy

1 *A Dictionary of Methodism in Britain and Ireland*, John A Vickers (ed.), Epworth Press, Peterborough, 2000, p. 24
2 *John Wesley's Sunday Service of the Methodists in North America*, with an Introduction by James F White, United Methodist Publishing House, Nashville TN, 1984, p. 17
3 Letter to James Harvey, 20 March 1739, John Telford, *The Letters of John Wesley*, Vol 1, Epworth Press, London, 1931 (1960), p. 284
4 Ted A Campbell, *John Wesley and Christian Antiquity: Religious Vision and Cultural Change*, Abingdon Press, Nashville TN, 1991, p. 2
5 Thomas A Langford (ed.), *Doctrine and Theology in the United Methodist Church*, Abingdon Press, Nashville TN, 1991, p. 86
6 W Stephen Gunter *et al.*, *Wesley and the Quadrilateral: Renewing the Conversation*, Abingdon Press, Nashville TN, 1997, p. 142
7 Frank Baker, *John Wesley and the Church of England*, Epworth, London, 1970, p. 159
8 *The Journal of the Rev John Wesley*, June 27, 1740, Nehemiah Curnock (ed.), Charles H Kelly, London, 1909

9 *The Works of John Wesley*, Vol 10, *The Methodist Societies: The Minutes of Conference*, Henry D Rack (ed.), Abingdon Press, Nashville TN, 2011, pp. 855–856
10 *Hymns on The Lord's Supper*, Bristol, 1745, No 64
11 Copy of a Letter from Charles Wesley to his brother: *Proceedings of the Wesley Historical Society*, Vol XXIII, p. 11
12 *The Works of John Wesley*, Vol 10, *The Methodist Societies: The Minutes of Conference*, Henry D Rack (ed.), Abingdon Press, Nashville TN, 2011, p. 646
13 Gordon Rupp, *Thomas Jackson: Methodist Patriarch*, Epworth Press, London, 1954
14 Thomas Jackson, *Wesleyan Methodism a Revival of Apostolic Christianity*, T Mason and G Lane, New York, 1839, p. 35
15 Benjamin Gregory, *The Holy Catholic Church, The Communion of Saints*, Wesleyan Conference Office, London, 1873, p. 159
16 *Ibid.*, p. 209
17 Thomas Jackson, op cit, p. 210
18 Benjamin Gregory, op cit, p. 239
19 W B Pope, *A Compendium of Christian Theology*, Wesleyan Methodist Book Room, London, 1880, pp. 358–359
20 H B Workman, *The Place of Methodism in the Catholic Church*, Epworth Press, London, 1921, pp. 97f
21 Martin Wellings, *From The Soul of Dominic Wildthorne to the Wesleyan Guild of Divine Service: some Methodist Responses to Anglo-Catholicism in Victorian and Edwardian England*, Anglo-Catholic History Society Lecture 2011, p. 22
22 Daniel Hone, *Corrupted Methodist Worship*, Ipswich, n.d.
23 Sir Henry Lunn, *Chapters From My Life: With Special Reference to Reunion*, Cassell & Co, London, 1918
24 *A Dictionary of Methodism in Britain and Ireland*, John A Vickers (ed.), Epworth Press, Peterborough, 2000, p. 214

25 Gordon S Wakefield, *Methodist Devotion: The Spiritual Life in the Methodist Tradition 1791–1945*, Epworth Press, London, 1966, p. 102

26 Sir Henry S Lunn, *The Secret of the Saints*, Heffer, Cambridge, 1933, p. x

27 *The Unveiled Heart: Private Prayers of the Late Rev Walter James*, E Theodore Carrier (ed.), Robert Culley, London, 1909

28 David W James, *Brothers in the Ministry: The Story of Walter and Francis Bertram James*, World Methodist Historical Society (British Section), 1982

29 *A Dictionary of Methodism in Britain and Ireland*, John A Vickers (ed.), Epworth Press, Peterborough, 2000, p. 58

30 Samuel Chadwick, *The Way to Pentecost and The Path of Prayer*, Hodder & Stoughton, London, 1948, p. 179

31 Thomas H Barratt, 'The Place of the Lord's Supper in Early Methodism' in *Methodism: Its Present Responsibilities*, Epworth, London, 1929, pp. 72–73

32 Paul Chilcote, 'The Legacy of J Ernest Rattenbury' in *Doxology: Journal of the Order of St Luke*, Vol 3, Rutland VT, 1986, p. 11

33 Robert Currie, *Methodism Divided: A Study in the Sociology of Ecumenicalsim* (sic), Faber and Faber, London, 1968

34 J Ernest Rattenbury, *The Sacrament of the Lord's Supper*, Epworth Press, London, c 1920, p. 5

35 *Ibid.*, pp. 11–12

36 Ole E Borgen, *John Wesley on the Sacraments: A Theological Study*, Publishing House of the United Methodist Church, Zurich, 1972, p. 17

Chapter 2: Gregorian Voices

1 Letter from R C Simmonds to Miss Wainwright, MSF Archives, File 1934

2 Gordon S Wakefield, *T S Gregory*, WMHS Publications, Emsworth, 2000, p. 32

3 *Ibid.*, p. 8

4 *MSF Bulletin*, No 96, All Saints 1975, pp. 5–6
5 T S Gregory, *The Unfinished Universe*, Faber and Faber, London, 1935
6 *Methodist Recorder*, 28th August 1975
7 T S Gregory, 'Preaching is Praying,' *The Preacher's Quarterly*, Volume 9, March 1963, p. 70
8 T S Gregory, *A Week of Prayers*, Methodist School of Fellowship, Privately Printed, 1965
9 T S Gregory, *According to your Faith*, Epworth Press, London, 1966, pp. 74–75
10 Gordon S Wakefield, *T S Gregory*, WMHS Publications, Emsworth, 2000, p. 40
11 *Ibid.*, 2000, pp. 46–47
12 *Methodist Recorder*, 28th August 1975
13 *Ibid.*
14 T S Gregory, 'Newman and Liberalism' in *A Tribute to Newman: Essays on aspects of his Life and Thought*, Michael Tierney (ed.), Browne and Nolan, Dublin, 1945, pp. 112–113
15 Cyclostyled *Report* issued from 33 Rutland Road, Bedford by A Kingsley Lloyd, dated December 1932, MSF Archives, File 1932
16 A S Gregory, *Retreat at Sidcup September 1932 – Suggested Basis of Discussion and Questions*, carbon copy of typed notes drawn up for Sidcup Retreat and initialled by the author, MSF Archives, File 1932
17 Cyclostyled *Report* issued from 33 Rutland Road, Bedford by A Kingsley Lloyd dated December 1932, MSF Archives, File 1932
18 There are hand-written notes on A S Gregory's copies of the *Proposed Basis*, indicating that it was drawn up before the Uniting Methodist Conference had adjourned and that it was written by T S Gregory. MSF Archives, File 1932
19 MSF Archives, File 1932
20 *Ibid.*

21 Manuscript 'Notes' of Retreat at Epsom, 1st May 1933, MSF Archives, File 1933
22 MSF Archives, File 1934
23 Summary of Discussion at Ministers' Retreat held at Oxford Hall, Manchester on 11th June 1934, MSF Archives, File 1934
24 MSF Archives, File 1934
25 *MSF Bulletin*, No 59, Lent 1960, p. 7
26 MSF Archives, File 1934
27 *Ibid.*
28 *Ibid.*
29 MSF Archives, File 1935
30 *Ibid.*
31 Proposed Methodist Sacramental Fellowship, February 1935, MSF Archives, File 1935
32 Proposed Methodist Sacramental Fellowship, March 1935, MSF Archives, File 1935
33 Methodist Sacramental Fellowship meeting of Manchester and Liverpool sympathisers, June 1935, MSF Archives, File 1935
34 Letter to A S Gregory, 6th May 1935, MSF Archives, File 1935
35 *Minutes of Methodist Conference 1938*, Obituaries, p. 192
36 *The Discipline and Culture of the Spiritual Life: A Memorial Volume* compiled from the writings of A E Whitham, Hodder & Stoughton, London, 1938, p. 9
37 *Ibid.*, pp. 106–108
38 *Methodist Devotion: The Spiritual Life in the Methodist tradition 1791–1945*, Gordon S Wakefield, Epworth Press, London, 1966, p. 104
39 *A Dictionary of Methodism in Britain and Ireland*, John A Vickers (ed.), Epworth Press, Peterborough, 2000, p. 393
40 August Correspondence, MSF Archives, File 1935
41 Inaugural Conference Calling Paper, MSF Archives, File 1935
42 Rules, Pledge and Offices, MSF Archives, File 1935

43 Inaugural Conference Agenda, pp. 1–2, MSF Archives, File 1935
44 *Ibid.*
45 Inaugural Conference Agenda, pp. 1–2, (A S Gregory's Copy), MSF Archives, File 1935

Chapter 3: Organised Opposition

1 September Circular of 1935, MSF Archives, File 1935
2 *Methodist Sacramental Fellowship: An Appeal to Facts and First Principles*, The Protestant Truth Society, London, n.d.
3 *Methodist Recorder*, 18th June 1936
4 A Private Report from the MSF Treasurer, MSF Archives, File 1936
5 Copy of Letter to R C Simmonds, MSF Archives, File 1936
6 Letter to A S Gregory, MSF Archives, File 1936
7 *Ibid.*
8 *Churchman's Magazine*, June 1937, p. 163
9 Letter from Robert Bond to A E Whitham, MSF Archives, File 1937
10 Printed Circular from R C Simmonds, 15th June 1937, MSF Archives, File 1937
11 *Ibid.*
12 Agenda of the Methodist Conference 1937, pp. 3–5
13 *MSF Bulletin*, No 5, November 1937, p. 3

Chapter 4: Second Spring

1 Copy of Statement by Rev Dr Rattenbury to the Conference Committee of Enquiry, 2nd June 1938, MSF Archives, File 1938, p. 3
2 *Ibid.*, p. 5
3 Agenda of the Methodist Conference 1938, p. 493
4 *Ibid.*, p. 494
5 *Ibid.*, p. 495

6 *In Defence of the Methodist Sacramental Fellowship at the Conference of the Methodist Church at Hull, 1938 – The Speech of the Rev J E Rattenbury with Notes*, MSF Pamphlet No 7, 1938, passim
7 *Ibid.*, pp. 1–2
8 MSF Archives, File 1938
9 Minutes of a meeting at the Charing Cross Hotel, MSF Archives, File 1938
10 *MSF Bulletin*, No 113, Epiphany 1985, p. 10
11 *An Appeal to all Christian People*, Clause 9, Lambeth Conference 1920

Chapter 5: Eucharistic Faith

1 See Frank Baker, 'Approaching a Variorum Edition of *Hymns on the Lord's Supper*' in *Proceedings of the Charles Wesley Society*, Volume 2, 1995, pp. 7ff
2 Geoffrey Wainwright, 'Our Elder Brother Join: The Wesley's Hymns on the Lord's Supper and the Patristic Revival in England' in *Proceedings of the Charles Wesley Society*, Volume 1, 1994, pp. 13ff
3 *Ibid.*, pp. 13ff
4 W F Flemington, *The Holy Communion – in Prayer and Worship*, Cambridge University Sermons 1945, Hodder and Stoughton, London, p. 78
5 *Hymns on the Lord's Supper*, No 125
6 *Hymns on the Lord's Supper*, No 59
7 *Hymns on the Lord's Supper*, No 116
8 *Hymns on the Lord's Supper*, No 72
9 *The Holy Communion: A Symposium*, Hugh Martin (ed.), SCM Press, London, 1947, p. 125
10 J Ernest Rattenbury, *The Eucharistic Hymns of John and Charles Wesley*, Epworth Press, London, 1948, pp. 116–117
11 John C Bowmer, *The Sacrament of the Lord's Supper in Early Methodism*, Dacre Press, London, 1951, p. 167
12 *Ibid.*, p. 186

13 A Raymond George, 'The Lord's Supper' in *The Doctrine of the Church*, Dow Kirkpatrick (ed.), Epworth Press, London, 1964, pp. 149–160
14 Franz Hildebrandt, *I offered Christ: A Protestant Study of the Mass*, Epworth Press, London, 1967, pp. 162ff
15 *Ibid.*, p. 203
16 Ole E Borgen, *John Wesley on the Sacraments: A Theological Study*, Methodist Publishing House, Zürich, 1972, p. 282
17 Geoffrey Wainwright, *Eucharist and Eschatology*, Epworth Press, London, 1971, p. 56
18 Gordon Wakefield, 'John and Charles Wesley: A Tale of Two Brothers' in *The English Religious Tradition and the Genius of Anglicanism*, Geoffrey Rowell (ed.), IKON, Wantage, 1992, p. 165
19 Gordon Wakefield, 'The Wesley *Hymns on the Lord's Supper* (1745) in History and Eucharistic Theology' in *Like a Two-Edged Sword: Essays in honour of Canon Donald Gray*, Martin R Dudley (ed.), The Canterbury Press, Norwich, 1995, pp.149–150
20 *Ibid.*, p. 156
21 *MSF Bulletin*, No 138, Epiphany 2011, p. 11
22 Christopher J Cocksworth, *Evangelical Eucharistic thought in the Church of England*, CUP, Cambridge, 1993, pp. 69–70
23 T S Gregory, *According to Your Faith*, Epworth Press, London, 1966, p. 108
24 Arnold H Cooper, *Divine Compassion: The Intercession of Our Lord: Charles Wesley's Eucharistic hymns for Today*, Privately Printed, 1998. p. 36
25 Daniel B Stevick, *The Altar's Fire: Charles Wesley's 'Hymns on the Lord's Supper' 1745 Introduction and Comment*, Epworth Press, Peterborough, 2004

Chapter 6: Constant Communion

1 *The Journal of Rev. John Wesley*, Standard Edition, Curnock (ed.), Charles H Kelly, London, 1909, Vol I, p. 466
2 Frank Baker, 'John Wesley and the *Imitatio Christi*' in *London Quarterly and Holborn Review*, January 1941, pp. 74–87
3 Frank Baker, MS. Catalogue: *Wesley's Works*, Section 36, p. 45. Copy in Wesley College Library, Bristol
4 *Wesleys' Works*, Vol VII, Conference Office, London, 1872, p. 147
5 *John Wesley*, Albert Outler (ed.), OUP, Oxford, 1964, p. 333
6 Ole E Borgen, *John Wesley on the Sacraments: A Theological Study*, Methodist Publishing House, Zürich, 1972, p. 23
7 Richard P Heitzenrater, 'John Wesley's Early Sermons' in *Proceedings of the Wesley Historical Society*, Vol XXXVII, June 1969, p. 114
8 *The Duty of Constant Communion*, A Sermon by John Wesley, MSF Booklets, Southport, 1936, New Edition 1960(?)

Chapter 7: Vital Elements

1 *MSF Bulletin*, No 8, May 1939, pp. 3 and 17
2 Nathaniel Micklem (ed.), *Christian Worship: Studies in its History and Meaning by Members of Mansfield College*, OUP, Oxford, 1936
3 *MSF Bulletin*, No 13, June 1942, p. 3
4 *MSF Bulletin*, No 17, June 1946, p. 5
5 MSF Archives, File 1946
6 Pamphlet *Kingsway 1946*, MSF Archives, File 1946
7 *MSF Bulletin*, No 18, January 1947, p. 2
8 Gregory Dix, *The Shape of the Liturgy*, Dacre Press, Adam & Charles Black, London, 1945, p. xvi

9 *MSF Bulletin*, No 18, January 1947, pp. 58
10 Rattenbury's other books on the Christian Year are: *The Adoration of the Lamb* – for Lent and Holy Week (1950), *O'er Every Foe Victorious* – for Easter to Trinity (1951), *The Throne, The Cradle and The Star* – for Advent and Epiphany (1952), *The Seven Windows of Calvary* – for Good Friday (1953) and *The Spirit and The Bride* – Whitsun Meditations (1955)
11 MSF Archives, File 1947, Cyclostyled Minutes of the Annual Conference
12 *MSF Bulletin*, No 21, June 1948, p. 2
13 *Ibid.*, p. 3
14 *Ibid.*, p. 6
15 *MSF Bulletin*, No 22, October 1948, p. 2
16 *Ibid.*, p. 2
17 *MSF Bulletin*, No 23 (24), April–June 1949, p. 25
18 *Ibid.*, pp. 10–11
19 *MSF Bulletin*, No 24, October 1949, p. 3
20 *MSF Bulletin*, No 29, June 1951, p. 2
21 *MSF Bulletin*, No 34, September 1952, p. 1
22 *Ibid.*, p. 4
23 *MSF Bulletin*, No 35, December 1952, p. 2
24 *Ibid.*, p. 9
25 *MSF Bulletin*, No 37, June 1953, pp. 45
26 *MSF Bulletin*, No 38, September 1953, p. 3
27 *MSF Bulletin*, No 39, December 1953, pp. 1 and 2
28 *MSF Bulletin*, No 41, June 1954, pp. 34
29 *The Churchman's Magazine*, J A Kensit (ed.), September 1954, Vol 108, No 1299, p. 133
30 *Ibid.*, p. 134
31 *MSF Bulletin*, No 44, July 1955, p. 2
32 J Ernest Rattenbury, *The Witness of the MSF*, 1955, p. 1
33 *MSF Bulletin*, No 45, All Saints-tide 1955, p. 3
34 *Ibid.*, p. 8
35 *MSF Bulletin*, No 46, Epiphany 1956, p. 5
36 *Ibid.*, p. 9

37 *MSF Bulletin*, No 48, Trinity-tide 1956, p. 6
38 Donald Soper, *All His Grace*, Epworth Press, London, 1957, p. 114
39 *MSF Bulletin*, No 51, Trinity-tide 1957, p. 3
40 *MSF Bulletin*, No 55, All Saints-tide 1958, p. 3
41 *MSF Bulletin*, No 56, Lent 1959, p. 2
42 *MSF Bulletin*, No 57, Michaelmas 1959, p. 3
43 *Ibid.*, pp. 5 and 6
44 Francis B Westbrook, *The Holy Communion Service: Explanatory Notes – A Manual of Membership Preparation and a Devotional Commentary on the 1936 Communion Office*, Epworth, London, 1958
45 *MSF Bulletin*, No 60, Summer 1960, p. 13
46 *MSF Bulletin*, No 58, Advent 1959, p. 10

Chapter 8: Ecumenical Odyssey

1 *MSF Bulletin*, No 59, Lent 1960, p. 4
2 *Ibid.*, p. 5
3 *Ibid.*, p. 6
4 *Ibid.*, p. 7
5 *MSF Bulletin*, No 60, Summer 1960, p. 1
6 *Ibid.*, p. 7
7 *Ibid.*, p. 8
8 *Ibid.*, p. 14
9 *MSF Bulletin*, No 64, Advent 1961, p. 1
10 *MSF Bulletin*, No 65, Lent 1962, p. 11
11 *MSF Bulletin*, No 66, Summer 1962, p. 1
12 *Ibid.*, p. 7
13 *MSF Bulletin*, No 67, Michaelmas 1962, p. 1
14 *Ibid.*, p. 2
15 *MSF Bulletin*, No 69, Trinity 1963, p. 3
16 *Ibid.*, p. 4
17 *Ibid.*, p. 8
18 *Ibid.*, p. 9
19 *MSF Bulletin*, No 70, Epiphany 1964, p. 2
20 MSF Archives, File 1964

21 *MSF Bulletin*, No 69, Trinity 1963, p. 16
22 *MSF Bulletin*, No 70, Epiphany 1964, p. 2
23 *Ibid.*, p. 3
24 *Ibid.*, p. 5
25 MSF Archives, File 1965
26 *MSF Bulletin*, No 71, Pentecost 1967, p. 1
27 MSF Archives, File 1967
28 *MSF Bulletin*, No 72, Epiphany 1968, p. 5
29 *MSF Bulletin*, No 73, Trinity 1968, p. 7
30 *MSF Bulletin*, No 75, Trinity 1969, p. 2
31 *Ibid.*, p. 23
32 *Ibid.*, p. 8
33 MSF Archives, File 1969
34 *MSF Bulletin*, No 76, All Saints 1969, p. 4
35 *Ibid.*, p. 5

Chapter 9: Catholic Society

1 *MSF Bulletin*, No 80, Pentecost 1970, p. 7
2 *MSF Bulletin*, No 81, All Saints 1970, p. 1
3 *MSF Bulletin*, No 82, Passiontide 1971, p. 4
4 *Ibid.*, p. 8
5 *MSF Bulletin*, No 86, Pentecost 1972, p. 12
6 *MSF Bulletin*, No 82, Passiontide 1971, p. 13
7 *MSF Bulletin*, No 85, Lent 1972, p. 7
8 *MSF Bulletin*, No 86, Pentecost 1972, p. 5
9 *Ibid.*, p. 17
10 *MSF Bulletin*, No 88, Lent 1973, p. 4
11 *Ibid.*, p. 4
12 *MSF Bulletin*, No 89, Pentecost 1973, p. 3
13 *Ibid.*, p. 4
14 *Ibid.*, p. 6
15 *Ibid.*, p. 14
16 *MSF Bulletin*, No 92, Pentecost 1974, p. 5
17 *MSF Bulletin*, No 93, All Saints 1974, p. 7
18 *MSF Bulletin*, No 92, Pentecost 1974, p. 17
19 *MSF Bulletin*, No 93, All Saints 1974, p. 6

20 *MSF Bulletin*, No 95, Pentecost 1975, p. 1
21 *Ibid.*, p. 1
22 *Ibid.*, p. 1
23 *Ibid.*, p. 1
24 G E Radford, *My Providential Way: A Biography of Francis Brotherton Westbrook*, G C Brittain & Sons Ltd, Derby, n.d., p. 92
25 *MSF Bulletin*, No 96, All Saints 1975, p. 8
26 *Ibid.*, p. 26
27 *MSF Bulletin*, No 97, Lent 1976, p. 4
28 *MSF Bulletin*, No 98, Pentecost 1976, p. 3
29 *Ibid.*, p. 17
30 *Ibid.*, p. 22
31 Donald Rogers, *Methodists and the Retreat Movement*, Methodist Home Mission Division, London, 1976, pp. 4 and 5
32 *MSF Bulletin*, No 99, All Saints 1976, p. 12
33 *MSF Bulletin*, No 100, Lent 1977, p. 17
34 *MSF Bulletin*, No 101, Pentecost 1977, p. 7
35 *MSF Bulletin*, No 102, Christmas 1978, p. 3
36 *Ibid.*, p. 3
37 *Ibid.*, p. 14
38 *Ibid.*, p. 15
39 *MSF Bulletin*, No 102, Christmas 1978, p. 16
40 *Ibid.*, p. 16
41 *MSF Bulletin*, No 103, Pentecost 1979, p. 3
42 John Newton, *Heart Speaks to Heart*, DLT, London, 1994, p. 95f
43 *MSF Bulletin*, No 103, Pentecost 1979, p. 7
44 *Ibid.*, p. 3
45 *MSF Bulletin*, No 104, Christmas 1979, pp. 13–14

Chapter 10: Methodist Fellowship

1 *MSF Bulletin*, No105, Advent 1980, pp. 14–15
2 *MSF Bulletin*, No107, Pentecost 1981, p. 15
3 *MSF Bulletin*, No 109, Pentecost 1982, p. 16

4 *MSF Bulletin*, No 110, Epiphany 1983, p. 1–2
5 *Ibid.*, p. 11
6 *Ibid.*, p. 19
7 *MSF Bulletin*, No 111, Pentecost 1983, p. 7
8 *MSF Bulletin*, No 115, Lent 1986
9 MSF Archives, File 1984
10 MSF Archives, File 1985
11 *MSF Bulletin*, No 115, Lent 1986, pp. 4–10
12 MSF Archives, File 1986
13 *MSF Bulletin*, No 115, Lent 1986, pp. 10–25
14 *Ibid.*, p. 25
15 *MSF Bulletin*, No 116, Epiphany 1987, p. 11
16 *MSF Bulletin*, No 117, 1988, pp. 10–25
17 *Ibid.*, pp. 7–10
18 Letter to Norman Wallwork, Summer 1963
19 *MSF Bulletin*, No 122, 1993, p. 19
20 Letter to John Kellaway, *MSF Bulletin*, No 112, p. 20
21 Letter to John Kellaway, *MSF Bulletin*, No 112, p. 21
22 Tribute by Donald Rogers, MSF Archives, File 1974
23 Gordon S Wakefield, *A tribute to The Reverend the Lord Soper, President Emeritus of the Fellowship*, April 1999, MSF Archives, File 1999
24 *MSF Bulletin*, No 128, 1999, pp. 56 and 57
25 *MSF Bulletin*, No 102, Christmas 1978, p. 14
26 Gordon S Wakefield, *Robert Newton Flew 1886–1962*, Epworth Press, London, 1971
27 Gareth Powell, *A Tribute to The Reverend Gordon S Wakefield DD*, 2001, MSF Archives, File 2001
28 Gordon S Wakefield, *Medicines for the Heart*, Church in the Market Place, Buxton, 1999, p. 3
29 Gordon S Wakefield, *My Providential Way*, Church in the Market place, Buxton, 1999, p. xxiii

Chapter 11: Glorious Company

1 Mervyn Davies (ed.), *A Thankful Heart and a Discerning Mind: Essays in Honour of John Newton*, Lonely Scribe, Gloucestershire, 2010, p. 25
2 Donald Rogers, MSF Annual Conferences Record 1965–2007, MSF Archives
3 *The Grace Given You in Christ: Catholics and Methodists reflect further on the Church*, The World Methodist Council, Lake Junaluska, North Carolina, 2006, p. 62, para 144

Chapter 12: Liturgical Tradition

1 *MSF Bulletin*, No 126, 1997, pp. 6–8
2 Neil Dixon, *Wonder Love and Praise: A Companion to The Methodist Worship Book*, Epworth Press, London, 2003, p. 9
3 *MSF Bulletin*, No 124, 1995, pp. 34–35
4 A M Allchin, *Participation in God: A Forgotten Strand in Anglican Tradition*, Darton, Longman and Todd, London, 1988, p. 25
5 *Exciting Holiness*, Canterbury Press, Norwich, 1977
6 Gordon S Wakefield, *On the Edge of Mystery*, Epworth, London, 1969, p. 59
7 *MSF Bulletin*, No 138, Epiphany 2011, pp. 33–34

Chapter 13: Marian Pilgrimage

1 Jackson (ed.), *Wesley's Works*, Wesleyan Conference Office, London, 1872, Vol X, p. 129
2 *Ibid.*, p. 133
3 *Ibid.*, p. 86
4 *Ibid.*, p. 105
5 *Ibid.*, p. 105
6 *Ibid.*, p. 103
7 *Ibid.*, p. 103

8 Jackson (ed.), *Wesley's Works*, Wesleyan Conference Office, London, 1872, Vol IX, p. 224
9 Jackson (ed.), *Wesley's Works*, Wesleyan Conference Office, London, 1872, Vol X, p. 147
10 *The Journal of the Rev. John Wesley*, Standard Edition, Curnock (ed.), Charles H. Kelly, London, 1909, Vol VI, p. 339
11 *The Letters of Rev. John Wesley*, Telford (ed.), Epworth Press, London, 1931, Vol III, p. 190
12 J Neville Ward, *The Use of Praying*, Epworth Press, London, 1967, p. 117
13 Carbon Copy typescript kept with the Rosary at The Leys School
14 Ditto
15 Michael Rear, *Walsingham: Pilgrims and Pilgrimages*, St Paul's Publications, London, 2011, p. 178
16 Vincent Taylor, *The Historical Evidence for the Virgin Birth*, Oxford University Press, Oxford, 1920, pp. 127–130
17 J Neville Ward, *Five for Sorrow, Ten for Joy: A Consideration of the Rosary*, Epworth Press, London, 1971, pp. xi and xii
18 J Neville Ward, *The Following Plough*, Epworth Press, London, 1978, p. 121
19 Neville Ward, *Mary: Intercessor*, The Ecumenical Society of the Blessed Virgin Mary, 1982, p. 7
20 *Mother of Jesus Pamphlets No 1*, The Ecumenical Society of the Blessed Virgin Mary, 1967, p. 10
21 *Ibid.*, p. 11
22 C K Barrett, *The Holy Spirit and the Gospel Tradition*, SPCK, London, 1947, pp. 23–24
23 *Mother of Jesus Pamphlets No 7: Magnificat*, The Ecumenical Society of the Blessed Virgin Mary, 1969, p. 1
24 *Mother of Jesus Pamphlets No. 8: Intercession*, The Ecumenical Society of the Blessed Virgin Mary, 1969, p. 5
25 *MSF Bulletin*, No 92, Pentecost 1974, p. 10

26 Geoffrey Wainwright, *The Ecumenical Moment: Crisis and opportunity for the Church*, William B Eerdmans, Grand Rapids, MI, 1983, p. 182
27 Geoffrey Wainwright, Review of John McHugh, *The Mother of Jesus in the New Testament* (Darton, Longman and Todd, London, 1975) in *One in Christ*, Vol 12, 1976, p. 193
28 Papers of the International Ecumenical Conference, The Ecumenical Society of the Blessed Virgin Mary, Oxford, 1979, p. 5
29 Short Hymns on Selected Passages of Scripture, *Poetical Works of J & C Wesley*, Osborn (ed.), 1871, Vol XII, p. 92
30 *MSF Bulletin*, No 108, Pentecost 1982, p. 10
31 Frances Young, *Face to Face: A Narrative Essay in the Theology of Suffering*, T & T Clark, Edinburgh, 1990, p. 93
32 *MSF Bulletin*, No 111, Pentecost 1983, p. 18
33 *Ibid.*, p. 19
34 Frank Topping, *An Impossible God*, Fount Paperbacks, Collins, Glasgow, 1986, p. 39
35 *MSF Bulletin*, No 116, Epiphany 1987, pp. 4–5
36 Eamon Duffy, 'The Place of the Blessed Virgin Mary in Roman Catholicism' in *Epworth Review*, Vol 16, No 1, January 1989, p. 66
37 David Chapman, *Mary, Icon of the Covenant – A Methodist Perspective*, The Ecumenical Society of the Blessed Virgin Mary, Pamphlet, 1996, p. 9
38 David Carter, 'Mary, Servant of the Word' in *Mary is for Everyone: Essays on Mary and Ecumenism*, William McLoughlin and Jill Pinnock (eds), Gracewing, Leominister, 1997, p. 167
39 Richard Clutterbuck, 'Helpmate of a self-sufficient God: the Servanthood of Mary in dialogue with Karl Barth' in *Mary for Time and Eternity*, William McLoughlin and Jill Pinnock (eds), Gracewing, Leominister, 2007, p. 285

40 Norman Wallwork, 'Mary – Mother of all God's Children' in Mervyn Davies (ed.), *A Thankful Heart and a Discerning Mind: Essays in Honour of John Newton*, Lonely Scribe, Gloucestershire, 2010, pp. 207–208

41 Margaret Barker, 'Mary and the Temple,' in *Mary in Pilgrimage*, Peter Marr (ed.), Ecumenical Marian Pilgrimage Trust, Plymouth, 2011, pp. 7–21

Chapter 14: Arminian Testimony

1 Gordon S Wakefield, *Catholic Spirituality Reconsidered*, MSF Jubilee Lecture, 1985, p. 21

2 Philip Blackburn, *Altars and Altar Calls: A Catholic Evangelical in the Circuit Ministry*, MSF Annual Lecture, Portsmouth, 1987, p. 3

3 *Ibid.*, p. 3

4 *Ibid.*, p. 4

5 *Ibid.*, p. 4

6 John Newton and Donald Soper, *What I Owe to the Wesleys*, MSF Lecture, 1988, p. 5

7 *Ibid.*, p. 5

8 *Ibid.*, p. 24

9 Gordon S Wakefield, *Kindly Light*, Epworth Press, London, 1984, pp. 66–67

10 Michael J Townsend, *Whatever Happened to Heaven? Worship, Prayer and the Communion of Saints*, MSF Annual Lecture, Leicester, 1989, p. 19

11 Janet Morley, *All Desires Known*, Movement for the Ordination of Women, London, 1988, p. 17

12 Norman Wallwork, *Norah and Her Ark: The Dilemma of Inclusive Language for Humans and God*, MSF Annual Lecture, Cardiff, 1990, p. 24

13 Michael Austin, *An Hour to Raise the Dead: The Art of Performance in Sunday Worship*, MSF Annual Lecture, Bolton, 1991, p. 8

14 Kenneth Cracknell, *Protestant Evangelism or Catholic Evangelization? A Study in Methodist Approaches*, MSF Annual Lecture, Newcastle-upon-Tyne, 1992, p. 3
15 *Ibid.*, p. 8
16 *Ibid.*, p. 11
17 Michael Townsend, *Our Friends in Light: Praise and Prayer in the Communion of Saints*, MSF Annual Lecture, Derby, 1993, p. 3
18 *Ibid.*, p. 10
19 *Ibid.*, p. 15
20 Frances Young, *Presbyteral Ministry in the Catholic Tradition or Why shouldn't Women be Priests?* MSF Annual Lecture, Leeds, 1994, Cover Comment
21 *Ibid.*, p. 14
22 Leslie Griffiths, *The Far Side of the Cross: The Spirituality of R S Thomas*, MSF Annual Lecture, Blackpool, 1996, p. 4
23 *Ibid*, pp. 17–18
24 David Chapman, *The Fragrance of the Spirit: Towards the Sacramental Use of Oil in Methodism*, MSF Annual Lecture, London, 1997, p. 15
25 Neil Dixon, *At Your Service Again! Some Comments on The Methodist Worship Book*, MSF Annual Lecture, Southport, 1999, pp. 21–22
26 George Guiver CR, *A Sense of Déjà Vu? Eighteenth Century Liturgical Reforms on the Continent and some Food for Thought about Ourselves*, MSF Annual Lecture, Huddersfield, 2000 in *MSF Bulletin*, No 130, Advent 2000, p. 5
27 *Ibid.*, p. 9
28 *Ibid.*, p. 10
29 Kenneth Wilson, *The Eucharistic Community: The Community of Saints*, A Sermon preached at the MSF Conference Public Meeting in Ipswich 2001 in *MSF Bulletin*, No 131, Pentecost 2003, p. 4

30 Susan White, *Whatever Happened to God the Father? The Jesus Heresy in Modern Worship*, MSF Lecture, Wolverhampton, 2002, p. 14
31 *Ibid.*, p. 24
32 John Swarbrick, *'Jesus the Soul of Musick Is:' Music and the Methodists*, MSF Annual Lecture, Llandudno, 2003, p. 4
33 Present author's note – Neither the Wesleyan texts nor the Lutheran tune were able to cross the cultural chasm into contemporary Methodist hymnody!
34 Jackson (ed.), *Wesley's Works*, Vol VI, London, 1872, p. 205
35 Richard Watson, *Theological Institutes*, Vol II, London, 1877, p. 261
36 W B Pope, *A Compendium of Christian Theology*, Vol I, Wesleyan Conference Office, London, 1880, pp. 284–285
37 Geoffrey Wainwright, *Doxology*, Epworth Press, London, 1980, pp. 23 and 29
38 Jackson (ed.), *Wesley's Works*, Vol 12, London, 1872, p. 293
39 Norman Wallwork, *The Forgotten Trinity in Contemporary Methodism*, MSF Annual Lecture, Loughborough, 2004, p. 7
40 Kenneth Cracknell, *Resisting the Tyranny of Genesis Three: Frederick Denison Maurice, John and Charles Wesley and a Eucharist of Creation*, MSF Annual Lecture, Torquay, 2005, p. 10 (from Hymn number 28 in Charles Wesley, *Hymns of Petition and Thanksgiving for the Promise of the Father*, London, 1746)
41 Kenneth Cracknell, *Resisting the Tyranny of Genesis Three: Frederick Denison Maurice, John and Charles Wesley and a Eucharist of Creation*, MSF Annual Lecture, Torquay, 2005, p. 14 (from *The Methodist Worship Book*, Trustees for Methodist Church Purposes, London, 1999, pp. 124, 154 and 169)

42 Thomas à Kempis, *The Imitation of Christ*, translated by Robert Jeffrey, Penguin Classics, London, 2013

43 Robert Jeffrey, *Imitating Christ: Wesley's Christian Pattern and Spirituality for Today*, MSF Annual Lecture, Edinburgh, 2006, p. 18

44 John Lampard, *Theology in Ashes: How the churches have gone wrong over cremation*, MSF Annual Lecture, Blackpool, 2007, pp. 25–26

45 Inderjit Bhogal, *Immense, Unfathomed, Unconfined: Gospel Grace in the Methodist Mode*, MSF Annual Lecture, Scarborough, 2008, p. 19

46 Ruth Duck, *Finding Words for Worship*, Westminster John Knox Press, Louisville, KY, 1995, p. 10

47 Helen Dixon Cameron, *The Extempore Sacrament: Finding words in and for the present*, MSF Annual Lecture, Wolverhampton, 2009, p. 11

48 *Ibid.*, p. 15

49 William J Abraham, *Crossing the Threshold of Divine Revelation*, Eerdmans, Grand Rapids, MI, 2006, pp. 6–9 and Daniel Pratt Morris-Chapman, *Whither Methodist Theology Now? The Collapse of the 'Wesleyan Quadrilateral,'* MSF Annual Lecture, Portsmouth, 2010, p. 20

50 Daniel Pratt Morris-Chapman, op cit, p. 23

51 Samuel McBratney, *Look, No Mitres! A Conversation on Bishops and Leadership in British Methodism*, MSF Annual Lecture, Southport, 2011, p. 21

52 Paul Kybird, *Belonging and Believing: The Dilemma of Methodist Identity*, MSF Annual Lecture, Plymouth, 2012, p. 17

Index